American Power in
the Twenty-First Century

American Power in the Twenty-First Century

*Edited by David Held and
Mathias Koenig-Archibugi*

polity

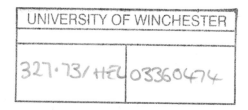

Contents

About the Contributors

Robert Cooper is Director General for External and Politico-Military Affairs at the General Secretariat of the Council of the European Union. He joined the Diplomatic Service in 1970 and from 1989 to 1993 he was Head of the Policy Planning Staff. Later in the 1990s he was Director for Asia and was then Deputy Secretary for Defence and Overseas Affairs in the Cabinet Office. Before moving to Brussels in 2002 he was Special Representative for the British Government on Afghanistan. He has published a number of essays and articles on international affairs and, most recently, a book of essays, *The Breaking of Nations* (2003).

Michael Cox is Professor in the Department of International Relations of the London School of Economics and Political Science. He is the author and editor of several books and currently he is working on two studies of the United States: *America at War* and *The New American Empire*. Professor Cox was editor of the *Review of International Studies* between 1998 and 2001, Senior Fellow at the Norwegian Nobel Institute in 2002, and is currently Chair of the United States Discussion Group at Chatham House.

Zhiyuan Cui is a Professor at the School of Public Policy and Management, Tsinghua University, Beijing. During 2003–4 he is a Fellow of the Institute for Advanced Studies in Berlin. In addition to his many publications in Chinese, he is author of the forthcoming book in English *Wrestling with the Invisible Hand*.

Abdelwahab El-Affendi is a Senior Research Fellow at the Centre for the Study of Democracy, University of Westminster, and co-ordinator of the Centre's Project on Democracy in the Muslim World. He is author of *Turabi's Revolution: Islam and Power in Sudan* (1991), *Who Needs an Islamic State?* (1991), *Revolution and Political Reform in Sudan* (1995), *Rethinking Islam and Modernity* (2001), and *For a State of Peace: Conflict and the Future of Democracy in Sudan* (2002), and of many contributions to journals and edited volumes. Dr El-Affendi is a member of the Consultative Council of the Arab Human Rights Organisation in the UK, and a trustee of the International Forum for Islamic Dialogue.

David Held is Graham Wallas Professor of Political Science at the London School of Economics and Political Science. He is the author of *Democracy and the Global Order: From the Modern State to Cosmopolitan Governance* (1995), *Models of Democracy* (2nd edn, 1996) and *Global Covenant* (2004), coauthor of *Global Transformations: Politics, Economics and Culture* (1999) and *Globalization/Anti-Globalization* (2002), and editor or coeditor of *Prospects for Democracy: North, South, East, West* (1993), *Cosmopolitan Democracy: An Agenda for a New World Order* (1995), and *Re-imagining Political Community* (1998).

G. John Ikenberry is the Albert G. Milbank Professor of Politics and International Affairs at Princeton University in both the Woodrow Wilson School and the Politics Department. He is the author of *After Victory: Institutions, Strategic Restraint and the Rebuilding of Order after Major War* (2001), which won the Schroeder/Jervis Award for best book in History and International Politics by the American Political Science Association. He is also coauthor of *State Power and World Markets* (2002) and editor of *America Unrivaled: The Future of the Balance of Power* (2002).

Robert Kagan is Senior Associate at the Carnegie Endowment for International Peace. His most recent book, *Of Paradise and Power* (2003), was on the *New York Times* bestseller list for 10 weeks and the *Washington Post* bestseller list for 14 weeks. It has been translated into over 20 languages including French, German,

Italian, Spanish, Greek, Dutch, Danish, Polish, Czech, Portuguese, Hebrew, Korean, Finnish, and Japanese. He is also the author of *A Twilight Struggle: American Power and Nicaragua, 1977–1990* (1996) and is coeditor with William Kristol of *Present Dangers: Crisis and Opportunity in American Foreign Policy* (2000). Kagan writes a monthly column on world affairs for the *Washington Post*, and is a Contributing Editor at both the *Weekly Standard* and the *New Republic*.

Mary Kaldor is Professor of Global Governance and Director of the Centre for the Study of Global Governance at the London School of Economics and Political Science. She has researched and written extensively about security and civil society. Her latest books include *New & Old Wars* and *Global Civil Society: An Answer to War* (2003). She is also coauthor of the annual publication *Global Civil Society*.

Mathias Koenig-Archibugi is Lecturer in Global Politics in the Departments of Government and International Relations of the London School of Economics and Political Science. He is the author of several articles in scholarly journals and coeditor of *Taming Globalization: Frontiers of Governance* (2003) and *Global Governance and Public Accountability* (2004).

Michael Mann is Professor in the Department of Sociology of the University of California, Los Angeles. He is the author of *The Sources of Social Power* (vol. 1, 1986; vol. 2, 1993) and has recently finished two books: *Fascists* and *The Dark Side of Democracy: Explaining Ethnic Cleansing*.

Joseph S. Nye, Jr, is the Sultan of Oman Professor of International Relations at the Kennedy School of Government. Nye has been on the Harvard faculty since 1964, during which time he also served as Assistant Secretary of Defense for International Affairs, Director of the National Intelligence Council, and Assistant Secretary of State for Security Assistance, Science, and Technology. He was dean of the Kennedy School of Government from 1995 to 2004. His most recent publications are *Soft Power: The Means* *to Success in World Politics* (2004); *Power in the Global Information Age* (2004), an anthology of essays; and *Understanding International Conflicts* (5th edn, 2004).

Thomas Risse is Professor and Chair of International Politics at the Free University of Berlin's Department of Political and Social Sciences. He currently serves as Dean of the Social and Political Science Division at the Free University and as Director of its Center for Transatlantic Foreign and Security Policy. He has previously taught at several universities in Europe and the US, including the European University Institute, Florence, Italy, the University of Konstanz, Germany, Cornell, Yale, and Stanford Universities, and the University of Wyoming. He is the author of *Cooperation among Democracies: The European Influence on U.S. Foreign Policy* (1995) and the coeditor of *The Handbook of International Relations* (2002), *Transforming Europe: Europeanization and Domestic Change* (2001), and *The Power of Human Rights: International Norms and Domestic Change* (1999).

Editors' Preface

Most of the chapters of this book are revised versions of the Miliband Lectures on American Power in the Twenty-First Century given at the London School of Economics and Political Science (LSE) in 2003. Contributions by other distinguished authors, and an introduction, have been added to the collection in order to round out the exploration of this important topic.

The nature and the use of American power raise questions of crucial significance. At stake is the future character of global governance and its capacity to promote international peace and justice. The chapters of this book provide a broad range of views on American foreign policy – what drives it, what it can achieve, and how Americans and people in other countries might relate to it. We think that presenting these diverse perspectives in the same book contributes to the vital public debate about the future of international order.

The Miliband Programme honors the memory of Ralph Miliband, who taught at the LSE from 1949 to 1972, and is funded through a generous bequest of a former LSE Ph.D. student, who was inspired by Ralph Miliband's critical vision. This bequest has made the lecture series possible, and we are grateful to all those who supported the initiative; in particular, we wish to thank Anthony Giddens, Fred Halliday, Ayse Kaya, Marion Kozak, Chun Lin, David Miliband, Edward Miliband, Henrietta Moore, and Salome Van Jaarsveld.

D. H. and M. K.-A.

Introduction: Whither American Power?

David Held and Mathias Koenig-Archibugi

Few political issues today elicit such strong and diverse responses as the role of the United States of America in shaping world affairs. 9/11, the reaction to it, and the wars in Afghanistan and Iraq have intensified the debate about the nature and prospects of American power. Views range from the celebration of the United States' achievements in bringing liberty, democracy, and prosperity to every corner of the world to the condemnation of America's pursuit of empire and its attempt to impose a single economic system and a narrow set of moral beliefs on other peoples. Whatever the interpretation of the causes and consequences of the United States' actions on the world stage, most agree that the history of the twenty-first century will be determined to a large extent by the way American power is used, and by the way in which non-Americans react to it.

This volume aims to present a broad range of views about the nature, the impact, and the future of American power. While several dimensions of this power are considered by the contributors to this book, most notably America's economic, ideological, and cultural influences, the focus is on the dimension of power that is most concentrated in the hands of American leaders: the capacity to project coercive power globally. In this introduction, we consider this capacity, and sketch some possible scenarios about the development of American power and its implications for international order. Introducing the debate about American power in this way provides a useful mechanism for mapping different conceptions of US power and drawing together the contributions of the book.

Broadly speaking, two kinds of change can be conceived in relation to the exercise of power by states in the global system. The first involves shifts along a dimension from the highly centralized to the highly diffuse: that is, from a situation in which the actual and threatened use of force is carried out by one political actor to a situation in which more states participate actively in deterrence and are prepared to intervene militarily abroad. Of course, it is also conceivable that the international system will maintain the current level of centralization for a long time. The second type of change involves movement along a dimension in which the exercise of coercive power may become more discretional, or more constitutionalized. The exercise of coercive power would become more discretional if the existing rules about the use of force were to be increasingly ignored, or if new rules were to be imposed unilaterally. A constitutionalization of coercive power means, by contrast, that such power is exercised in accordance with precise and binding rules that are collectively agreed by the participants in the system. Combining these two dimensions, it can be shown that, depending on whether the exercise of coercive power is becoming more centralized or diffused, and discretional or constitutionalized, the international system is moving towards empire, a balance of power system, a system of collective security, or a democratic world government – global democracy for short (see figure 1.1). Each of these scenarios is explored in greater detail below. Each captures a possible trajectory of the distribution of international power, and each carries with it a different constellation of opportunities and costs.

Scenario 1: Toward Empire

In the first scenario, the global order of the twenty-first century will be defined by two trends. The first is the trend toward the

The exercise of coercive power becomes:

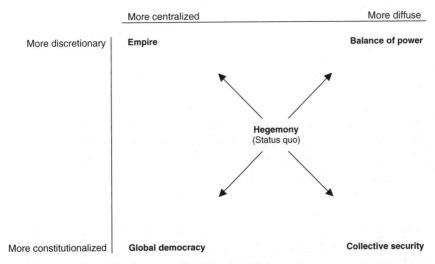

More centralized   More diffuse

More discretionary | **Empire**   **Balance of power**

Hegemony
(Status quo)

More constitutionalized | **Global democracy**   **Collective security**

Figure 1.1 Coercive power and global orders

further concentration of crucial power resources in the hands of the governments of the United States. The current US National Security Strategy states that "our forces will be strong enough to dissuade potential adversaries from pursuing a military buildup in hopes of surpassing, or equaling, the power of the United States."[1] This goal may be extended to achieve the military capacity to impose US policies on a large number of states in different parts of the globe at the same time. G. John Ikenberry notes in chapter 3 that America spends on its armed forces more than the next 14 countries combined and by 2007, if current trends continue, US military expenditure will be equal to the rest of the world combined. Paul Kennedy notes elsewhere that it is already the case that all the other navies in the world combined could not dent American maritime supremacy.[2] And another commentator suggests that the command of the commons enjoyed by the United States – that is, command of the sea, space, and air – is "the key military enabler of the U.S. global power position."[3] If American economic growth rates remain high, the concentration of world military power may continue for several decades. Even at the current level of US capabilities, many think, as Robert Kagan puts it in chapter 5, that "the United States can shoulder the burden of maintaining global security without much help from Europe" – or anybody else.[4]

The second trend in this scenario is an increasing willingness by American administrations to take decisions about the use of force in defiance of international norms and procedures – much like the current Bush administration. The United Nations Charter and similar international legal documents may be perceived by American decision-makers to be more and more irrelevant, and foreign policy goals may be pursued more frequently without multilateral or collective authorization. In addition, the benefits of traditional alliances such as NATO may no longer be considered sufficient to offset the cost in terms of autonomy, flexibility of response, and speed of action. Kagan argues that American leaders are not, and should not feel, constrained by their European allies: "Europe is not really capable of constraining the United States." Kagan belongs to an influential group of decision-makers and policy analysts usually referred to as "neoconservatives." In chapter 8, Thomas Risse describes their main tenets. According to his account, the neoconservatives believe America should use its superior capabilities to reshape the international order in line with American values and interests; it should act pre-emptively against challengers; it should promote "regime change" in "rogue" states; and it should comply with international law and procedures only when it is demonstrably in the American national interest. As Mary Kaldor notes in chapter 7, neoconservatives do not accept the principle of sovereignty as a barrier to external intervention in the political and economic affairs of other states.[5] If neoconservative prescriptions became the guiding principles of US foreign policy in the decades to come, the exercise of power by America (and presumably by other states as well) would become entirely discretional. The United States would aim at being not only the world's policeman, but also the lawmaker and judge. This would amount to a deconstitutionalization of the international order.

The combination of the centralization of power in one state and the lack of significant institutional constraints on its exercise is a distinctive mark of imperial orders. It is a matter of controversy if America's current position in the world justifies calling it an "empire." If one adopts a narrow definition of empire – for instance, the "direct administration of different communities from an imperial centre"[6] – then it seems difficult to call America an empire, and the establishment of an imperial world order would seem a very unlikely prospect in this century. But if one adopts a broader definition of empire – such as "relationships of political control imposed by some political societies over the effective sovereignty of other political societies"[7] – then the prospect of a world dominated by an imperial center in Washington is much less far-fetched. As shown by Michael Cox in chapter 1, some neoconservatives now speak openly about building an American empire – a "benign" empire that promotes freedom, democracy, and the market economy worldwide. Even neoconservatives who do not use the vocabulary of empire, such as Kagan, believe that the establishment of a benign American empire-like supremacy is possible. As Michael Mann notes in chapter 2, the empire advocated by the neoconservatives is indirect and informal: territorial occupation is only the last resort and a temporary measure – what is envisaged is "temporary territorial imperialism."

Most contributors to this volume are skeptical about the idea that the world is moving toward a new imperial order. This development is considered unlikely because they see the United States as lacking the motivation and/or the capacity to establish an empire. Ikenberry emphasizes the lack of motivation: America is unlikely in the future to reject multilateralism and a rule-based international order, essentially for three reasons. First, as global economic interdependence grows, the need for multilateral coordination of policies also grows. Second, it is rational for dominant powers to accept some limitations to their freedom of action in the form of multilateral institutions; if the stronger state accepts some restrictions on how it can use its power, weaker states are more likely to cooperate willingly and have less reason to resist the hegemony of the stronger state. Finally, American political culture stresses the importance of the rule of law as a foundation of political order, and this tradition provides significant support for a multilaterally oriented foreign policy. Further, in chapter 8 Risse indicates the role of domestic coalitions and values in constraining foreign policy. In the current Bush administration, neo-conservatives nurturing an "imperial ambition" are to some extent balanced by traditional conservatives who are wary of undermining alliances and multilateralism. Whether the US pursues "imperialist" policies is not determined by inexorable structural factors, but by a domestic political game whose outcome is far from certain. Moreover, Risse argues that economic interdependence between America and Europe and a commitment to shared values work against US unilateralism.

Other contributions to this volume maintain that, whatever the intentions of its leaders, the United States has not sufficient capabilities to establish an imperial order. Mann argues that a bid for empire requires four kinds of power – economic, military, political, and ideological – and that, overall, the United States possesses less power than the major empires of history. US leaders are unable to use their nation's wealth to implement imperialist policies, as American voters and taxpayers are not prepared to bear the economic costs involved in building an empire. In addition, despite the activities of the IMF and the World Bank, the ability of the US government to determine the economic policies of other countries is limited, as most governments retain a substantial degree of economic sovereignty and accountability to their own electorates. Regarding military power in particular, Mann notes that America has overwhelming offensive capabilities and firepower, which give it an unprecedented global offensive reach. However, American capabilities by themselves are insufficient to patrol the whole world and deliver imperial pacification. Imperial domination requires the collaboration of local allies, but America lacks political power – that is, the capacity to bind local allies to itself and to control them. For Mann, this is partly due to the fact that today nationalist ideologies are predominant and imperialism is thoroughly delegitimized at the ideological level. Americans simply cannot persuade other peoples that imperial rule is just and beneficial, as traditional empires once did.[8]

Adding to the skepticism about the United States' imperial capacity, Kaldor points at the gap between the destructive capacity of the American military machine and the actual results it can achieve. American power is much less effective than is generally assumed, not least because today military force is largely unsuitable to achieve political goals. Kaldor argues that the increasing destructiveness of all weapons means that it is more difficult to win an outright military victory as a result of technological superiority. Even full military command of the air does not confer the capacity to control territory. Kaldor points to the effectiveness of unconventional warfare in present-day Iraq as evidence that military occupation of territories is increasingly costly. In chapter 10 of this book, Abdelwahab El-Affendi stresses the limits of American power in the Middle East. He argues that the Middle East has a crucial importance for the American imperial project, as it had for previous Western empire builders from Alexander the Great to the British. But in this region American power has been remarkably ineffective. It attempts to "shock and awe," but it is unable to exert significant influence even on allies such as the governments of Saudi Arabia, Egypt, and Israel. El-Affendi writes: "What we see here is the powerlessness of power in its most spectacular and paradoxical manifestation."

Scenario 2: Toward a Multipolar Balance of Power System

Many scholars of world politics maintain that a universal feature of international relations is the tendency of weaker states to resist the hegemonic aspirations of stronger states by forming coalitions and augmenting their own military capabilities. Shortly after the end of the Cold War, some of these scholars predicted that the end of the bipolar international system would lead to a reconfiguration of existing alliances and alignments.[9] The unipolar distribution of power engendered by the collapse of the Soviet Union is considered but a transitory state of affairs. This "unipolar moment" will inevitably be replaced by a multipolar international system, in which a limited number of states will cooperate and compete with an eye to preventing any of them from gaining or retaining the upper hand. In this scenario, the emergence of a multipolar balance of power system would be the result of two trends. First, a number of states would improve or acquire the capacity to project military power regionally or globally, by spending more on their armed forces and/or by pooling efforts with other states. The exercise of coercive power would thus become more diffuse. Second, each of the "poles" in the system would use or threaten to use force with greater discretion than is now the case.[10] Relations between the great powers would become more competitive, and they would be reluctant to limit their freedom of action by entering into and complying with international agreements. The United Nations Charter would, as in scenario 1, become obsolete in this international order.

The development of multipolarism may be propelled mainly by two factors. First, the attempt by US administrations to establish imperial relationships with other states may raise concerns even in states that are not immediate targets of US action.[11] The costs of occupying a subordinate position in the emergent imperial system may be seen as outweighing the benefits, and this may prompt a reaction by the affected states. In the case of Europe, for instance, this reaction may be the result of an increased influence of the politicians and policy advisers that Risse calls European "Gaullists," who are concerned about American "hyper-power."[12] In chapter 9, Zhiyuan Cui notes as well that China has adopted a range of counterbalancing strategies: from using China's power in the UN Security Council to supporting the euro and promoting economic cooperation with other East and Central Asian countries, including Russia. For Cui, emerging signs of Chinese–European cooperation may be the most significant response to American assertiveness.

However, the transition to multipolarism may result not only from the perception that America is too strong, but also from a relative decline in its power. In this volume, Mann is confident that in the long run we will see relative American decline, and points out that American economic power has already declined relative to Europe and Japan, and will soon do so in relation to China and India. Mann notes that "the world may return to a version of 19th century world order, now characterized by a leading Power (the US), embedded in a multilateral Concert of Powers and a transnational capitalism."

There is also a bleaker version of the balance of power scenario: multipolar politics may lead not to a Concert of Powers that aims at preserving a degree of international order, but to a situation in which tensions and armed conflicts proliferate at the periphery of the international system (and no major power is prepared to intervene to restore peace and order) – or even a state of the world in which great power competition fuels regional wars and civil strife. The decentralization and deconstitutionalization of the use of force may, in other words, lead to a further bifurcation of the world: a prosperous region in which deterrence and balancing practices preserve the peace between the main powers, and a vast region in which poverty, political instability, and great power competition combine to generate a spiral of international and domestic armed conflicts.[13] Furthermore, "weak states on America's hit list may increasingly conclude that weapons of mass destruction joined to terror tactics are the only feasible equalizer to its power."[14] While this conclusion may generate a degree of reciprocal deterrence in the relationship between the United States and a number of developing countries, it also limits the capacity of powerful states to placate local conflicts and address humanitarian crises.

Just as with the imperial scenario, the balance of power scenario has raised significant objections. Ikenberry points out that there is no evidence that major states – neither allies such as Western Europe and Japan nor former adversaries such as Russia and China – are balancing the power of the United States. He explains this behavior by pointing to four facets of American power that reduce incentives to resist or check the United States. First, there are traditional power assets: the extent of American advantage in the military domain makes it difficult if not impossible for a group of states to develop capabilities that could balance those available to the United States. Moreover, America provides protection to many states against potential or actual regional rivals, and any anti-US balancing strategy could mean forgoing this protection. Also the desire to retain access to the

American market reinforces American hegemony. Second, the geographical remoteness of the United States makes it less threatening to the rest of the world; most states see American power less as a source of domination and more as an asset that can be used to defuse local security dilemmas. Third, institutions matter: American democracy and transparency reassure leaders of other states and particularly the leaders of other democratic states about American intentions; US institutions offer opportunities for access to foreign governments and give them the possibility of influencing decision-making in Washington; and the United States is entangled in a web of international institutions that makes its foreign policy more predictable and malleable. Finally, Ikenberry argues that American power is more acceptable to the rest of the world because the American "model" is congruent with the deeper forces of economic, political, and cultural modernization. Together, these facets of American power suggest that no balancing coalition is likely to emerge.[15]

Similarly, with reference to the relations between America and Europe, Risse stresses that two fundamental elements of the transatlantic security community are intact. First, there is a collective identity based on common values. Despite the recent (2003–4) war in Iraq, there is no widening gap in the worldviews and the general foreign policy outlook between Americans and Europeans. Second, the transatlantic region is highly integrated economically and common material interests provide a basis for a security community. While growing US unilateralism and imperial ambitions put the transatlantic relationship under considerable strain, for Risse these conflicts are unlikely to lead to the strengthening of the European Union as a counterweight to the United States, especially given the need to accommodate the positions of the United Kingdom and the new EU member states in Central Europe. "A European common foreign policy will fail immediately and split Europe further apart if it is constructed as a counter-hegemonic project."

Parallel arguments apply also to other regions of the world. In chapter 4, Joseph Nye describes how Americans may preserve their predominance by devoting to soft power – that is, the ability to get others to want what you want – at least as much attention as that devoted to hard power, that is, economic and military power that works through inducements and threats. If the United States retains or rebuilds a strong reservoir of soft power, which Nye equates with attractive power, then other states will not seek to check and delimit it. A similar line of argument is pursued by Robert Cooper in chapter 6.

Scenario 3: Toward a Collective Security System

Movement towards a pluralistic collective security system implies the unfolding of two processes. First, the exercise of military power becomes more decentralized: armed intervention is increasingly carried out by a plurality of states, rather than prevalently by the United States. Second, military power becomes more constitutionalized: it is exercised on the basis of rules that are precise, impartial, and legally binding. Individual states relinquish the capacity to decide autonomously when armed intervention is justified. Any change to the rules is made on the basis of participative procedures and not as a result of unilateral decisions.

Compared to the present situation, moving toward a genuine collective security system is likely to require a thorough reform and reinforcement of the United Nations. The UN, like the League of Nations before it, was built as the fulcrum of a global collective security system, but it has never been able to perform this function effectively.[16] While peacekeeping operations authorized and coordinated by the UN have contributed to pacifying and stabilizing a number of regional conflict zones, the logic of collective security has been regularly trumped by the logic of superpower competition, aided in this by the veto power wielded by the permanent members of the Security Council.

One path that may conceivably lead toward a collective security system can be set out as follows. Liberal internationalists, strongly committed to a rule-based multilateral order, come to power in the United States, possibly in the wake of electoral successes of the Democratic Party. Liberal internationalists pay much attention to maintaining and gaining soft power, and they regard multilateral legitimacy as a crucial part of soft power, as

Nye elaborates in chapter 4. As a result of their multilateral orientation and perhaps of tight budgetary constraints, liberal internationalists could come to reject decisively the idea that the
United States should shoulder the burden of peace enforcement
and could try to persuade other powers (notably other rich countries and larger states in all continents) to participate in the task
of "policing of the world." Liberal internationalists in Europe (as
described by Risse) and in other regions of the world are willing
to increase their "capability for intervention" in crisis situations,
but they also demand a stronger system of rules and procedures
that would regulate the "if" and the "how" of armed intervention.
Washington may relinquish the right to intervene unilaterally
in exchange for sharing the costs of security provision. In this
scenario, decisions about the use of force are legalized and
centralized (e.g. in a reformed Security Council), while the
implementation of those decisions is decentralized. This process,
which at the start might involve rich countries alone, may progressively extend to other states and eventually cover all regions
of the world.

Risse observes that in the past Europeans have responded to
transatlantic conflicts by strengthening their institutional ties with
the United States rather than trying to counterbalance it, and
this is still likely to be the most successful strategy for promoting
European values and interests. Similarly, the emergence of a global
collective security system would represent a process of "binding"
the United States in a tighter web of commitments and cooperation. Risse notes that American public opinion holds views much
closer to European outlooks than to those of US neoconservatives.
If this continues to be the case, then in the longer run the
prospects of a transatlantic bargain based on collective security
and "burden-sharing" may be good.

Like the other scenarios, the idea that the world may be moving
toward a collective security system evinces considerable skepticism. Some authors, like Kagan in chapter 5, stress the differences
between the strategic worldviews of two essential components
of such a system, the United States on the one hand, and the
European governments on the other. Given the existence of fundamental disagreements on the best way to achieve security in the

contemporary world, the constitutionalization of the use of force is considered very unlikely in the foreseeable future. Similarly, skeptics see it as improbable that the "burden" of enforcing world order with military means will be more evenly shared among the great powers. The reluctance to shoulder greater responsibilities on the part of wealthy countries such as Germany or Japan is variously attributed to an antimilitaristic political culture or to the benefits of a strategy of "free riding," that is, exploiting the provision of security by the United States without contributing to its economic and political costs.

While advocates of American primacy and interventionism tend to stress the shortcomings of America's potential partners, critics of current US foreign policies are often skeptical about the prospect of collective security in the light of their understanding of American foreign policy objectives. If the paramount goal is to achieve "world dominance,"[17] then any attempt to establish a collective security system is bound to founder as a result of American opposition. Paul Kennedy, for instance, asks:

> Can one have a reasonably balanced UN Security Council when there now exists, in addition to the gap between its five permanent veto members and the non-permanent members, a tremendous and real gulf in the power and influence of one of the five and the other four? Even before the present victories, the US played the game of using international organizations when it suited its own interests and paralyzing them when it disapproved.[18]

Those who stress the imperialist motives of the American leaders are often skeptical about the alleged differences among US administrations and about the capacity of electoral outcomes to change the thrust of American foreign policy. In this book, Cui notes that Chinese policymakers and analysts tend to emphasize the continuity between the policies of the Clinton administration and those under President George W. Bush: the "Bush Doctrine" is seen as the culmination and maturation of the US post–Cold War grand strategy. In this perspective, the establishment of a collective security system based on a durable alliance between liberal internationalists in the United States, Europe, Japan, and other powerful states is unlikely.

Scenario 4: Toward Global Democracy

The vision of a world polity that would end international anarchy and war is a recurring theme in political thought, which in the West dates back at least to Dante Alighieri's *De monarchia* and which was linked to republican and constitutionalist political principles by the thinkers of the Enlightenment.[19] Especially since the end of the Cold War, there has been an upsurge in thinking about the desirability and feasibility of a global polity organized around principles that may be considered democratic.[20] Moving towards such a form of political organization would involve a two-sided process of constitutionalization and centralization. On the one hand, a global rule of law would be entrenched in the normal practices of states and other actors in the global system.[21] This would aid the "domestication" of international relations, in the double sense of a taming of the forces driving coercive politics and of making international politics more akin to the domestic politics of constitutional and democratic states. On the other hand, global polity formation would require a centralization of military might, that is, a "permanent shift of a growing proportion of a nation state's coercive capability to regional and global institutions."[22] This does not necessarily mean the superseding of national armed forces by a single global army, but it does mean that the organization of force would take on a global element, that is, decisions to authorize and sanction the use of coercive power for peacemaking and peacekeeping would be monopolized by one (collective) entity.

The vision of a democratic world polity is often linked to a cosmopolitan ethical outlook. As Kaldor notes in chapter 7, cosmopolitans are committed to humanist norms and the principle of human moral equality, while recognizing difference as a legitimate and indeed valuable part of the human condition. However, the advocates of "cosmopolitan democracy" eschew the utopianism of earlier theorists of "world government," and they are careful not to present the progress toward global political integration as inevitable.[23] They maintain that global political integration is promoted by important processes in political, economic, and cultural domains.[24] The globalization of markets and production makes national economies more dependent on each other, and this creates a demand for the international coordination of trade, monetary, and regulatory policies. Moreover, the need to respond effectively to global problems such as climate change, the spread of HIV/AIDS and other infectious diseases, and the proliferation of weapons of mass destruction strengthens the interest in deeper forms of transnational and supranational cooperation on the part of a variety of social and political groups. Among the actors that are most vocal in demanding stronger global political institutions, many are part of global civil society, that is, the realm of transnational advocacy networks, social movements and nongovernmental organizations that negotiate or renegotiate social contracts between the individuals and the centers of authority at the global level.[25] The transnational campaign for the creation of an international criminal court is an important example of the contribution that global civil society can make to global polity formation.[26]

The possibility that the world may be moving toward a global polity organized according to democratic principles is greeted with considerable skepticism by commentators belonging to several traditions of analysis.[27] Scholars belonging to the "realist" school of international studies dismiss the idea of global democracy as inappropriate to the international realm, which is necessarily governed by the rules of power politics. Any global polity that might emerge in the foreseeable future would be simply an expression of the power of the strongest state in the international system, that is, a mask for American imperial domination. In the realist interpretation of world politics, most likely is the prospect that any such attempt would be blocked by a coalition of states intending to preserve their independence.[28] Marxist authors point out that the logic of capitalist globalization undermines international democratization.[29] And a variety of authors hold, sometimes from a "communitarian" perspective, that several prerequisites of democratic governance are largely absent beyond the level of individual nation-states: most notably, a sense of collective identity and common values, the willingness to share burdens and

exercise solidarity with other members of the political community, the existence of channels of political communication that are
not excessively biased in favor of educated elites, and chains of
political delegation and authorization that are not so stretched as
to render individual political participation inconsequential.[30]
Some economists also argue that international economic integration promotes political disintegration, rather than political integration, since large states are no longer required for the sake of
efficiency when economic activities are less and less limited by
state boundaries.[31]

Scenario 5: Continuation of the Status Quo

The four previous scenarios are based on arguments about the relative importance of various political, economic, and social forces.
Some of these forces support the centralization of the exercise of
coercive power, while other forces push in the opposite direction,
toward its diffusion. Similarly, some forces promote the constitutionalization of power, while other forces tend to make it more
discretionary. It may well be possible that these forces will balance
each other out, and that as a result the status quo will enjoy a
substantial degree of stability. It is conceivable that during the
twenty-first century the relations between the United States and
the rest of the world will not become more imperial than they
are at present, that emerging states will not challenge US military
supremacy, that genuine collective security will not be realized,
and that the world will not experience the emergence of a democratic global polity. In this scenario, military force will continue to
be used, often unilaterally, against states that, from time to time,
will be declared "rogue" and a threat to national or international
security, and American hegemony will continue to arouse intense
passion and discussion.

The essays in this volume analyze and debate the nature of
American power in the twenty-first century. While there is no
consensus about what might or should happen to America's role
in the world, there is agreement that the power of the United
States will determine the shape of global order in the decades

ahead. US citizens or not, we are all stakeholders in this debate, and stakeholders in a struggle to decide which scenario will actually predominate.

Notes

1 President of the United States, *The National Security Strategy of the United States of America* (Washington, DC: White House, September 2002), p. 30.

2 Paul Kennedy, "The Greatest Superpower Ever," *New Perspectives Quarterly*, 19 (2002).

3 Barry R. Posen, "Command of the Commons: The Military Foundation of U.S. Hegemony," *International Security*, 28 (2003), pp. 5–46, quotation at p. 8.

4 On the durability of US supremacy see William C. Wohlforth, "The Stability of a Unipolar World," *International Security*, 24 (1999), pp. 5–41.

5 At the same time, neoconservatives are often "sovereignists" when it comes to the question of joining international institutions that may constrain American policy autonomy. See, for instance, the contributions to the "AEI Conference: Trends in Global Governance – Do They Threaten American Sovereignty?" *Chicago Journal of International Law*, 1 (2000), pp. 205–490. On American "exemptionalism," see also John Gerard Ruggie, *American Exceptionalism, Exemptionalism and Global Governance*, Regulatory Policy Program Working Paper RPP-2003-20 (Cambridge, MA: Center for Business and Government, John F. Kennedy School of Government, Harvard University, 2003).

6 Adam Watson, *The Evolution of International Society* (London and New York: Routledge, 1992), p. 16. Watson conceived a continuum from independent statehood to empire, where intermediate stages are hegemony, suzerainty, and dominion.

7 Michael W. Doyle, *Empires* (Ithaca, NY: Cornell University Press, 1986), p. 19, quoted by Barry Buzan and Richard Little, *International Systems in World History* (Oxford: Oxford University Press, 2000), p. 176. In a similar vein, Paul W. Schroeder writes that "Imperialism means simply and centrally the exercise of final authority and decision-making power by one government over another government or community foreign to itself. Empire does not require the direct annexation and administration of a foreign territory or its

people." Schroeder, "Iraq: The Case Against Preemptive War," *American Conservative*, 1 (October 21, 2002), pp. 8–20.

8   In addition, while the United States may enjoy undisputed command of the sea, space, and air, its capacity to prevail over its adversaries is much more uncertain in what Posen calls "contested zones," that is, "arenas of conventional combat where weak adversaries have a good chance of doing real damage to U.S. forces." Posen, "Command of the Commons," p. 22. As the case of Somalia shows, large numbers of men of military age, favorable terrain, and plentiful basic infantry weapons may create serious problems for the US military.

9   Kenneth N. Waltz, "The Emerging Structure of International Politics," *International Security*, 18 (1993), pp. 44–79; Christopher Layne, "The Unipolar Illusion: Why New Great Powers Will Arise," *International Security*, 17 (1993).

10 The doctrine and practice of preventive war adopted by the Bush administration may contribute to the undermining of the norms that limit the use of force among the members of international society. See Schroeder, "Iraq." Writing after the war against Iraq, Stanley Hoffmann laments the Bush administration's "destruction of some of the main schemes of cooperation that have been established since 1945 and are aimed at introducing some order and moderation into the jungle of traditional international conflicts." Hoffmann, "America Goes Backward," *New York Review of Books*, 50 (June 12, 2003).

11 Jack Snyder, "Imperial Temptations," *The National Interest*, 71 (Spring 2003).

12 In a speech delivered in November 1999, French President Jacques Chirac said that "The European Union itself [must] become a major pole of international equilibrium, endowing itself with the instruments of a true power"; quoted by Charles A. Kupchan, "Hollow Hegemony or Stable Multipolarity?" in G. John Ikenberry, ed., *America Unrivaled: The Future of the Balance of Power* (Ithaca, NY: Cornell University Press, 2002), p. 72. According to Kupchan, the European Union is emerging as the main competitor of the United States in a future multipolar international system.

13 A "zone of peace" and a "zone of turmoil," in the words of Max Singer and Aaron Wildavsky, *The Real World Order: Zones of Peace, Zones of Turmoil* (Chatham, NJ: Chatham House Publishers, 1993).

14 Snyder, "Imperial Temptations."

15 On the absence of sustained attempts to balance the United States see also Stephen M. Walt, "Keeping the World 'Off-Balance': Self-Restraint and U.S. Foreign Policy," in Ikenberry, *America Unrivaled*, pp. 121–54.

16 Inis L. Claude, *Power and International Relations* (New York: Random House, 1962); George W. Downs, ed., *Collective Security Beyond the Cold War* (Ann Arbor: Michigan University Press, 1994).

17 Noam Chomsky, *Hegemony or Survival: America's Quest for World Dominance* (London: Hamish Hamilton, 2003).

18 Kennedy, "Greatest Superpower Ever."

19 Derek Heater, *World Citizenship and Government* (Basingstoke: Macmillan, 1996); Cornelius F. Murphy, Jr, *Theories of World Governance: A Study in the History of Ideas* (Washington, DC: Catholic University of America Press, 1999).

20 James A. Yunker, *World Union on the Horizon: The Case for Supranational Federation* (Lanham, MD: University Press of America, 1993); David Held, *Democracy and the Global Order* (Cambridge: Polity, 1995); Daniele Archibugi, "Principles of Cosmopolitan Democracy," in Daniele Archibugi, David Held, and Martin Koehler, eds, *Re-Imagining Political Community: Studies in Cosmopolitan Democracy* (Cambridge: Polity, 1998); Richard Falk and Andrew Strauss, "On the Creation of a Global Peoples' Assembly: Legitimacy and the Power of Popular Sovereignty," *Stanford Journal of International Law*, 36 (2000).

21 Daniele Archibugi and Iris Marion Young, "Toward a Global Rule of Law," *Dissent* (Spring 2002), pp. 27–32.

22 Held, *Democracy*, p. 279.

23 But see the argument of Alexander Wendt, "Why a World State is Inevitable," *European Journal of International Relations*, 9 (2003), pp. 491–542.

24 David Held, Anthony McGrew, David Goldblatt, and Jonathan Perraton, *Global Transformations* (Cambridge: Polity, 1999).

25 Mary Kaldor, *Global Civil Society: An Answer to War* (Cambridge: Polity, 2003), p. 78.

26 Marlies Glasius, "Expertise in the Cause of Justice: Global Civil Society Influence on the Statute for an International Criminal Court," in Marlies Glasius, Mary Kaldor, and Helmut Anheier, eds, *Global Civil Society 2002* (Oxford: Oxford University Press, 2002), pp. 137–68.

27 See the contributions in Daniele Archibugi, ed., *Debating Cosmopolitics* (London: Verso, 2003).

28 Waltz, "Emerging Structure of International Politics."

29 Christoph Görg and Joachim Hirsch, "Is International Democracy Possible?" *Review of International Political Economy*, 5 (1998), pp. 585–615.

30 See for instance Robert A. Dahl, "Can International Organizations Be Democratic? A Skeptic's View," and Will Kymlicka, "Citizenship in an Era of Globalization: Commentary on Held," both in I. Shapiro and C. Hacker-Cordon, eds, *Democracy's Edges* (Cambridge: Cambridge University Press, 1999), pp. 19–36 and 112–26 respectively; Robert O. Keohane, "Global Governance and Democratic Accountability," in David Held and Mathias Koenig-Archibugi, eds, *Taming Globalization: Frontiers of Governance* (Cambridge: Polity, 2003), 130–59.

31 Albert Alesina and Enrico Spolaore, *On the Size of Nations* (Cambridge, MA: MIT Press, 2003).

1

Empire? The Bush Doctrine and the Lessons of History

Michael Cox

"Empire – Sure! Why Not?"[1]

It is either the privilege of the influential, or their enormous egos, that allows them to reflect more frequently than most on the condition of their existence; and certainly long before the 2004 presidential election turned the United States into an even more self-obsessed nation than it had been before, three large questions had animated intellectual debate about that perennially fascinating topic: American power.

The first, given academic definition by an English import,[2] and stimulated by what seemed at the time to be serious problems facing the Reagan administration, asked whether or not the United States could even be compared to other major powers; and, assuming that it could, whether, then, it was likely to decline in (more or less) the same fashion as all other powerful states in the past? The answer provided by many writers – though by no means all – was that the US, though still in possession of several unique assets, had reached the limit of its influence. Challenged on the one hand by what Paul Kennedy famously termed "imperial overstretch," and on the other by dynamic economic change that was rapidly undermining the nation's capacity to compete in world markets, the United States was entering dangerous times – and unless it took some critical decisions, and took them soon, it would face the direst of consequences. Difficult days lay ahead. The era of Pax Americana, at last, was over.[3]

The collapse of the communist project, followed in quick succession by a stunning American victory in the first Gulf War, the implosion of the USSR, and the quite unexpected failure of Japan and Europe to realize their potential in the 1990s, not only undercut the intellectual case for decline, it compelled critics to face, and ask, an even more revisionist kind of question: namely, that if the United States was not in fact going the way of all other great imperiums, then should we not accept that there was something very special about the American system of power; and that much as one might have resisted the idea before, should we not concede, reluctantly perhaps, that the United States was, in effect, the exception to the golden rule of great power decline and would continue for the indefinite future to write the rules of the global game from an unrivaled position of self-evident strength?[4] The answer provided was a clear and emphatic "Yes" that spelt academic doom for those who had once foreseen a dire future for America. As one of the new triumphalists noted in a tough attack on the pessimists of old, those who had earlier anticipated (and looked forward to) US decline had been proved completely wrong. The country had recovered its nerve, proved its economic mettle, and entered the new millennium in fine shape. The "American Century" was here to stay.[5]

The third moment in this great debate came with the election of George W. Bush, followed by September 11 and the brilliantly successful ground and air wars conducted against the Taliban regime in Afghanistan and Saddam in Iraq. Now the question of American power was posed more sharply still by those who later went on to provide theoretical justification for the so-called Bush doctrine.[6] In an era of unchallenged US military supremacy they argued, where the United States effectively spent more on security than the rest of the world put together, in an international system where its reach was becoming more extensive than ever, why not accept that America was either becoming, or in fact had already become, something more than just another great power: that is, an Empire? Admittedly, it was an Empire with a democratic imperative; and its actions were more governed by good intentions than bad ones. But that did not make it any the less of an imperial power with all the essential features of an Empire, including the capacity to set the larger rules of the game.[7] Thus why not take the extra step and admit what was self-evident to most outsiders, if not to all Americans? Indeed, what else was one supposed to call the United States? As one of the more celebrated (non-American) theorists of the modern era was to remark – in some frustration – what word other than Empire better described this extensive system that was the American international order with its host of dependent allies, its vast intelligence networks, its five global military commands, its more than 1 million men- and women-at-arms on five continents, its carrier battle groups on watch in every ocean, and its 30 percent control of the world's economic product? None at least that he could think of.[8]

The "imperial turn" in the age of Bush was by any stretch of the imagination a most extraordinary phenomenon, particularly in a country where, as Williams pointed out many years ago, "one of the central themes of American historiography" was that there was "no American Empire,"[9] and woe betide the writer who suggested otherwise. As another American academic remarked in 2002, "a decade ago, certainly two," the very idea of Empire would have caused "righteous indignation" amongst most US observers. But not any longer it would seem.[10] As Ronald Wright has noted, "how recently we believed the age of empire was dead," but how popular the idea had now become in an era of international terrorism.[11] But something interesting, and strange, was to happen along the way. For whereas in the 1960s the term was the monopoly of the left,[12] by the turn of the century, it had become all the rage on the neoconservative right; and what many of them appeared to be suggesting was quite startling: in effect, that under conditions of international anarchy, where order remained the prime concern, the United States had to learn the most important and self-evident lesson of history – if there was to be any form of order at all, it had to act in the same imperial fashion as the

British and Romans had done in the past. In fact, it was precisely because the United States had been insufficiently assertive in the 1990s that 9/11 happened in the first place.[13] Such inertia was no longer an option. In a fragmenting postmodern world, where small bands of fanatics could cause havoc and mayhem, there was only one possible solution. Politicians might want to call it something else; and no doubt President Bush would repeat the old mantra that "America" had no "Empire to extend."[14] But that is precisely what the United States would have to do. Other existing methods had been tried and found wanting. Now, in a new era, where old forms of deterrence and traditional assumptions about threats no longer held, it was up to America to impose its own form of "peace" on a disorderly world: to fight the savage war of peace (to quote one of the new gurus) so as to protect and enlarge the empire of liberty.[15]

Of course, the new imperialists were careful to make some important distinctions. The American Empire they conceded had its own very distinct, American characteristics. As others were to point out, there was something distinctly "virtual," "funny," almost "incoherent" about this particular Empire.[16] But this was no reason not to use the term at all. It was – according to the new cohort – more suggestive than the obvious intellectual competitors in the form of "superpower" and "hegemon"; it certainly forced people to think more historically about the nature of American power; and it compelled people to act. And in these new, more disturbed times, this was absolutely vital. As one of the new theorists of Empire put it, American policymakers could do a lot worse than turn to the chroniclers of the Greek, Roman, and British empires "for helpful hints about how to run American foreign policy."[17] And what such wise men taught was simple and blunt: that the only way for an imperial power to remain great was by acting assertively and ruthlessly. Such a policy had worked for others in the past, and there was no reason it should not work for America now. "The logic of neo-imperialism" was, in the last analysis, simply "too compelling to resist."[18]

Naturally, not everybody agreed. Most American academics in fact – liberals and realists alike – remained decidedly cool about the idea that one could achieve security through expansion.[19] Furthermore, these voices were to grow louder as the easy war in Iraq gave way to a deeply uneasy peace. Yet as another writer remarked, "whether or not the United States" now viewed itself "as an empire," an increasingly large number of people (including "many foreigners") had arrived at the not illogical conclusion that if it looked, talked, and walked like an Empire, then that is most decidedly what it was.[20] The modern imperialists could not have agreed more. Indeed, they were not only convinced of the correctness of their own cause, but were keen to convince others too; and they were in a position to do so. One for example was, or at least had been, an influential writer on the *Wall Street Journal*;[21] another was a popular pundit with a well-established reputation for capturing the American mood;[22] a third had already made his name in the earlier neoconservative intervention on multiculturalism;[23] and a fourth was a regular columnist for the *Washington Post*, who like many of his peers probably felt he was only expressing in public what many in the White House had been talking about in private.[24] Some of the talk was not even that confidential, as the famous 2002 National Security Strategy document revealed only too graphically.[25] One thing was clear, though. In the shadow of 9/11 many new ideas were circulating within the foreign policy community, but the most radical, by far, was that in an age of "unparalleled global dominance" the United States had every right to arrogate to itself the international role of setting standards, determining threats, using force, and meting out justice.[26] Call it unilateralism; call it the necessary response to new threats: it was imperialism by any other name. The idea that had "dared not speak its name" for at least a generation had been thrust back on to the agenda.[27]

In what follows I want to reflect on the theory and practice of the "new" American Empire – the Bush Doctrine by any other name – by dealing in an abbreviated and I hope provocative fashion with three very specific issues: the sources of the new debate about Empire, the more general applicability of the term, and the obvious limits of the American Empire as a real world phenomenon. I make a number of claims.

The first is that Empire is not really new at all in US grand narratives; in fact one can trace the debate back to the very foundations of the American republic. Furthermore, while the more modern version of the discussion only really began in earnest after 9/11, one can detect powerful rumblings on the conservative right long before the attack itself. To this extent September 11 is probably better understood as a catalytic converter for a debate that was already under way, rather than the direct cause of the debate itself. This in turn leads to a second issue: about the appropriateness of the term itself. It is evident that the idea of Empire as applied to the United States can be questioned on several grounds.[28] But as the new conservatives have pointed out, the concept (ambiguous warts and all) does have its uses as a comparative tool of analysis, one which has not been fully exploited in the past, partly for methodological reasons – the term after all is open to different meanings – but largely because it has for so long been associated with a radical critique of American foreign policy.[29] This has been particularly unfortunate and has made it virtually impossible for other commentators to employ the concept at all.[30] My argument here is that it is now time to rescue the idea and put it back where it belongs, at the centre of the discussion of what in fact has become the most extensive international system in history.

Finally, I want to explore the future of the American Empire. Here I argue that this may be less problematic than has been implied by a number of writers (most forcefully by Michael Mann in this volume) but more serious than has been suggested by the new triumphalists – including the modern neoconservative imperialists – who, as we have seen, have been predicting an extraordinarily bright time ahead for the United States. It may well be the case that the twenty-first century will turn out to be just as American as the twentieth.[31] But this does not mean it will be roses all the way. The American Empire retains many obvious assets and for the foreseeable future will play the central role at the heart of the world order.[32] However, it confronts some very serious challenges – some increasingly of its own making – and it might find these very difficult to resolve in the turbulent years that undoubtedly lie ahead.[33]

Empire of Liberty[34]

It is an empire without a consciousness of itself as such, constantly shocked that its good intentions arouse resentment abroad. But that does not make it any the less of an empire, with a conviction that it alone, in Herman Melville's words, bears "the ark of liberties of the world."[35]

The concept of Empire in the United States was of course first employed by the Founding Fathers to describe a political mission linked to a geographical aspiration in which liberty and continental expansion were intimately connected. In effect one could not exist without the other. Thus the conquest of America required a people yearning to be free, while freedom, as Frederick Jackson Turner later noted in one of the more important essays ever written on American history, demanded an ever expanding frontier.[36] This influential, and very American notion combined in turn with another equally powerful set of ideas about American exceptionalism, a condition which described the obvious fact (at least obvious to most Americans) that the United States was both distinctive and superior to all other nations. This not only rendered it immune to criticism from abroad – always useful for a nation with global ambitions; it also meant it had the God-given duty to spread the dream and promise of America beyond its own shores. Indeed, as many Americans readily admitted, if the American way was good enough for the United States then it was certainly good enough for the rest of the world.[37] But in no way should this be confused with imperialism of the more traditional kind. After all, even though the US might have used force outside of its borders on no less than 101 occasions between 1801 and 1904, its mission – at least in its own mind – was not to conquer other peoples but to liberate them from despotism, in much the same way as it had liberated itself from British rule in the late eighteenth century. In this fashion, the US managed to carve out a special position for itself in the long history of aspiring world powers. Not for America the ideological embarrassment of trying to defend the institution of colonialism, or the costs involved in occupying other countries, but the more noble purpose of bringing a better way of life to others less fortunate than itself.

Naturally, such an outlook inevitably infused US foreign policy with a particularly moralistic and idealistic tone, much to the great chagrin of later realist critics like Morgenthau and Kennan. But it also permitted it the rare privilege of pursuing policies designed to advance its own interests while all the time believing, or at least claiming, that it was doing so for the benefit of mankind. J. R. Seeley once wrote that the British acquired an Empire in a fit of absentmindedness. When the United States acquired one of its own it would be in a state of "deep denial."[38]

The rise of the United States as a world power by 1898, and its more complete emergence as a superpower in two stages at the end of World War I and then World War II, is one of the great American stories with its assortment of European deadbeats, perfidious but heroic Brits, internationalist paragons, and isolationist villains, all playing their various walk-on parts in a play of epic proportions that in the end left only one serious actor standing on the stage of history. Yet to read many of the less reflective tales told about this spectacular but deeply uneven process, one could easily come away thinking the United States never really wanted to become a major international player in the first place. It was, to use that most useful of phrases, a most "reluctant superpower," one that feared "entangling alliances" which was only enticed out of its natural state of self-imposed isolationism by the threat posed by others. It is all very comforting. But brute facts still remain brute facts – as Chris Brown has rather nicely put it – and the fact of the matter is that by 1945 this most innocent of countries, with apparently little liking for the idea of power, and even less for running the world, happened to be in charge of most of the world's economic resources, the majority of its military capabilities and a network of bases stretching across two oceans and four continents. No doubt it was helped in this endeavor by the foibles of others; moreover, there were many Americans who actively strove to keep the United States at home. Nonetheless, when the guns fell silent, this retiring wallflower with apparently few ambitions of its own, found itself in a position of influence unparalleled in history. Little wonder that Washington now came to be known by some as the new Rome, and its Chief Executive spoken of more often than not as the "Imperial" President.[39]

Nor did the Cold War do much to halt America's upward mobility. If anything, this often dangerous and costly conflict afforded the United States many important opportunities; and in this, ironically, it was much helped by the activities of its chief rival, the Soviet Union. The Soviet threat was real enough. That much is obvious from any reading of the new primary sources.[40] Yet the USSR's often brutal and sometimes ill-judged actions not only did little to weaken the West but in many vital respects helped shape and define it.[41] As Truman readily conceded, Stalin was in his own way as much a Western asset as he was an American enemy. Indeed, Soviet actions not only helped US leaders mobilize America's vastly superior capabilities against what turned out to be a most incomplete superpower rival, but over time provided them with almost the most perfect of all imperial ideologies. For if the Soviet Union was a menace to the whole of the free world – as Cold Warriors claimed – then this demanded nothing less than a global response. Moreover, if the menace took several forms, then the US would have to develop the capabilities and policies needed to counter this, from building extensive international alliances and extending military aid to the far corners of the globe, to reconstructing the global economy and taking the lead role in those various multilateral institutions that would ensure its healthy development. In these various overlapping ways, the United States managed to extend its reach to every part of the free world. Of course, Pax Americana did not manage to penetrate everywhere. Nor did its economic position go unchallenged. In fact, for most of the 1970s and 1980s, many pundits assumed it was rapidly falling behind its more competitive allies in Europe and Japan.[42] No matter. By the time the edifice of the Cold War came tumbling down, the United States – and the United States alone – still possessed what others lacked: a series of embedded assets that gave it true global reach.[43]

It is at this precise point in time that we can begin to trace the sources of what is now referred to as the "new" American Empire. It is an act in two parts. Part one, of course, was played out in the 1990s, a period according to the conventional wisdom that was marked by drift, indecision, and a lack of grand strategy; but as we have already shown, this was a really quite innovative decade that saw the United States experiencing an enormous economic boost at home accompanied by increased freedom to act abroad.[44] Yet in spite of this, there were some who still felt the US could do much better – or more precisely, could do far more to exploit all its various assets and turn them to American advantage.[45] Reaganite by background, hegemonist by inclination, and keenly aware that there existed a growing gap between US military capabilities and America's ever-expanding global role, the new ideologues on the right were determined to remove all the constraints that they felt had been imposed on the last remaining superpower by the "international community" in the post–Cold War period.[46] Primacy was the name of the game and a new American century the prize.[47] However, the former would mean nothing and the latter remain a pipe dream without a much greater projection of US hard power. As Charles Krauthammer put it, "after a decade of Prometheus playing pygmy" the United States now had to act.[48]

Some even drew lessons from the late nineteenth century to make their case for them. By the end of the 1880s the US, they argued, was economically powerful but internationally irrelevant. Something therefore had to be done, and in the end it was, first by more resolute state intervention and then by some very determined presidential leadership. The lesson was clear: decisive political action was essential again if the United States wanted to realize its full potential. This in the end is why Clinton was such a disaster. He may have talked about US leadership. But at heart he was a born-again multilateralist who was prepared to stake all on the ability of international institutions to achieve world order. This was a road to nowhere. Indeed, in the neoconservative vision of an America unchained, even such bodies as NATO could no longer be regarded as being unambiguously useful assets. There was also the difficult problem of Europe. Since it was unwilling and incapable of building a serious military capacity of its own, America – it was argued by the new right – had for too long been far too sensitive to the continent's needs. Not any more. In a world where the key threats to global security emanated from outside of Europe, and in which the Europeans were more often than not likely to get things wrong than right (note here their collective failure in Bosnia), there was no need to buy into the shibboleth known as the transatlantic security community. And to be blunt, there were very good reasons for not doing so given the European inclination to resolve problems in just the sort of ways – through recourse to international law and global regulation – that were bound to tie the American Gulliver down.[49]

Long before 9/11 therefore the intellectual ground was already shifting on the right. However, it took the quite unexpected election of a particular kind of President, followed by the even more unexpected tragedy of September 2001, for the balance of argument to shift decisively towards those who had for some time been arguing for a more determined policy. Naturally, forging what amounted to a neo-imperial foreign policy for a post-communist world would be no easy task.[50] And as we now know, during its first few months in office, the Bush team ran into a barrage of international opposition to its policies.[51] This is why 9/11 was so important, not because it reduced criticism from abroad (though for a brief moment it did) but because it created an acute sense of crisis which made previously controversial policies now seem far more acceptable at home. If nothing else 9/11 certainly proved in the most dramatic fashion possible that the world was still a very dangerous place, and that unless decisive action was taken things could easily get much worse. Indeed, the so-called "war against terror" – which soon metamorphosed into something much wider – provided the neoconservatives, as they readily conceded, with an opportunity of unparalleled importance. For if, as it was now claimed, America was threatened by a transnational and undeterrable enemy with hidden cells here and shadowy allies there who were prepared to use weapons of mass destruction to achieve their theological ends, then Washington quite literally had no alternative but to intervene robustly and ruthlessly abroad. The fact that this might cause resentment in other countries was unfortunate. But this was of much less concern to certain Americans than achieving results. Ultimately, the new right took a quite philosophical view of all this foreign noise. In the end, they reasoned, what would shape international attitudes would not be weasel words but decisive action backed up by overwhelming military power. Situations of strength not diplomatic niceties would determine how friends and enemies responded to the new Bush Doctrine.[52]

To Empire or not Empire?

Over the last two millennia the word "empire" has meant many different things to different people from different countries at different times.[53]

9/11 therefore not only marked a significant watershed in its own right, but was successfully used by those who had earlier "spotted" what one British admirer of American neoconservatism referred to later as "an historic opportunity" to exploit the possibilities already present in a post–Cold War world.[54] This does not mean the attack was of little importance or that the Bush team did not view the threat of terrorism as being real. Nor is it meant to imply that every member of the Bush administration was now won over to the idea of Empire. What it does point to however is a connection – between a very real trauma on the one hand and a larger game plan on the other. Nor should this kind of opportunism come as a great surprise to those who know their diplomatic history. Indeed, there has been a very long American tradition of genuine crises being tapped to serve a wider foreign policy purpose. The Cold War was full of them. The very real Czech coup of 1948 for example helped "sell" Marshall aid to a reluctant Congress, the Berlin blockade then convinced them of the necessity of NATO, Korea persuaded a skeptical Truman of the virtues of NSC-68, and nearly thirty years later the Soviet invasion of Afghanistan and martial law in Poland helped justify the Reagan military buildup. It is certainly not the first time in the history of American grand strategy when significant events outside of anybody's control have been used to great effect by those with a preexisting set of policy preferences. And, no doubt, it will not be the last.

But even if we accept this, and even agree with the judgement that the real issue now is "not whether the United States has become an imperial power" but "what sort of empire" (the citizenry of America) "intends theirs to be,"[55] this still does not answer the question as to whether or not we should really be employing the term Empire at all. It might capture the current mood. It might even have much to recommend it as a metaphor. But none of this addresses the important issue of appropriateness: and there are some very serious intellectual objections to the idea. One concerns the very obvious fact that the United States controls very little territory itself, another is that if America were an Empire then why has it championed the principle of self-determination, and a third is that if it had the kind of power some now claim it does, then why does it sometimes appear to have less influence over world affairs than one would imagine? A number of critics would also argue that it makes little sense to talk of an American Empire under what Anthony Giddens has termed modern "runaway" conditions; and if it did, then how do we account for the fact that the United States not only seems unable to control financial markets but cannot even "extend democracy to other regions, to impose its own system on the rest of the world"?[56] These are all fair questions, and cannot be dismissed as some of the more conspiratorially-minded might like to, by accusing those who advance them of supping with the devil.

Let us deal firstly with the issue of territory. It is obviously the case that most Empires in the past, from the Greek to the Spanish, the Ottoman to the Russian, have been defined as such because they brought vast swathes of land belonging to other people under their control. It is equally true that the United States in the main has not practiced such forms of annexation beyond its current boundaries. And to some therefore this is proof that the United States is not an Empire in any meaningful sense of that word. This is a fair point even though it might be considered a rather narrow definitional base upon which to discuss and compare all Empires. But even if we were prepared to – just for the moment – this still ignores one rather important historical fact: that America has indeed done more than its fair share of land grabbing. In fact, those who would claim that the United States is not an Empire because it has never acquired other people's territory seem to forget that the nation we now call the United States of America only became

the United States of America because it annexed a great deal
during the nineteenth century: from France and Russia (through
purchase), Spain and Mexico (by military conquest), from Britain
(by agreement), and, most savagely, from those 3 million Native
Americans who were nearly all eliminated in the process.
Admittedly, this tells us little about how it then used its massive
geographical power base in the global arena. Nor can we assume
that what it did in the process of conquering the American inte-
rior, it would do, or would want to do, to the rest of the world.
But it does at least hint at the possibility that ruthlessness and
ambition in the pursuit of power and the American experience
are not quite so alien to each other as some would have us
believe.[57]

Then there is the small matter of Latin and Central America.
Admittedly, neither was ever formally colonized by the US. But
should that preclude us from thinking of the US relationship with
its immediate South in imperial terms? Perhaps so, if you are an
American from the United States. But that is not the way most
Latin Americans look upon their own problematic connection
with their very large and extraordinarily powerful neighbor to the
North. Nor to be blunt do many North Americans. As even the
more uncritical of them would readily concede, the whole
purpose of the famous Monroe Doctrine was not to limit
American influence in the region but to embed it. Moreover, the
story thereafter is not one of US disengagement from the region
but of the latter's more complete integration into an American-
led system – one which presupposed a definite hierarchy of power,
was sometimes brutally exploitative in character, and was constructed around some fairly typical racial stereotypes of the
"other." More than that. It was built on the good old-fashioned
ideology – much beloved by European colonials – which assumed
that certain areas should, of right, fall within the sphere of influence of one of the great powers. In fact, it was precisely because
the Americans thought in such terms that policymakers in
Washington (even more liberal ones) rarely felt any compunction
in intervening in the region whenever and wherever they saw fit.
If this was not imperialism by any other name, then it is difficult
to think what might be.[58]

However, there still remains the more general question about territory and the degree to which America's overall lack of territorial ambition means we should either not use the term or only do so in the most qualified fashion possible. There is no unambiguously straightforward answer. In the end it very much depends on whether or not territory, and territory alone, constitutes the basis of Empire. Many would insist that it does. Dominic Lieven, for example, has argued that "there has to be some sort of direct rule over the dominion for a power to be classified as an empire."[59] Others however would point to the complex forms which all Empires have taken through time; indeed, a study of the most developed would indicate that they have invariably combined different forms of rule, none more successfully than America's presumed predecessor, Great Britain. As the famous Gallagher and Robinson team showed in their justly celebrated work, British imperialism entertained both formal annexation and informal domination, direct political rule and indirect economic control. The real issue for the British therefore was not the means they employed to secure the outcomes they wanted, but the outcomes themselves.[60] Thus if one could create a system overall that guaranteed the right results – which for Britain meant a stable international space within which its goods could find a market and its capital a profitable home – then that was perfectly fine. And what was fine for the British, it could be argued, has been equally fine for the Americans. In fact, not only did they adopt a similar set of criteria after 1945 by which to measure success; many of its more able leaders like Dean Acheson were great admirers of the British Empire. The British, he felt, had done a very good job in the nineteenth century defending the world trade system by pumping their surplus capital into other countries; and there was no reason why the United States with it vast wealth and enormous power after World War II should not do the same. In many ways, it had no real alternative in his view. For as he argued at the time, global order presupposed power, power resided with states, and it was up to the strongest state – the hegemon to use the jargon – to pay the bills and enforce the rules of the game. And if it did not do so (as it had failed to do in the interwar period) then the international system was doomed.[61]

Of course, nobody would be so foolish as to suggest that the United States achieved total control of the whole world as a result. Nor did it always get its own way, even with the most dependent of its allies.[62] Nonetheless, it still achieved a very great deal and did so in a quite conscious fashion. Indeed, in a relatively short space of time, following what amounted to a 30-year crisis, it managed to construct the basis for a new international order within which others – old enemies and traditional rivals alike – could successfully operate. But not only did they manage to operate; the international economy as a whole flourished, to such an extent that between 1947 and 2000 there was a 20-fold increase in the volume of world trade and a 700 percent rise in gross world product. And the US achieved all this under the most testing of political conditions with all sorts of ideological "barbarians" constantly trying to pull down what it was attempting to build.[63] So successful was it in fact that, after several years of costly standoff, it even began to push its various rivals back – initially in the contested and unstable Third World, then in Eastern Europe, and finally in the enemy's heartland itself. Not for it therefore the Roman fate of being overrun by the Mongol hordes or the British experience of lowering the flag in one costly dependency after another. On the contrary, by the beginning of the 1990s, the American Empire faced neither disintegration nor imperial overstretch, but found itself gazing forth upon a more open, seemingly less dangerous world in which nearly all the main actors (with the exception of a few rogue states) were now prepared to accept its terms and come under its umbrella. Clearly, there was to be no "fall" for this particular Empire.[64]

But this still leaves open the problem of how we can legitimately talk of an American Empire when one of the United States' primary objectives in the twentieth century has involved support for the right of self-determination. The objection is a perfectly reasonable one and obviously points to a very different kind of Empire from those which have existed in the past. But there is a legitimate answer to this particular question – that if and when the US did support the creation of new nations in the twentieth century, it did not do so out of pure idealism but because it realistically calculated that the breakup of other Empires was likely to decrease the power of rivals while increasing its own weight in a reformed world system. As the great American historian William Appleman Williams noted many years ago, when and where the US has combated colonialism – both traditional and communist – it has done so for the highest possible motive. But the fact remains that it only acted in this fashion (and then not always consistently) in the full knowledge that it would win a host of new and potentially dependent allies as a result.[65] Imperialism, as others have pointed out, can sometimes wear a grimace and sometimes a smile; and in the American case nothing was more likely to bring a smile to its face than the thought that while it was winning friends amongst the new states, it was doing so at the expense firstly of its European rivals (which is why so many of Europe's leaders disliked Wilson and feared FDR) and then, after 1989, of the USSR.[66]

This brings us then to the issue of influence and the capacity of the United States to fashion outcomes to its own liking under contemporary conditions. The problem revolves as much around our understanding of what empires have managed to do in the past, as it does about what we mean by influence now. Let us deal with both issues briefly – beginning with the first question about influence.

As any historian of previous Empires knows, no Empire worth the name has ever been able to determine all outcomes at all times within its own imperium. All Empires in other words have had their limits. Even the Roman Empire, to take the most cited example, was based on the recognition that there were certain things it could and could not do, including, by the way, pushing the outer boundaries of its rule too far.[67] Britain too was well aware that if it wanted to maintain influence it had to make concessions here and compromises there in order not to provoke what some analysts would now refer to as "blowback."[68] How otherwise could it have run India for the better part of 200 years with only 50,000 soldiers and an army of administrators? Much the same could be said about the way in which the United States has generally preferred to rule its Empire. Thus like the British Empire it has not always imposed its own form of government on other countries; it has often tolerated a good deal of acceptable dissent;

and it has been careful, though not always, not to undermine the
authority of friendly local elites. In fact, the more formally independent they were, the more legitimate its own hegemony was
perceived to be. There was only one thing the United States asked
in return: that those who were members of the club and wished
to benefit from membership had to abide by the club's rules and
behave like gentlemen. A little unruliness here and some disagreement there was fine; so long as it was within accepted
bounds. In fact, the argument could be made – and has been –
that the United States was at its most influential abroad not when
it shouted loudest or tried to impose its will on others, but when
it permitted others a good deal of slack. It has been more secure
still when it has been invited in by those whose fate ultimately
lay in its hands. Indeed, in much the same way as the wiser Roman
governors and the more successful of the British viceroys conceded when concessions were necessary, so too have the great
American Empire builders of the postwar era. Far easier, they reasoned, to cut bargains and do deals with those over whom they
ultimately had huge leverage rather than upset local sensitivities.
It was only when the locals transgressed, as they did on occasion
by acting badly abroad or outside the bounds of acceptable behavior at home, that the US put its foot down firmly to show who
was really in charge.[69]

Yet the skeptics still make a good point. Under modern conditions, it is extraordinarily difficult for any single state to exercise
preponderant influence at all times, a point made with great force
in both a recent radical attempt to theorize the notion of Empire[70]
and a liberal effort to rubbish it.[71] The argument is well made. In
fact it is obvious: under conditions of globalization where money
moves with extraordinary speed in an apparently borderless
world, it is very difficult indeed for any state – even one as powerful as the United States – to exercise complete control over all
international relations. There is also the question of its own economic capabilities. The United States might have a huge military
capacity. However, in the purely material realm it is far less powerful than it was say 20 years ago – before Europe and China
became more serious economic actors – or immediately after the
war when it controlled 70 percent of the world's financial

resources. All this much is self-evident and any honest analysis of the "new" American Empire would have to take this on board. But one should not push the point too far. After all, the US economy continues to account for nearly 30 percent of world product, it is roughly 40 percent bigger than any of its nearest rivals, the dollar still remains mighty, and Wall Street is still located at the heart of the international financial system. Furthermore, as the better literature on modern globalization shows, the world economic system is not completely out of control; governments still have a key role to play; and the enormous resources at the American government's disposal not only give it a very large role in shaping the material environment within which we all happen to live, but also provide it with huge influence within those bodies whose function it is to manage the world economy. America's control of these might not be complete, and the outcomes might not always be to its liking. But they get their way more often than not. As one insider rather bluntly put it, "IMF programmes are typically dictated from Washington."[72] Furthermore, as Robert Wade has convincingly shown, by mere virtue of its ability to regulate the sources and supply routes of the vital energy and raw material needs of even its most successful economic competitors, the US quite literally holds the fate of the world in its hands. This in the end is why the war in Iraq will prove to be so important, not just because it will allow the world to enjoy lower oil prices – though it should – but because it will prove once again that the United States alone has the ability to determine the fate of the region, and by so doing reinforce its central role in the wider world system.[73]

Finally, any assessment as to whether or not the United States is, or is not an Empire, has to address the problem of perception, or more concretely of how US leaders view America's role and how the world in turn looks upon the United States. It is difficult to make easy generalizations. Nonetheless, it would not be a million miles away from the truth to suggest that most members of the Washington foreign policy elite do tend to see themselves as masters of a larger universe in which the United States has a very special part to play by virtue of its unique history, its huge capabilities, and its accumulated experience of running the world for the last 50 years. At times they may tire of performing this onerous task. Occasionally they falter. However, if it was ever suggested that they give up that role, they would no doubt throw up their hands in horror. Being number one does have its advantages after all. It also generates its own kind of imperial outlook in which other states are invariably regarded as problems to be managed, while the United States is perceived as having an indispensable role to perform, one of such vital importance that there is no reason why it should always be subject to the same rules of the international game as everybody else. This is why the United States, like all great imperial powers in the past, is frequently accused of being "unilateral." The charge might be just, but basically it is irrelevant. Indeed, as Americans frequently argue (in much the same way as the British and the Romans might have argued before them), the responsibilities of leadership and the reality of power mean that the strong have to do what they must – even if this is sometimes deemed to be unfair – while the weak are compelled to accept their fate. So it was in the past; so it has been, and will continue to be, with the United States.

But how then do others look upon the United States? With a good deal of loathing in some quarters to be sure; and rather jealously in others no doubt. But this is by no means the whole story. For while many may resent the metropolitan center, most are conscious of the fact that the benefits of living under the American imperium normally outweigh any of the disadvantages. In fact, this is one of the reasons why the American Empire has been so successful. After all, given the choice of living within its compass or trying to survive outside it, most nations – and most people – have invariably chosen the former over the latter. If nothing else life is likely to be safer and conditions more prosperous. As one of the more surreal examinations of one former Empire illustrated only too graphically, even the more discontented are well aware that life under imperial rule may not be quite so bad as some would have us think. Recall the famous scene in *Life of Brian*. The anti-imperialist leader, trying to stir up revolt, asks his rather small band of followers the following: "Tell me then, what has the Roman Empire ever done for you?" No doubt he later wished he had not asked the question in the first place, for the reply was simple and arrestingly honest, "Well, actually, quite a lot in fact" – from building straight roads to keeping the Huns and the Visigoths at bay, to constructing a decent sewage system through to maintaining law and order. This surely is the issue. Many Empires, including the American, have not always been benign; and they have not always been sensitive. However, the more successful including the American have lasted not just because they were feared, but because they performed a series of broader political and economic functions that no other state or combination of states was willing or able to undertake. Indeed, one suspects that the US still has a very long way to go. For whereas other more formal Empires in the past failed in the end because they could not withstand progressive change, the United States will go on and on – or so some feel – precisely because it embraces and celebrates change. Not for it therefore the ignominy of being outflanked by history but the very real chance of being in its vanguard. If the optimists are to be believed, the sun may never set on this modern Empire.[74]

The Limits of Empire

Not since Rome has one nation loomed so large above the others.[75]

The American era appears to be alive and well. That encapsulates the conventional wisdom – and it is woefully off the mark.[76]

This essay began with a reflection on the ongoing debate about American power and went on to do three things: one, explain how and why so many influential figures on the right today are prepared to make the case for a new American Empire; two, suggest that there may in fact be nothing particularly new about the idea of Empire in the United States; and finally try to argue that in spite of its possible imperfections as a concept, the notion of Empire has a good deal to recommend it. Nowhere of course have I tried to insist that the idea is without its flaws. Nor have I attempted to understate the differences between America as a democratic Empire with very special features and other kinds of Empire. What I have tried to suggest, though, is that by employing the term in a creative rather than dogmatic fashion, it does at least make it possible for us to make useful – and not necessarily misleading – comparisons between the United States and other "great powers" in history. To this extent I very strongly disagree with those who would argue that the term does not enrich our understanding of the United States.[77] Indeed, it is only by making such comparisons that we are able to challenge one of the more restrictive and stultifying concepts that has made intelligent discussion of America so difficult in the past: namely the notion that it is so exceptional that it is impossible to compare it with anything at all. If nothing else, the idea of Empire drags the United States back into the historical mainstream where it should be, and hopefully will remain.

Recognizing the utility of the idea of Empire however is one thing; speculating about the future of Empires is quite a different matter, especially in the American case where so much of this in the past appears to have been so wide of the mark with its predictions of its imminent decline. But it is still something we need to do – most obviously because many writers now appear to think that the new century is likely to be just as "American" as the old one. It may well be the case, as the *Economist* put it, that "the United States" now "bestrides the globe like a colossus."[78] We might even concede that "American hegemony is here to stay."[79] But that does not mean the hegemon is without its limits.

The first limit has to do with the character of American power itself. Nearly everybody agrees that the United States has an enormous amount of the hard stuff; and no doubt most Americans think this is just fine and dandy. Yet if history teaches us anything – and if the events since 9/11 teach us anything at all – it is that those who possess vast power are just as likely to be resented as feared; and if recent polls are to be believed, then over the last two years there has never been quite so much resentment of the United States as there is today. This began to manifest itself in various forms before 9/11, but it took off with a vengeance as the US prepared and then went to war with Iraq. As one American commentator admitted, never had the country gone into battle (with the sole exception of Vietnam back in the 1960s) with so few allies actually prepared to back it enthusiastically.[80] In fact, never had such a war, even before it began, generated so much global opposition, the overwhelming bulk of it caused less by any sympathy that people might have had towards America's intended target, and more by what many regarded as the dangerously aggressive policies of an overpowerful state led by a President with little concern for global opinion.[81] As one friendly European critic remarked, rarely in history had one nation mobilized so much hard power in such a short space of time: and never had it lost so much soft power in the process.[82]

The first problem facing the United States therefore revolves around the issue of power and the extent to which its own imperial behavior is already beginning to generate various forms of resistance. This in turn raises a second question about the conditions under which the United States exercises its power. As Nye amongst others has pointed out, America may be the world's only superpower, but this does not necessarily mean it can always go it alone, and at the same time hope to maintain friendly or amicable relations with other countries. Coalitions are wonderful things, and coalitions of the very willing even better. But when coalitions are compelled into being by fear rather than consent, then something is not quite right. Of course, the new hegemonists in Washington take a typically hard-nosed view of all this. As they point out, the US still managed to build an alliance of sorts against Iraq; former critics meanwhile are now running for cover; so why all the fuss? The answer should be obvious: because the more secure Empires in history have been those that could lead rather than coerce, inspire affection rather than suspicion. And while the United States might still have more than its fair share of friends around the world, it is currently testing their loyalty to the utmost.[83]

A third challenge concerns the United States itself. Views about the last remaining superpower have always been deeply divided and will almost certainly remain so. Nonetheless, for most of the post–Cold War period when the nation was at peace with itself, and liberals of both a Republican and Democratic persuasion were defining the political agenda, international attitudes towards the

United States – with some obvious exceptions – tended to be positive. This however has changed since September 11, and has done so in large part not just because of what America has been doing abroad, but because of what has been happening on the home front. Indeed, in the process of securing the nation against further terrorist attacks, America appears to have become a decidedly less open and welcoming society. One should not exaggerate. To talk of a new "empire of fear," as some on the left have already done, might be going too far. However, there are some deeply worrying signs, and if the American state becomes ever more intrusive, and many of its people less and less tolerant, in a world that seems to be more and more threatening, then in the years ahead the great shining city on the hill is going to look anything but – especially in those European countries where anti-Americanism is already on the rise.[84]

This in turn raises a question about the domestic sources of the "new" American Empire and the policies currently being pursued by the Bush administration. Thus far the Bush team have been brilliantly successful in maintaining a high level of support for its current strategy of assertion – it may even win the 2004 election. However, there is no guaranteeing Bush's support will last forever. A series of setbacks abroad (most obviously in Iraq), another attack on the United States itself, or the feeling that all this is costing far too much treasure and aggravation abroad, could easily see the mood swing back in either a more isolationist or even a less unilateral direction. Significantly, according to another survey, the American people even now seem to have little stomach for going it alone, and this could have consequences over the longer term for the conduct of US foreign policy, especially if the policy fails to tackle the original reasons for going imperial in the first place – namely the threat of international terrorism.[85]

Finally, the success of Empires in general, and, it could be argued, of the American Empire in particular, has in the end rested on its ability to deliver a bundle of public goods in the form of improved living standards, economic opportunity, and growth worldwide. This in large part brought it victory in the Cold War and self-confidence for most of the 1990s. However, as recent economic events have revealed only too graphically, none of this can any longer be taken for granted. Naturally, we should beware crying wolf.[86] The US capitalist system continues to have huge reserves and an even greater capacity for regenerating itself. Yet the warning signs are there; and to make matters worse, Europe is beginning to show clear signs of challenging the United States.[87] This will not necessarily undermine America's position of material (let alone strategic) privilege within the wider international system; if anything, under conditions of crisis, its position is likely to be augmented rather than weakened simply because it has greater political capacity and market space. Nonetheless, the economic dominance it once enjoyed can no longer be taken for granted, especially in an age when it is becoming increasingly dependent on the financial largesse of others to manage its growing debt.[88] America and Americans live, in other words, in deeply troubling times where the old economic truths are coming under challenge. In some ways, the modern imperialists in Washington could not have thought of a more inauspicious time to start building their "new" American Empire.

Notes

1   Quoted in Christopher Hitchens, "Imperialism, Superpower Dominance, Malignant and Benign" (December 10, 2002), at http://slate.msn.com/id=2075261.
2   Paul Kennedy, *The Rise and Fall of the Great Powers: Economic Change and Military Conflict from 1500–2000* (London: Unwin Hyman, 1988).
3   See my "Whatever Happened to American Decline? International Relations and the New United States Hegemony," *New Political Economy*, 6, 3 (2001), pp. 311–40.
4   See, for example, G. J. Ikenberry, ed., *America Unrivaled: The Future of the Balance of Power* (Ithaca, NY, and London: Cornell University Press, 2002).
5   Bruce Cumings, "Still the American Century," in Michael Cox, Ken Booth, and Tim Dunne, eds, *The Interregnum: Controversies in World Politics, 1989–1999* (Cambridge: Cambridge University Press, 1999), pp. 271–99.
6   For a pre-Bush analysis of the dangers of Empire see the remarkably prescient Chalmers Johnson, *Blowback: The Costs and Conse-*

quences of American Empire (London: Little, Brown and Company, 2000).

7   Clyde Prestowitz, *Rogue Nation: American Unilateralism and the Failure of Good Intentions* (New York: Basic Books, 2003), pp. 19–50.

8   Michael Ignatieff, "Empire Lite," *Prospect*, 83 (February 2003), p. 36.

9   William Appleman Williams, "The Frontier Thesis and American Foreign Policy," *Pacific Historic Review*, 24 (November 1955), p. 379.

10 Charles S. Maier, "An American Empire," *Harvard Magazine*, 105, 2 (November–December 2002), pp. 28–31.

11 Ronald Wright, "For a Wild Surmise," *Times Literary Supplement* (December 20, 2002), p. 3.

12 See Alex Callinicos, "The Grand Strategy of the American Empire," *International Socialism*, 97 (Winter 2002), pp. 3–38.

13 Ivan Eland, "The Empire Strikes Out: The 'New Imperialism' and its Fatal Flaws," *Policy Analysis*, 459 (November 26, 2002), pp. 1–27.

14 George Bush speeches to cadets at West Point (June 2002) and to veterans at the White House (November 2002).

15 Max Boot, *The Savage Wars of Peace: Small Wars and the Rise of American Power* (New York: Basic Books, 2002).

16 See Martin Walker, "America's Virtual Empire," *World Policy Journal* (Summer 2002), pp. 13–20; Victor Davis Hanson, "A Funny Sort of Empire," *National Review Online* (November 27, 2002); and Michael Mann, *Incoherent Empire* (London: Verso Books, 2003).

17 Robert Kaplan, *Warrior Politics: Why Leadership Demands a Pagan Ethos* (New York: Random House, 2002), pp. 152–3.

18 Sebastian Mallaby, "The Reluctant Imperialist: Terrorism, Failed States, and the Case for American Empire," *Foreign Affairs*, 81, 2 (March–April 2002), p. 6.

19 See Jack Snyder, *Myths of Empire: Domestic Politics and International Relations* (Ithaca: Cornell University Press, 1991); and David C. Hendrickson, "Toward Universal Empire: The Dangerous Quest for Absolute Security," *World Policy Journal*, 19, 3 (Fall 2002), pp. 1–10.

20 Dimitri K. Simes, "America's Imperial Dilemma," *Foreign Affairs*, 82, 6 (November–December 2002), pp. 91–102.

21 Max Boot, "The Case for American Empire," *Weekly Standard* (October 15, 2001).

22 Robert Kaplan. See also Preston Jones, "The World According to Robert Kaplan," *Ottawa Citizen* (March 3, 2002).

23 Dinesh D'Souza, "In Praise of American Empire," *Christian Science Monitor* (April 26, 2002).

24 Sebastian Mallaby. For a pre-9/11 argument in favour of an American Empire see also Thomas E. Ricks, "Empire or Not? A Quiet Debate over the U.S. Role," *Washington Post* (August 21, 2001).

25 John Lewis Gaddis, "A Grand Strategy of Transformation," *Foreign Policy* (November–December 2002), pp. 1–8.

26 G. John Ikenberry, "America's Imperial Ambition," *Foreign Affairs*, 81, 5 (September–October 2002), p. 44.

27 See Niall Ferguson, "The Empire that Dare Not Speak its Name," *The Sunday Times*, New Review (April 13, 2003).

28 See for example Martin Shaw, "Post-Imperial and Quasi-Imperial: State and Empire in the Global Era," *Millennium*, 31, 2 (2002), pp. 327–36.

29 "Those who by virtue of age and sobriety can remember the 1960s may recall the term 'American empire' as a bit of left-wing cant," Wright, "For a Wild Surmise," p. 3.

30 Though see the useful piece by Tarak Barkawi and Mark Laffey, "Retrieving the Imperial: *Empire* and International Relations," *Millennium*, 31, 1 (2002), pp. 109–27.

31 For an example of the new triumphalism see Alfredo Valladao, *The Twenty First Century Will Be American* (London: Verso, 1996).

32 See Thanh Duong, *Hegemonic Globalisation: U.S. Centrality and Global Strategy in the Emerging World Order* (Aldershot: Ashgate, 2003).

33 On this see the useful David Campbell, "Contradictions of Lonely Superpower," in David Slater and Peter J. Taylor, eds, *The American Century: Consensus and Coercion in the Projection of American Power* (Oxford: Blackwell, 1999), pp. 222–42.

34 See Walter A. McDougall, *Promised Land: Crusader State – The American Encounter with the World* (Boston, MA: Houghton Mifflin Company, 1997).

35 Michael Ignatieff, "Empire Lite," p. 36.

36 Frederick Jackson Turner, *The Significance of the Frontier in American History* (1893).

37 See Pierre Hassner, *The United States: The Empire of Force or the Force of Empire?* Chaillot Papers, Paris, 54 (September 2002), p. 14.

38 Michael Ignatieff, "Empire Lite," pp. 36–43, and Niall Ferguson, "The Empire that Dare Not Speak its Name," p. 3.

39 The best short description of the US power position in 1945 is by Donald W. White, "The Nature of World Power in American History: An Evaluation at the End of World War Two," *Diplomatic History*, 11, 3 (1987), pp. 181–202.

40 See the 13 Bulletins of the important *Cold War International History Project* based at the Woodrow Wilson Center, Washington DC.

41 A point made often by George F. Kennan, the architect of containment. See my "George F. Kennan: Requiem for a Cold Critic, 1945–1950," *Irish Slavonic Studies* (1990).

42 See my "Whatever Happened to American Decline? International Relations and the New United States Hegemony," *New Political Economy*, 6, 3 (2001), pp. 311–40.

43 See, for example, Susan Strange, "The Future of the American Empire," *Journal of International Affairs*, 42, 1 (1988), pp. 1–18, and Stephen Gill, *American Hegemony and the Trilateral Commission* (Cambridge: Cambridge University Press, 1990).

44 Andrew J. Bacevich, *American Empire: The Realities and Consequences of U.S. Diplomacy* (Cambridge, MA: Harvard University Press, 2002).

45 This section draws heavily from the excellent firsthand description provided by Nicholas Lemann, "The Next World Order: The Bush Administration May Have a Brand-New Doctrine of Power," *The New Yorker* (4 April 2002), at www.newamericancentury.org.

46 See the publications of the *Project for a New American Century* at www.newamericancentury.org. Key conservative figures associated with this very important pressure group included Max Boot, Frank Carlucci, Midge Decter, Elliot Abrams, Robert Kagan, Donald Kagan, R. James Woolsey, William Kristol, William J. Bennett, Aaron Friedberg, Dick Cheney, Donald Rumsfeld, Dan Quayle, Lewis Libby, Paul Wolfowitz, Fred C. Ikle, Jeb Bush, Peter W. Rodman, and Norman Podhoretz.

47 See in particular Fareed Zakaria, *From Wealth to Power: The Unusual Origins of America's World Role* (Princeton, NJ: Princeton University Press, 1998).

48 Charles Krauthammer, "The New Unilateralism," *Washington Post* (June 8, 2001), p. 29.

49 See Robert Kagan, *Paradise and Power: America and Europe in the New World Order* (London: Atlantic Books, 2003).

50 William Kristol and Robert Kagan, "Towards a Neo-Reaganite Foreign Policy," *Foreign Affairs*, 75, 4 (July–August 1996).

51 I discuss European criticism of the early Bush policies in my "Europe and the New American Challenge after September 11: Crisis – What Crisis?" *Journal of Transatlantic Studies*, 1, 1 (2003), pp. 37–55.

52 As Secretary of Defense Donald Rumsfeld put it following the war with Iraq: "Being on the terrorist list" of states "is not some place I'd want to be." Quoted in *The Times* (April 14, 2003).

53 Dominic Lieven, *Empire: The Russian Empire and its Rivals* (London: Pimlico, 2003), p. 3.

54 Andrew Roberts, "Americans are on the March," *The Times* (April 12, 2003).

55 Quote from Andrew Bacevich cited in Ferguson, "The Empire that Dare Not Speak its Name."

56 Mary Kaldor, "American Power: From 'Compellance' to Cosmopolitanism," *International Affairs*, 79, 1 (January 2003), pp. 1–2.

57 I discuss this in my "America and the World" in Robert Singh, ed., *Governing America: The Politics of a Divided Democracy* (Oxford: Oxford University Press, 2003), pp. 13–31.

58 The presidential champion of self-determination, Woodrow Wilson, sanctioned the use of military force to the "South" on nearly ten occasions during his period in the White House.

59 Dominic Lieven, "The Concept of Empire," *Fathom: The Source for Online Learning*, at www.fathom.com/feature/122086.

60 See John Gallagher and Ronald Robinson, "The Imperialism of Free Trade," *Economic History Review*, 2nd ser., 6, 1 (1953), pp. 1–25.

61 This point is outlined in terms of IR theory by Robert Gilpin, *Global Political Economy: Understanding the International Economic Order* (Princeton, NJ: Princeton University Press, 2001), pp. 97–102.

62 See G. John Ikenberry, "Rethinking the Origins of American Hegemony," *Political Science Quarterly*, 104 (1989), pp. 375–400.

63 Figures from Martin Wolf, "American and Europe Share the Responsibility for World Trade," *Financial Times* (April 23, 2003).

64 See "Imperial Anticolonialism" in William Appleman Williams, *The Tragedy of American Diplomacy* (Cleveland, OH: World Publishing, 1959).

65 On the uses of self-determination as a means of advancing US influence see Michael Cox, G. John Ikenberry, and Takashi Inoguchi, eds, *American Democracy Promotion: Impulses, Strategies, Impacts* (Oxford: Oxford University Press, 2000).

66 On British suspicion of Wilson and Roosevelt see Niall Ferguson, *Empire: How Britain Made the World* (London: Allen Lane, 2003).

67 See John Wacher, *The Roman World*, 2 vols (London: Routledge, 1990), p. 139.

68   A term recently coined by Chalmers Johnson in his *Blowback.*

69   "Empire is the rule exercised by one nation over others both to reg-
     ulate their external behavior and to ensure minimally acceptable
     forms of internal behavior within the subordinate states." Quoted
     in Stephen Peter Rosen, "An Empire, If You Can keep It," *The
     National Interest*, 71 (Spring 2003), p. 51.

70   "The US does not and indeed no nation-state can today form the
     centre of an imperialist project." Cited in John Hardt and Antonio
     Negri, *Empire* (Cambridge, MA: Harvard University Press, 2000),
     pp. xiii–xiv.

71   Joseph Nye, Jr, *The Paradox of American Power: Why the World's
     Only Superpower Can't Go It Alone* (New York: Oxford University
     Press, 2002).

72   Joseph Stiglitz, *Globalization and its Discontents* (London: Penguin
     Books, 2002), p. 24.

73   Robert Wade, "The Invisible Hand of the American Empire," unpub-
     lished MS (15 February 2003).

74   For an alternative perspective see Donald W. White, *The American
     Century: The Rise and Decline of the United States as a World Power*
     (New Haven, CT: Yale University Press, 1996).

75   Nye, *The Paradox of American Power*, p. 1.

76   Charles A. Kupchan, "The End of the West," *The Atlantic Online*
     (18   April   2003),   at   www.theatlantic.com/issues/2002/11/
     kupchan.htm.

77   See Philip Zelikow, "The Transformation of National Security:
     Five Redefinitions," *The National Interest*, 71 (Spring 2003),
     p. 18.

78   "America's World," *The Economist* (October 23, 1999), p. 15.

79   John M. Owen, "Why American Hegemony is Here to Stay,"
     symposium: *Pax Americana or International Rule of Law* (16
     January 2003), at http://fesportal.fes.de/pls/portal30/docs/FOLDER/
     POLITIKANALYSE/paxamericana/eingangsseite1.htm.

80   Fareed Zakaria, "Arrogant Empire," *Newsweek* (March 2003).

81   On forms of anti-Americanism see Richard Crockatt, *America
     Embattled* (London: Routledge, 2002), esp. pp. 39–71.

82   Charles Grant, comment at the Centre for European Economic
     Reform (May 2003).

83   See for example the chapter by Thomas Risse in this volume.

84   On German and French anti-Americanism assessed even before
     9/11 see D. Diner, *America in the Eyes of Germans: An Essay on Anti-
     Americanism* (Princeton, NJ: Markus Wiener, 1996) and Philippe

Roger, *L'Ennemi américain: Généalogie de l'antiaméricanisme français* (Paris: Seuil, 2002).

85 On this see Craig Kennedy and Marshall M. Boulton, "The Real Transatlantic Gap," *Foreign Policy* (November–December 2002).

86 As does Robert Brenner, "The Crisis in the US Economy," *London Review of Books*, 25, 3 (February 6, 2003), pp. 18–23.

87 For the most radical scenario concerning the European challenge – written by an American – see Charles A. Kupchan, "The Rise of Europe: America's Changing Internationalism, and the End of U.S. Primacy," *Political Science Quarterly*, 118, 2 (2003), pp. 205–25.

88 On some of the economic problems facing "Pax Americana" see John Gray, *Al Qaeda and What It Means to be Modern* (London: Faber and Faber, 2003), pp. 85–101.

2

The First Failed Empire of the Twenty-First Century

Michael Mann

American foreign policy has been recently dominated by the venture into Iraq. This has not gone well. Most criticism has focused on "mistakes" – there were not enough US troops, or they were of the wrong type, the Iraqi army was mistakenly disbanded after it surrendered, looting was not anticipated, oil expectations were unreal, the US depended too much on Iraqi exile claims, and so on. Indeed, these were mistakes. Two hundred and fifty thousand troops trained also in police roles would have made a difference. So might Iraqi soldiers turned into policemen. So might better planning all round. But the mistakes were only the surface phenomena of a more profound American failure. The Iraq venture was doomed from the outset by the attempt made by American neoconservatives to create what some of them styled a "New American Empire." This exaggerated American powers, made facile historical comparisons with previous Empires, and misidentified the century we live in. So this early twenty-first-century attempt at Empire is failing.

From my previous research, it was firstly obvious that effective power requires a combination of four more specific powers: ideological, economic, military, and political. Most regimes wield unequal combinations of them, and some regimes may be quite light on one or two of them. But the new imperialists relied overwhelmingly on military power alone – and indeed on only one part of military power, offensive firepower – and this is insufficient to create Empire. Second, it was obvious that the world has moved politically and ideologically in the late twentieth century from an Age of Empires (and imperialism) to an Age of Nation-States (and nationalism), and this is damaging to any contemporary attempt to found Empire.

Neither point seemed evident to many others, however. American neoconservatives, breaking with the traditional American aversion to the word "empire," proclaimed the coming of a New American Empire. "The fact is," said Pulitzer Prize-winning journalist Charles Krauthammer, "no country has been as dominant culturally, economically, technologically and militarily in the history of the world since the late Roman Empire." The writer Robert Kaplan compared the US to Rome after the Second Punic War. It was a second "universal power" and it must deploy "warrior politics" to achieve a Pax Americana. Dozens of American conservatives endorsed the imperial noun (though rarely the imperialist adjective). British historians resident in the US added their two cents' worth, playing Greeks to the American Romans. Niall Ferguson of Columbia University urged the US to take on the global imperial burden formerly shouldered by Great Britain.[1] Paul Kennedy of Yale University went even further in flattering his hosts, as revealed by the title of his article "The Greatest Superpower Ever."[2]

Philip Bobbitt is Professor of Constitutional Law, and a former adviser to both the CIA and the Clinton administration. Though a Texan, he is not a neoconservative. But he is an imperial academic, the author of a massive book on the history of states, warfare, diplomacy, and international law which culminates in a global benevolent American Empire able to finally end what he calls "The Long War" raging over the last few centuries between sovereign states. His "constitutional theory" rates democracy and human rights above state sovereignty (which, he says, was responsible for the Long War). If a state is not democratic and does not protect human rights (like Iraq), then its "cloak of sovereignty" should no longer protect it from military intervention. The United States, being immensely powerful, democratic, *and* committed to human rights, is the only Power which combines the might and the right to attack Iraq and others. For the same reason, he says

the US has the right to take preemptive action against weapons
of mass destruction (WMD), and to have immunity from international law for its own military forces.[3] Since half the states
in the world are neither genuinely democratic nor respectful of
human rights, Bobbitt's constitutional theory would seemingly
place much of the world at risk of American invasion. This is a
theory doing imperial service.

At the other end of the political spectrum many also stress
American power. Leftists have long denounced US imperialism –
"imperialism" is really their term. Yoking together the power of
the US and of capitalism, they blame most of the world's ills on
the US, thus crediting it with enormous powers. They agree with
the neoconservatives that this is imperialism, they just see it as a
bad thing. Perry Anderson sees no significant challenge to US
power and hegemony anywhere. Other Powers grumble, but they
acquiesce. Even the consent of victims can be bought by American capitalism, he says. Robert Wade writes elegantly of the
"Unipolar" and "empire-like power" of a US-dominated world
economy. His call for a more multipolar world is an ethical
demand, not a product of any "balancing" that he sees in the actual
workings of the economy, since he sees virtually none.[4] The "anti-
globalization" movement repeatedly denounces American domination of the world economy, which it blames for poverty,
exploitation, and environmental degradation around the world.
French intellectuals snipe on the sidelines, employing former
French Foreign Minister Hubert Védrine's term *hyperpuissance* to
capture the sense of a hyperactive, antisocial child – who is also
unfortunately a Superpower. Left and right agreed: this is the Age
of American Empire.

"World systems theorists" and other advocates of "hegemonic
cycles" have also compared American power to British, Roman,
and Chinese power in earlier centuries. But they differed in also
foreseeing hegemonic decline, and some said the US had already
begun that decline.[5] The preeminent world systems theorist
Immanuel Wallerstein has offered trenchant criticism of recent
American imperial ventures.[6] Of course, world systems' hegemonic analogies can be criticized. Patrick O'Brien rightly observes
that they greatly overstate the supposed British "hegemony" in the

nineteenth century, while he ridicules the notion that the Dutch might have exercised comparable powers earlier. He says there has never been a Superpower like the US.[7] I agree. In volume 2 of *The Sources of Social Power*, I also argued that the rather precarious world order during the nineteenth century was a product not only of British leadership in matters industrial, financial, and naval, but also of a multilateral "Concert of Great Powers," and of a capitalism that had strongly transnational as well as national powers. As we shall see below, O'Brien is also right when he goes on to enumerate the far greater dominance which the US has in many ways in relation to its main rivals than Britain ever enjoyed. But we must be careful not to deduce too much from this. For imperialism it is not the relationship between Great Powers which is crucial here, but their relationship to the rest of the world. This has changed fundamentally, in principle to the detriment of all Great Powers and of all direct, territorial imperialism, but in practice to the detriment of any American Empire.

But amid this supportive intellectual environment, in which so many said the US *could* achieve Empire, the administration of Bush the younger acted. Senior administration figures like Dick Cheney, Donald Rumsfeld, and Paul Wolfowitz, plus second-tier assistant secretary figures like Douglas Feith, John Bolton, and J. D. Crouch, plus supportive Republican congressmen and senators, did their best to fulfill these ambitious goals. They believed the US had the power to remake Iraq, restructure the whole Middle East, and eliminate terrorism and weapons of mass destruction across the world. They saw the problem confronting them was that terrorism and the proliferation of weapons of mass destruction offered a fundamental and potentially enduring threat to American power. These "weapons of the weak" seem to permit small groups of malcontents and rather puny Powers to remain invulnerable to American threats and even perhaps to launch attacks on the American homeland – as happened on 9/11. Nuclear, and more especially chemical and biological, weapons have been slipping downstream, spreading from the greatest to the lesser Powers. Fluid terrorist networks, often operating from the weakest states of all, "failed states," threaten our homeland security. Since they violate sovereignty, so should we. The new imperialists felt now was the time to strike against their threat, for another decade might be too late. American global domination might be short-lived if they did not act.

Their goals were quite limited. They did not want to rule over foreign lands permanently or directly. In normal times they are content with an indirect and informal Empire, able to pressure and threaten, but only in the last resort to invade foreign "rogue" states. The US would effect regime change and then leave with a more friendly regime in place. So conquest was intended only to found a *temporary territorial imperialism*. It would also be confined to a few specific places. The prosperous North of the world contained neither disorder nor military rivals nor collective resistance. All that the US required was that the other Northern states stick to their own affairs and not interfere in American imperial projects elsewhere. It correctly expected they were too divided to interfere, and believed it could divide and rule among them. It was also cautious about interfering in sub-Saharan Africa and much of Southern Asia. For the moment only two regions were in its sights, the central core of the Muslim world, in the Middle East plus Western Asia, and Northeast Asia. This was where this temporary territorial imperialism focused, especially at first on the "axis of evil," "rogue states" North Korea, Iraq, and Iran, though with Syria sometimes also informally added. The expectation was that if mere threats did not work, all would in due course be subjected to temporary territorial imperialism. And if that was successful, another four rogues could be added to the firing lines.

After all, as the new imperialists reminded us in 2002–3, there had been successful historical examples. In 1945 the US occupied Japan and with its allies occupied Germany. The forces occupied the countries for several years, and then retired into large bases from which they continued to project force against the perceived outside enemy. Japan and Germany then built up their own armed forces and civilian administrations. They were generously showered with dollars, assisting economic recovery, and offered labour and welfare reforms to compromise the class conflicts that had initially brought the fascists and militarists into power in these countries. The locals were also desperate for peace. 1945 came after six years of war for the Germans, more for the Japanese. They had been losing the war for at least two years, their cities were in ashes, and they were merely trying to stay alive. They were relieved when the war ended, and almost no one wished to restart it. The new regimes were popular, the countries democratized, and they became loyal allies of the US.[8] The medicine could be repeated.

We must remain skeptical of American claims that the New Empire would be completely benevolent. Imperialists always say this but never are. But an Empire to which the ruled routinely consent is not unusual. This is what we call "hegemony," a word which indicates that the imperial power establishes "the rules of the game" by which others routinely play. They may come to also approve of the rules as well, so that hegemony becomes genuinely legitimate. But the basis of hegemony is more of a matter-of-fact acceptance of things "as they are." Then people's own everyday actions help reproduce the dominance without much thought. I will instance the role of the dollar as the world's reserve currency below. Hegemony should be an invisible hand, lying behind the accepted rules of the game. The catch is that to be hegemonic, the US might have to play by the rules. An Empire based on highly visible militarism abandons the rules and so risks losing hegemony. Joseph Nye expressed this as the pursuit of "hard" power threatening America's "soft" power.[9] But the new imperialists went ahead, saying that success would bring legitimacy afterwards.

I enumerate the power resources they commanded, and ask whether they were sufficient for this new form of "temporary territorial imperialism." They were not.

Economic Power

Though the US now dominates the world economy much less than it did in the first decades after 1945, it remains the main engine of global growth. It enjoys a slight lead in many high-tech industries, though the consumption and indebtedness of its citizens provide the main dynamic. In overall volume of production and trade the US has declined so that it is now only one of three major economic blocs, level with the European Union, somewhat ahead of Japan/East Asia. But since neither "rival" is a single state, unlike the US, they find it much more laborious to devise common policies. As a single state actor the US is more than double the size of any other, so it tends to initiate policy while its two rivals react. However, they can block its initiatives and force compromise. The US cannot act unilaterally in bodies like the WTO or the G-8 to dictate global economic policy. Any hegemony in production and trade would be more accurately called "Northern," since the three Northern blocs collectively provide over 80 percent of world production, trade, and finance, and over 95 percent of its R&D.

It is finance that adds more American hegemony. The dollar remains the world's reserve currency and Wall Street trades two-thirds of the value of the world's stocks and shares. Since values are ultimately denominated in dollars, much of other nations' reserves and savings are held in dollars. This security means it offers only low interest rates, so that foreigners are essentially lending money to the US. Thus American consumers can amass large debts and American governments can finance massive trade and budget deficits. The poorer countries subsidize the American economy far more than they ever receive in US development aid. The US is the biggest debtor nation, a sign of strength, giving it a unique degree of financial freedom.[10] It also aids the US to maintain an enormous military budget, year in, year out, without the strains that were manifest in all previous Empires. To maintain this hegemony and this disguised military subsidy obviously requires that foreign investors do not lose confidence in American stewardship. While some capital flight from the US has been evident over the last two years, it has been offset by the growing trade deficit of the US with China and other Asian economies, which spend their surpluses on investing in the US. Financial hegemony remains, and will probably endure a while yet.

The US tries to use these economic powers to further its strategic interests through three principal mechanisms – aid, trade, and loans. The mix has not changed greatly over the last two decades, since the new imperialists have not introduced a new economic policy – a sign of their obsession with military power.

US aid programmes remain closely geared to strategic goals. About one-third of US aid throughout the last decade has gone to its closest ally, Israel. A further fifth has gone to Egypt and Jordan so that they will not attack Israel. Most of the rest has gone to sundry small Power allies old and new (Colombia, Uzbekistan, Pakistan, etc.). These governments are grateful, more likely to be pro-American, and cooperate with US foreign policy. Yet the total volume of aid has been low, only around $10–15 billion per year, which in per capita terms has been the smallest foreign aid budget of any OECD country. Most African countries get less aid from the US than from Europe. In 2003 came the first major consequence of the new imperialism. After some increase in aid to poorer countries, US aid suddenly more than doubled as $21 billion was pumped into Iraq, plus a military budget of $66 billion for Iraq following hard upon another one of $75 billion. Congress (reflecting popular American feeling) grumbled that Iraqis should pay for their own reconstruction. It will probably insist on loans not grants if another major Iraqi request comes. This is not a good omen for American Empire. It is doubtful whether Americans want their leaders to pay for Empire, however temporary. Over the last decades Americans have consistently resisted tax increases even for increased services at home. It is unlikely they will support them for foreign imperial ventures. Americans believe they exist in a nation-state, not an Empire.

In the mid-nineteenth century Britain had comparable economic strength to the US today but was able to invest in Empire and then break even. By 1900 its military costs were only about 2.5 percent of GDP (gross domestic product), compared to 4 percent in the US today, and the Empire was breaking even financially. This is unlikely in the US case unless the US were to take more control of Iraqi oil production than seems possible. The Belgians made a large profit in Africa by focusing on valuable raw materials and by inflicting enormous sufferings on Africans. At their worst the British also looted their colonies, but at their best they made initial investments which paid off later in profits for themselves and in economic development for the colonies. The US has the wealth to do the same, but it seems unlikely that it can loot the world in the old imperial way, and it is doubtful whether American voters would support the initial investment for this. It is not so much the material resources that are lacking as the supportive ideologies to deploy them.

Yet aid is less important than trade, where American policy is more vigorous. Recent administrations have said they believe that global growth flows from freeing up markets and cutting back the role of government. This "neoliberalism" or "Washington Consensus" can be seen as indirect economic imperialism, though it is also claimed to be benevolent, leading to global economic growth. Neoliberalism was preached more under Clinton than Bush, and in any case has been more rhetoric than actual policy. Free trade is encouraged more for others than the US itself, which has consistently subsidized its own agriculture and intermittently subsidized industries threatened by imports (currently especially steel and textiles). But this is not really *American* imperialism. In these respects the US is no different from the European Union or Japan. Together the three dominated previous WTO rounds of partial trade liberalization, even imposing some free trade agreements on the poorer countries without their realizing how damaging these might be for themselves – as in the "intellectual property rights" agreement. The first serious threats to this Northern domination came from Southern countries at the Cancun meeting of the WTO in 2003. This challenge seems likely to be maintained, since the WTO has a fairly democratic constitution. For its part the US will try to meet the challenge by intensifying its policy of offering bilateral deals to individual Southern countries, typically offering limited access to US markets in return for support of US foreign policy. This remains a formidable inducement, since the US is the biggest economy under the control of a single government.

But the main bite of imperfect neoliberalism comes with international loans. Power in the main lending agencies – the IMF, the World Bank, and other international development banks – is not democratically distributed. This is distinctively American imperialism, principally because the US dominates the constitutions of these organizations, with the other Northern economies holding less power and the Southern countries virtually none. The US Treasury dominates their policies.

Note the parameters of this power, however. International loans become problematic only if a country falls into debt. So the US Treasury has virtually no lending powers over other Northern economies, or over successfully developing countries which do not need loans, like India and China. But the story has been different over much of the South. In the 1970s Northern banks had offered very low interest rates to Southern countries and they borrowed very large sums to finance economic development. But in 1979 US Federal Reserve chairman Paul Volcker suddenly raised US interest rates (for reasons unconnected to the South), which meant their interest payments shot up and they couldn't pay. A massive Southern debt crisis began and still exists, boosted through the East Asian financial crisis of 1997, with knock-on effects on Russia and Brazil. When any business falls into debt to a bank, the bank seeks to restructure the payment of the debt and it seeks to vet the firm's business plans. This also happens at the global level. The US Treasury controls the IMF and World Bank. If they refuse a loan, then all the other international lending organizations also refuse. So the US Treasury becomes effectively the world's creditor bank and presses neoliberal terms for debt repayment. These are the "structural adjustment programs" whose primary purpose is not economic development but to get the debts repaid. To achieve this, the US seeks to impose fiscal austerity (cut government spending and raise taxes), high interest rates, currency stabilization, privatization of government enterprises, and liberalization of trade, capital markets, and labor markets. This is fairly direct economic imperialism, since it clearly increases the control by the US government and American corporations and banks over the domestic economies of indebted countries. However, other Northern corporations and banks also benefit from this. The US is here the hegemonic leader of the North, against the indebted parts of the South.

Few of these programs have much helped debtor countries, while some have harmed them. Social inequality has been a more common outcome than growth, especially in poorer countries, and this has generated considerable discontent across the South. The IMF and World Bank have come under increasing attack even from economists.[11] The IMF defensively renamed its "structural adjustment" programs "poverty reduction and growth" programs, and the World Bank, which used to ignore or condemn states, now recognizes effective states as promoting growth. But the political backlash in the South has been considerable. Structural adjustment programs are widely denounced as global economic imperialism in which the rich exploit the poor, led by the US government.

Southern governments rule in a world of sovereign nation-states. They, not the US, implement their economic policies. They want reelection, oligarchies want to keep power, and even generals fear social unrest. A contradiction results between the demands of the American-led international financial community and the needs of local political leaders. Most democratic governments simply cannot produce short-term economic misery for the sake of some dubious neoliberal vision of the long term, for in the meantime they will lose the next election. The US cannot *force* reform on them, as is clear currently in the case of Argentina, which since 2002 has refused to comply with IMF directives, partially defaulting on its repayments and forcing the IMF to accept this. In the global economy, the US is only a backseat driver, nagging the real driver, the sovereign state, sometimes administering sharp blows to his head. But the US does not steer the automobile and hitting the driver makes a crash more likely. The US, through its banking surrogates, has some supporters among Southern elites, and some governments comply. But more often compromise ensues, which may not be the best way to steer an automobile. Latin American governments liberalize the more internationally visible banking and trade sectors, while dragging their heels on labor markets, and preserving social security provisions. When things go wrong, the US gets some of the blame. Though Europe and Japan are also heavily implicated in these policies, they get off lightly.

So these US actions are seen more as power than hegemony. Under the Bush administration, its actions (which in these matters are little different from the Clinton administration) have been reinforced by a hardening of its line on global environmental issues. Here neoconservatism has influenced US policy, though the hardening was driven principally by its domestic environmental and energy program, not by foreign policy needs. The only delegate to be jeered and heckled at the Johannesburg Earth Summit Conference in September 2002 was not some oppressive dictator, nor even some stonyhearted corporate CEO. It was Colin Powell, representing the United States of America, who is not a neo-conservative. President Bush had not dared attend. Al-Jazeera's website of cartoons drawn from across the Arab world reveals the war on Iraq characterized as primarily a grab for oil. This was a motive, though not the primary one (if it were, the policy would be to make friends with oil producers not attack or threaten them). But America's economic policies now incur resentment and suspicion around the world, which increases resistance to the new imperialism.

These are very mixed powers, though not greatly changed under the Bush administration. They permit US leadership and some financial hegemony, but neither domination nor legitimacy across much of the world. There are no effective Great Power economic rivals, for the other Northern economies also benefit from the main thrust of US policy. But US economic powers have not been systematically engaged in the new imperialism. Public opinion is also a restraint on committing more of the national treasure to imperialism. The US did attempt ad hoc threats and economic inducements in 2001–3. New bases were bought from poor countries like Uzbekistan and Djibouti, and Pakistani and some Eastern European cooperation was more expensively bought. A second ad hoc thrust came with the attempt to buy Security Council votes over Iraq in 2003, but this lamentably failed. American economic power, though relatively declining, is still formidable, but it has not been systematically used in the new imperialism, and it is doubtful it can be.

Military Power

Military resources dominated the minds of the neoconservatives. They correctly perceived that American military power has no rival. Japan and Europe do not pursue military power, the Soviet enemy collapsed, and Russia and China want entry into the capitalist world. Almost all the world's military budgets are declining, except that of America. Its military budget for 2003 is 40 percent of the world's total military spending, exceeding the spending of the next 24 states combined. It is 25 times greater than the combined spending of all seven "rogue states" identified by the US as its enemies. The gap is growing wider.[12] The US is the only military Superpower.

Its enormous nuclear arsenal is not decisive here. The growing number of nuclear states all possess defense by deterrent, though the US arsenal gives it alone almost absolute invulnerability to attack from any rational enemy dependent on fixed, targetable assets. This is a higher level of defense than any state has ever possessed throughout history. The new imperialists felt it was wise to strike before minor but hostile Powers might also acquire such weapons, but right now the rest of the world should worry about its own defenses. The Bush administration is developing the Star Wars antiballistic missile defense system and new battlefield nuclear weapons (at University of California–run laboratories), while threatening nuclear preemptive strikes. But nuclear weapons cannot be used to acquire Empire, unless we wanted a radioactive one.

Empires require conventional, not nuclear forces. US conventional forces are big but not overwhelming – 1.45 million men and women under arms, down from 2.2 million in the 1980s, less than China's 2.5 million, just greater than the 1 million plus of India, North Korea, and Russia. The US has only 5 percent of the world's soldiers, and they are obviously insufficient to patrol the whole world. In 2003 the Iraq operations revealed that the US has only about 250,000 fighting troops, and these need rotation in and out of combat zones. US fighting forces are fully engaged with 130,000 troops in Iraq, 8,000 in Afghanistan, and 36,000 supposedly combat-ready in South Korea. The rest are spread out over its global network of bases and fortified embassies. This is far fewer combat troops than either the British or Roman Empires possessed at their height.

The crucial military superiority is neither nuclear weapons nor weight of numbers but global deployment and firepower. Only the US has global reach, with military facilities in 132 countries, about half of them being genuine bases. Nor can any Power rival the strike power of American airplanes, missiles, ships, tanks, and other capital-intensive, technology-laden weapons. It has a virtual monopoly of "smart" (self-guided, once launched) and "brilliant" (completely robotic) weapons. These first emerged during the 1990s in the so-called "revolution in military affairs," the RMA, coined by Pentagon guru Andrew Marshall to refer to "a major change in the nature of warfare brought about by the innovative application of new technologies which, combined with dramatic changes in military doctrine and operational and organizational concepts, fundamentally alters the character and conduct of military operations."[13] It combined long-range precision radar-guided missiles and bombs with "information warfare" deploying satellites in space, airborne cameras, handheld global positioning systems, and robot sensors. RMA-equipped forces can inflict enormous damage on the enemy, with very low US casualties. Even the US infantryman's M-16/M4 rifle can now deliver 90 rounds a minute, disintegrating human beings 2,000 feet away – even without the attachable grenade-launcher.

The Afghan War of 2001–2 and the Iraq invasion of 2003 showed the offensive utility of the system. In both cases enemy forces were devastated before their own weapons could come within range of American troops. Significantly, most of the new imperialists refer to the RMA and the new weaponry as their greatest resource.

No comparable military Power had previously existed. This is true of relative military expenditures, capacity to deter attackers, global offensive reach, and level of offensive firepower delivered with minimum risk to oneself. The combination gives a massive intimidatory presence to the United States vis-à-vis any state which dares to stand up to it. Military defiance would be a very high-risk strategy. The lack of rivals is truly unique in the history of the world, just as the new imperialists say. The US dwarfs Britain's nineteenth-century military leadership. True, its Royal Navy was deliberately kept bigger than the next two largest navies combined, and in reality it sometimes exceeded the next four. This meant that Britain was also defensively invulnerable (since it comprised islands and there were no airplanes). It also possessed unrivaled striking power across the seas and along the coastlines of the world. But British army strength only ranked fifth in the world, behind Germany, France, Russia, and Austria-Hungary. So Britain could not coerce or conquer its own continent, and it had well-armed rivals spread right across the Northern hemisphere. Indeed all previous Empires, including those of Rome and China, always had neighbors whose military powers restrained their actions.

Yet though offensive firepower can achieve battlefield victory, it cannot unaided deliver imperial pacification. Empire, however temporary, requires mopping-up operations, the quelling of rebellions and riots, and a gradual transition from military to policing roles. This concerns the interface between military and political power, and I discuss it under the latter heading.

Political Power

American political power might be restrained by either international political institutions or by resistance from the countries in which it intends to intervene. There is little restraint from the former. Though the international order is premised formally on the sovereign equality of states, some are more equal than others. The United Nations Security Council still embodies inequalities of the late 1940s, allowing five permanent members (the US, the USSR/Russia, China, Britain, and France) veto powers. But in reality two Superpowers, and then only one, dominated the Council. During the 1990s the US dominated UN resolutions, sanctions, and military interventions. It used its veto more than all the other Security Council Powers combined. If the US opposed force, there was no force; and until 2003 whenever the US wanted force, it secured it.[14] American power explains why Iraq was never offered carrots, as well as sticks, to disarm.[15]

The US sometimes had to pursue laborious arm-twisting and bribing, but it almost always worked. From the Soviet collapse until late 2002 no powers got together to thwart the American will. The thought did not often occur to them, since American power was fairly hegemonic – routinized and mostly legitimate. It could rely on support from Britain and (usually) France on the Security Council, plus the rest of Western Europe and the other

Anglo-Saxon countries, and Japan and other East Asian allies, plus most of Latin America. The US and not the UN had offered security to most of the world. The other states of the North had been under American protection since 1945, unable to defend themselves against communism without American help. America dominated security organizations like NATO and SEATO (South East Asia Treaty Organization). Whatever their jealousies and resentments, states in the "free world" believed they had common interests with the US. After the collapse of the Soviet Union, NATO was expanded eastward and former communist countries scrabbled for American favors.

If this is called "multilateralism," why should the US want unilateralism? US intervention without the political mandate of the United Nations incurs costs in military, economic, and ideological power. The mandate brings unconditional permissions to use foreign bases, allied troops, the cash to fund the venture, and above all legitimacy. Europe, not the US, paid most of the costs of rebuilding the former Yugoslavia; Germany, Japan, and the Arab oil states paid for most of the 1991 Gulf War. UN legitimacy particularly allows states to support actions which are unpopular with their own people. They hide behind UN authority and say "We are reluctant, but it is the will of the world." Intervention goes well for the US when formally multilateral.

But in 2003 the new imperialism stripped away the multilateral fig leaves. The Bush administration was unable to assemble a UN Security Council vote to fully and explicitly back an invasion of Iraq. So it went ahead almost unilaterally, with troops coming only from the US, Britain, and Australia, plus 56 Polish Special Forces. The new imperialists believed they could do it virtually unilaterally, and they could. The UN, Europe, Russia, China, and Japan now remained irrelevant to the invasion and even to the first stages of the subsequent unraveling of American power up to the end of 2003. These supposed "rivals" were powerless to stop the invasion. They sat on the sidelines, first disconsolately, then with barely concealed gloating. In the very short period that the US thought the war was going well, menacing threats were made against Syria and Iran, though a sudden tactical silence had descended on US policy toward the tougher nut of North Korea.

But the new imperialists still believed that the US could remake the world, and the rival Powers would eventually be forced back on the American team, under American terms. They wanted Iraqi loans repaid and Iraqi oil contracts. So the policy did not fail on abandonment of so-called multilateralism. Once again, there are no Great Power rivals.

It is different in the minnow states subjected to regime change. Previous Empires generally calculated that stable regime change through pacification of a conquered country needed at least two and one-half times the soldiers required by battlefield victory, since it involves dispersing, not concentrating troops. The imperial Power rarely provided these troops itself. It relied on local political allies. The European Empires (and the Romans before them) initially ruled indirectly, through local native allies. Their conquests were aided by local princes and potentates feeling oppressed by the local ruler, desiring to share in the imperial spoils. European troops focused their superior firepower on the capital and major cities, while larger native forces fanned out over the territories to repress any resistance.

After pacification the imperialists might continue ruling indirectly, through client native princes. But if the colony was valuable, they gradually increased control over the local allies, and soon integrated them as soldiers and administrators into their own colonial regimes. In European Empires, almost all officers remained Europeans, but the bulk of the rank-and-file and the NCOs were natives. In India, British troops provided only between 50,000 and 78,000 out of a force total of between 250,000 and 290,000. About 80% of both the army and the police force were usually Indians. In African colonies natives were even more numerous – usually about 90% in British colonies, and 98% in the Belgian Congo. The Germans used the most European soldiers (about 40%) and they were among the least successful and most repressive colonizers. Colonial troops also fought for their masters abroad. Over 130,000 Indian troops fought in Belgium and France in World War I and over 150,000 African troops fought for Britain in Asia in World War II. It seems extraordinary today – what concern were these wars of theirs?

Even "direct" imperial civilian administration usually worked through strengthening the authority of loyal princes, chiefs, and tribal and village councils, and ruling through them. A thousand British members of the Indian Civil Service were able to administer 250 million natives; 1,200 British civil servants administered a dozen African territories with a combined population of 43 million. Native allies were always better pacifiers, policemen, judges, and civil servants because they had local knowledge and control networks on the ground. This is how Empires ruled in the Age of Empires. By the early twentieth century their ranks included American imperialists, especially in the Philippines.[16]

As these Empires collapsed, the Cold War began. But the US kept up a comparable policy in its ensuing 50-year "informal Empire," dominating countries without the need of formal territorial controls. Because the Cold War was believed to be between rival economic and political ideologies, the US found "native allies" among elites who favored capitalism and liberal democracy over socialism. Given a little aid, these conservative elites usually proved more powerful than their leftist opponents. Only in a few cases, like Cuba and Vietnam, was the US confronted by leftist regimes successfully mobilizing most of the nation against it. But the Age of the Cold War is also over.

How did the new imperialists fare in their more recent ventures? In Afghanistan, an almost valueless country near the edge of their logistical reach on the ground (though not in the air), they maintained the historical tradition of Empire. They relied very heavily on local allies to actually conquer territory. Only about 300 Americans were on the ground as the Northern Alliance neared Kabul, and they were Special Forces spotters giving coordinates to US bombers, and CIA agents with suitcases brimming with dollars to buy Afghan warlords. After the conquest, US forces were strengthened to about 8,000 Americans plus several thousand other foreign allies. But the country outside of Kabul is mainly run by the Northern Alliance and other warlords, with the Karzai regime and the US only retaining very tenuous overall control. In fact, this is a typical case of indirect rule over a low-value colony. If the new imperialists had begun with higher aspirations, realities on the ground plus logistical pressures from Iraq forced them to settle for much less. If they thought Karzai could last for six months afterwards, they would withdraw – especially if they could capture or kill Osama bin Laden or Mullah Omar.

But in Iraq their ambition was much greater, while their resources were less proportionate to it. The US invaded without a political plan or political allies. Plan A was that Iraqi generals would desert, overthrow Saddam, and form a new client regime either before the invasion actually started or as it proceeded. Plan B was that US troops would be regarded simply as liberators and the various Iraqi factions would all assemble together and form a new, viable government in a peaceful environment. Both expectations were naive, a product of a Pentagon-run policy sidelining any experts familiar with Middle Eastern or Iraqi politics.

The real "unilateral" blunder of the US was not to ignore the UN and the Europeans, but to invade a country without local allies on the ground. There was one regional exception, for in the north the Kurdish allies already ran a de facto government and so after conquest the transition to a new regime was far smoother there. The exiled Iraqis on whom the US relied for the rest of Iraq had no effective organizations on the ground, the Shia used theirs for their own purposes, and at least some Sunni used theirs to kill Americans and Iraqi "collaborators." The bulk of Iraq would be an historic "first" – a country pacified with no local allies. It seemed unlikely it could be done. The Provisional Authority and the Iraqi National Council had little legitimacy among Iraqis, and they had inadequate infrastructures for transitioning through pacification to policing to effecting a stable, elected government. This was not a "mistake" of inadequate preparation, for (apart from the Kurds) there were no effective local allies available. Powerful Iraqis did not look to Americans to deliver them from Saddam Hussein. It had to be a largely unilateral invasion.

So in the six months after the US declared "victory" on May 1, 2003, more American troops were killed than during the invasion itself. Far more Iraqis were dying daily and the UN and international aid agencies were targeted and fled the country. The security situation is currently worsening, though some reconstruction is occurring and organized attacks remain sporadic outside the

Sunni/Saddam heartland. No one can accurately predict what will happen, given our lack of knowledge of rebel numbers and character. In fact, the remarkable dearth of US intelligence on them is not reassuring. The US capture of Saddam might not make much difference. US casualties will probably remain at one or two a day and Iraqis will continue to suffer much more. The US has long fought wars with a high regard for its own soldiers' lives and comforts, and has difficulty accepting such losses. It remains a largely unilateral enterprise and rebel tactics are to perpetuate this. The West European and other Powers, still smarting, refuse to commit real troops or substantial treasure, and the Turks, Pakistanis, and Indians drag their heels. The grants voted by the US and all other countries for Iraqi reconstruction up to the end of 2004 appear to total only about $22 billion ($18.5 billion from the US, $3.5 billion from the rest), yet the World Bank had estimated that $55 billion was required, and the US added on another $21 billion for security needs. Other countries have also offered nearly $10 billion in loans (mostly over a longer period) while the US Congress might only offer loans next time there is a budget request. Then Iraqis would have to pay for their own reconstruction. With what? Shall we take their oil in payment? Then the emperor would be without any clothes at all.

Invasions of Iran or Syria would encounter similar problems. "Reformists" in Iran and anti-Alawite factions in Syria are highly unlikely to seek Pentagon aid in their domestic squabbles. North Korea differs, since there is a major local ally, South Korea, though since its capital lies within artillery range of Northern forces, it would be a reluctant ally in any attack. Once again, the real "rivals" to the US are not Great Powers, but in matters of political power they are the minnow Powers on whom the US hoped to effect regime-change.

Some would-be nation-states are disorderly, some fail altogether. But the US must not exaggerate its chances of being able to do much about them.[17] Even its own client states are unreliable, pursuing their own goals, often to the detriment of American policy goals – as has been the case for Israel, Pakistan, and Saudi Arabia, for example. They are sovereign states, pursuing their own policies. In interventions inside nation-states, the US is

a political pygmy. After showering clients with aid, it cannot
control them, and it lacks the option of increasing controls on
them with military measures, as previous Empires did. After
inflicting military devastation on rogues, it cannot bring political
order – as both Afghanistan and Iraq reveal. The Age of Empire
has gone.

Ideological Power

Underlying this is a sea change in global ideologies. The Europeans
(like almost all imperialists before them) were greatly helped by
one important absence – nationalism. Conquered populations
rarely shared a sense of a common collective identity. The Europeans called them "Indians" and "Africans," but they themselves
did not, since their communities of attachment were much more
local – regional, or tribal, or sectarian. If they collaborated with
the imperialists, they were not called traitors to the nation. Rather
they were seen as advancing the interests of their local communities by sharing in the spoils of Empire. So, from Cortés securing
the alliance of the Tlaxcalans against the Aztecs, to the British and
French mobilizing rival networks of Indian princes, to the Belgians
ruling through Tutsi chieftains in Rwanda/Burundi, there was no
great ideological obstacle to Empire. When natives rose up in
rebellion, they confronted not just the Europeans, but also their
local allies.

The new imperialists and others say that American power is
much greater than that of Britain or France in the nineteenth
century. They are right if we compare individual countries. The
US is more powerful than Britain, much more powerful than
France. But Britain and France were not go-it-alone imperialists.
Despite fighting wars against each other, they were partners in a
much broader "civilizing mission" launched first by Europe, then
by the West, on the rest of the world. The US joined in at the end
of the nineteenth century in Cuba, the Philippines, China, and
elsewhere. This Western imperialism was much more formidable
than the US is today, militarily, politically, economically, and especially ideologically. From the point of view of the rest of the world,

Britain, France, Belgium, Russia, the United States, and other Empire builders all looked culturally the same. When viewed collectively, there was simply no escaping their power.

Culturally, the West represented modernity, progress, power. Its culture was so powerful that native elites all over the world knew they needed it even while they fought for liberation. The West also controlled the weapons of mass communication. In Africa the British, the French, the Belgians, the Portuguese, the Germans, and the Italians all communicated easily with each other; while the "Africans" (not their own term) in different regions of the continent could not easily communicate with each other, since they spoke many languages and few were literate. A Western communications monopoly prevented collective resistance at other than a local level. It also needed divisions among the imperialists themselves for news of colonial atrocities to get out.

But by the twentieth century the Western ideal of rule by the people was spreading to the colonies. Educating the natives for civil or military administration meant exposing them to liberal, socialist, and fascist notions of popular sovereignty. When Indian nationalists effectively adapted all these theories to local conditions, British rule in India was finished. The European Empires, weakened by their own nationalist hostilities, quickly collapsed in the face of native nationalisms. That was the end of the Age of Empires – though the Russian Empire got a short additional lease of life from communism which proclaimed an international brotherhood that slightly delayed the appeals of nationalism.

Nationalism is now the world's dominant ideology. Some facile theories of globalization assert that the nation-state dominated in the past, while transnational forces dominate today. True, before 1945 nation-states dominated Europe, but their Empires dominated the world. They were replaced by nation-states, from 1945 until the mid-1990s. All 191 of the world's states now claim to rule "in the name of the people." They sit together in a body called "the United Nations." True, Europe has moved slightly beyond the nation-state, some nations are disputed between rival ethnic, religious, and regional factions, and some states do not have effective sovereignty over their territories. But they aspire to sovereignty. Above all, there is no widespread ideology legitimizing anyone else ruling over a nation-state. Since only "the people" should rule, anti-imperialism is rampant across the world.

Complications arise where more than one collective identity compete as sources of nationalism and anti-imperialism. In the Middle East there are four: nationalism attached to a state (for example, Egyptian or Iraqi nationalism), pan-Arab nationalism, Islamism (popularly called fundamentalism), and Muslim sectarianism (mainly Sunni and Shia). The last two are not strictly nationalism, though they are certainly powerful anti-imperialisms. So Iraq is only a fragile, divided nation-state. There is distrust between Shia and Sunni, between secularists, conservatives, and Islamists, and between and within tribes and cities. But Iraqis distrust the alien occupiers even more. Iraq is for the Iraqis, they say, and so do Arabs and Muslims in general, for this is the dogma of nationalism everywhere.

To suppress resistance, the US must provide yet more militarism, as did all previous Empires. "Decimation" has entered the language after originating as the Roman practice of killing every tenth man or person in villages or towns that had revolted. Europeans – and Americans in the Philippines and Japanese in China – slaughtered civilians and burned villages and crops in similar retaliation. Thankfully, real Empires have departed from the world. Americans did commit some atrocities in Vietnam, and doubtless there have been some in Iraq. But Americans caused the deaths of an estimated 250,000 Filipinos in their last true imperial venture in the early twentieth century without causing much of an outcry. Global ideologies have changed since then to embrace ideals of racial equality and universal human rights. America claims to bring stability, freedom, and democracy to Iraq, not repression. It has to live up to this claim, not least in the eyes of the American public. Its imperial predecessors promised only "civilization," order imposed on people who were termed "savages," "barbarians," "heathens," or "lower races" (Americans coined the term "gooks" for Filipinos). Empires were skilled in repression, using means that would bring horrified denunciation everywhere today. American soldiers sometimes let slip derogatory stereotypes of Iraqis, but American reporters hover nearby, quoting and discrediting them back home when they do. Their officers then reprimand them.

Today the means of communicating such values as nationalism, anti-imperialism, racial equality, and human rights are enormously extended. Literacy and the media are global. Resistance to imperialism and its alleged atrocities are beamed globally. Al-Jazeera and Al-Arabiya beam them to 35 million Arabs, and increasingly to others. The weapons of mass communication are no longer controlled by the imperialists. Indeed, once things started going wrong in Iraq, the Bush administration could no longer control the media in the US. Now that the bombing has stopped, Iraqi rebel atrocities are probably worse than those inflicted by the Americans. But atrocities are interpreted within broader ideological frames. Westerners retain traces of old civilizational and racial ideologies in which they tend to see Iraqi rebels as less "civilized" than Western soldiers. But in other regions, and especially in Muslim countries, frames of anti-imperial struggles against foreigners, infidels, and Crusaders generate contrary stereotypes. In this ideological struggle, the US possesses a somewhat precarious advantage only in its own homeland, and among a few allies.

America does possess broader ideological advantages. It has long represented values of material plenty, individual freedom, and democracy to the world. The world tended in the second half of the twentieth century to see the US and not Europe as the exemplar of modernity. America also has the world's most powerful media, which sometimes express these values. The US was the first to develop efficient mass production of culture, and Hollywood and US television networks retain a global lead. But since over half Hollywood's profits now come from abroad, it counters the stilting effects of subtitles and dubbing by reducing the number of words per minute. Narrative drive, action, sex, and violence do not communicate much of a message. The major shows of the US television networks depict private life in an overwhelmingly apolitical and anodyne way, reinforcing the style of the commercials, which now occupy 22 minutes per hour of airtime. TV sales abroad declined as consumers turned to locally produced shows. A 2001 survey of 60 countries revealed that 7 of their top 10 programs were locally

produced. "The worldwide television market is growing," said the
president of Walt Disney Television, "but America's place in it is
declining." The US share of the worldwide web declined from a half
to a third during the 1990s. In 2003, 32% of Internet sites are
American, 28% European, and 26% Asian – Northern trilateralism
again.[18] In general American media powerfully convey values
of a commercial, material, and individual nature more than directly
political values.

Global annual surveys indicated that the world loves the
general values of democracy, freedom, and human rights and likes
the American version of them (though rather less strongly). It
also approves of globalization and free markets in principle. But
it likes "Americans" more than "the United States," and there has
been steadily rising criticism of US government policies. The US
is accused of worsening inequality, poverty, and the environment.
Majorities deplore American unilateralism and militarism, especially disliking US policy toward Israel and Iraq. In 2003 even
Israelis tended to see the US as favoring them rather than the
Palestinians, and only Americans out of all the countries surveyed
believed US policy was evenhanded. Even support for the war on
terrorism declined. The 2003 report said "the bottom has fallen
out of support for America in most of the Muslim world." Majorities in seven out of the eight Muslim countries surveyed (including Kuwait) said the US might become a military threat to their
country.[19] The US is losing the ideological struggle in the Muslim
world. Suicide bombers killing Americans are more often seen as
freedom fighters than as evildoers.

The new imperialists expected that Americans would be
greeted as liberators in Iraq. Yet US policies had alienated most
Iraqis, both as nationalists and as Muslims. The administration's
war against terrorism discriminated against Muslims. The
President blatantly and personally sided with Israel against the
Palestinians. Ten thousand Muslims were killed in Afghanistan for
no significant improvement in the country. The new imperialists
told a stream of lies about Iraq's supposed weapons of mass
destruction and terrorists. Iraqis suspected the US wanted their
oil, not without reason, since the 2001 Cheney Report on US
energy needs identified Saddam as America's main enemy and

urged the US to use all necessary means against him, "including military intervention."[20] Arab TV channels daily beamed such knowledge to Iraqis, enveloped in graphic video footage of Muslim suffering. Then Iraqis experienced it themselves. In 2003 the US killed over 15,000 Iraqis in six months, a rate of killing Saddam had not matched since 1991. Frightened US troops brandished lethal weapons, shouting "Stop!" in English at checkpoints – symbolizing their near complete ideological failure to communicate to Iraqis.

In the Age of Nationalism, aiding the US after it has invaded your country opens you to the charge of treason. The nations of the world are now held responsible for their own destinies. Outside intervention must be justified by extreme conditions, as the UN Charter states; and intervention must be quick and beneficent. This is a higher standard than the Roman or British Empires could have met. The first years of their conquests were usually mired in the blood of civilian casualties, but this mattered little to the rest of the world. Today the world's dominant ideologies, carried through mass media, contradict *any* imperialism. That is the fundamental ideological problem confronting the new imperialists. Even many in the supposed imperialist camp lack heart and soul for the task of repression.

Conclusion

Problems began to multiply for the new imperialists. New terrorists created by US policy moved into Iraq, now converted by the US into a failed state. Despite massive international cooperation which struck down many existing terrorists, new, younger terrorists struck in Casablanca, Riyadh, and probably in Iraq. The regimes in Iran and North Korea saw that Saddam was invaded because he lacked WMDs, so they rushed more quickly to acquire them while the US was bogged down in Iraq. The US was forced to rely on the UN to pressure Iran, and began to revert to the Clinton policy of offering inducements to North Korea to disarm. These revealed weakening of the new imperialists' resolve. The power struggle between the Pentagon and the State Department

began to tilt toward State for the first time since 9/11. Rumsfeld's
own doubts were leaked in a memo of October 24, 2003. He con-
fesses he does not "know if we are winning or losing the global
war on terror," asking whether we "need to fashion a broad, integrated plan to stop the next generation of terrorists," adding that
Afghanistan and Iraq "will be a long, hard slog."[21] The new imperialists were not yet defeated, though their apparent resolve continued to worsen the situation. There were suspicions across the
Middle East that the US might allow Israel to take out Iranian
nuclear plants, while the continuing policy of pressuring the
Palestinians but not Sharon worsened chaos there, worsened Arab
and Muslim alienation from the US, and increased the flow of terrorists. It was hard to think in recent times of a foreign policy that
was so counterproductive.

This is less a failed Empire than an Empire which never got
started. Will the Bush administration cut and run, or will it tough
it out, and for how long? Unless there is a remarkable and swift
turnaround in Iraq, the administration will have been so chastened
as to eschew imperial measures against other "rogues." I doubt its
pretensions to even a temporary territorial Empire will last past
November 2004, though whether they will be killed by a shift in
policy, by Iraqi fighters, or by American voters remains an open
question as I write.

What then? Provided a satisfactory policy or regime change can
be made in the White House, better policies could be restored.
Extraction from Iraq itself looks very difficult, though it would
probably involve handing over political authority to the UN. It
should be less difficult to shift back to a more effective policy of
anti-WMD proliferation which would offer carrots (security guarantees and economic inducements) as well as sticks. The shift
seems to be already beginning in policy toward North Korea.

Antiterrorist policy would have to make a more radical shift,
out from under the straitjacket term "terrorist." The US must distinguish between national and international terrorists, and accept
the moral equivalence of terrorism and state terrorism. International terrorists are ones like Al-Qaeda who target international
targets, including Americans and other Westerners. They are

enemies of America, and must be fought. But luckily they are much more exposed and easier to eliminate. They are émigrés, operating in alien environments, and their bombings usually kill more locals than Westerners. Thus almost all governments across the world cooperate in tracking them down. National terrorists are those like Hamas, Hezbollah, the Moro Liberation Front in the Philippines, and Chechen and Kashmiri groups, who only attack those they identify as their national oppressor. They are protected amid a "national liberation struggle" and a supportive people. In turn, their oppressor relies on an equally atrocious state terrorism to fight them. Since national liberation struggles are very deeply rooted in the Age of Nation-States and Nationalism, only rarely have national terrorists been completely eliminated in modern times. It is unwise of the US to attempt this, since it will likely fail and bring blowback in the form of terrorists shifting to international targets and attacking Americans. Here the US can bring its power to bear in pressuring both the national terrorists and their state terrorist opponents into settlement of their dispute – as, for example, in putting equal pressure on Sharon and Arafat, the legitimate leaders of their sides.

Additionally, the US might give more generous aid to Muslim countries to help repair the harm the new imperialism has done to US interests there. More generally, a greater commitment against world poverty and disease would help, as would a realization that effective economic policies across the world must be tailored by locals to their own distinctive portfolios of resources. The world also needs more positive collective action against environmental degradation. All of this would aid the spread of genuine democracy.

It would be overoptimistic to expect the US to do all of this. Yet some reaction against the disastrous imperial policies can be expected. They need not leave too harmful a legacy, for the realities of global power remain. The US would remain the global economic leader and the global political leader in "multilateral" organizations. It might easily regain global ideological leadership by reasserting traditional American virtues. It is also the only Power capable of projecting military power around the world. Any vigorous, concerted, global action in any of these policy directions requires American leadership. Little constructive can be done without it. The new imperialists pressured and then ignored their Great Power rivals, but they did not do them actual harm. Nor have they done harm to most countries of the world. If the US shifts policy, they will accept its leadership again, though some will do so grudgingly. Informal, indirect, imperial powers will return, with at least partial hegemony soon following.

Of course, the long run will see relative American decline. American economic power has already declined relative to Europe and Japan, and it will soon also decline relative to China and India. Some of these countries may become politically and even militarily more assertive. Then the world may return to a version of nineteenth-century world order, now characterized by a leading Power (the US), embedded in a multilateral Concert of Powers and a transnational capitalism – boosted perhaps by other transnational actors generated by the present phase of globalization. Let us hope that the twenty-first century does not end badly, as the nineteenth century did. The damage is harder to undo for Muslims and Arabs, the real sufferers from the new imperialism, as well as from their own terrible internal conflicts. But they can at least derive pride from the fact that it is through their sufferings, their conflicts, and their tenacity that the first would-be Empire of the twenty-first century was stopped dead in its tracks.

Notes

1   Niall Ferguson, *Empire: The Rise and Demise of the British World Order and the Lessons for Global Power* (New York: Basic Books, 2002).
2   Paul Kennedy, "The Greatest Superpower Ever," *New Perspectives Quarterly* (Winter 2002).
3   Philip Bobbitt, *The Shield of Achilles* (New York: Alfred A. Knopf, 2001), pp. 678ff.
4   Perry Anderson, "Force and Consent," *New Left Review*, New Series, 17 (September–October 2002); Robert Wade, "The Invisible Hand of the American Empire," *Ethics and International Affairs*, 17, 2 (2003).

5   Representative of the approach are essays in Volker Bornschier and Christopher Chase-Dunn, eds, *The Future of Global Conflict* (London: Sage, 1999).

6   Immanuel Wallerstein, "The Eagle Has Crash-Landed," *Foreign Policy* (July–August, 2002).

7   Patrick O'Brien, "The Governance of Globalization: The Political Economy of Anglo-American Hegemony, 1793–2003," *Center for Economic Studies and Ifo Institute for Economic Research*, Working Paper 1023 (September 2003).

8   Richard Merritt, *Democracy Imposed: US Occupation Policy and the German Public, 1945–1948* (New Haven, CT: Yale University Press, 1995); and John Dower, *Embracing Defeat: Japan in the Wake of World War II* (New York: Norton, 1999).

9   Joseph S. Nye, Jr, *The Paradox of American Power* (New York: Oxford University Press, 2002). A similar view underlies Andrew Bacevich's *American Empire: The Realities and Consequences of U.S. Diplomacy* (Cambridge, MA: Harvard University Press, 2002).

10 Peter Gowan, *Global Gamble: Washington's Faustian Bid for World Dominance* (London: Verso, 1999). Robert Wade gives a succinct account of these powers in his essay "The Invisible Hand".

11 For example, Joseph Stiglitz, *Globalization and its Discontents* (New York: Norton, 2002); and Ha-Joon Chang, *Kicking Away the Ladder* (London: Anthem Press, 2002). On inequality effects, see Samuel Morley, *The Income Distribution Problem in Latin America and the Caribbean* (Santiago, Chile: CEPAL/ECLAC, 2001); William Easterly "The Effect of IMF and World Bank Programs on Poverty," World Bank, unpublished paper (February 2001); and Branko Milanovic, "Can We Discern the Effect of Globalization on Income Distribution? Evidence from Household Budget Surveys," International Trade 0302004, Economics Working Paper Archive at WUSTL.

12 Data from Stockholm Peace Research Institute, and Center for Defense Information websites, and Carl Conetta's "The Pentagon's New Budget, New Strategy, and New War," Project on Defense Alternatives, Briefing Report 12 (June 2002).

13 Andrew W. Marshall, "Some Thoughts on Military Revolutions," Memorandum for the Record, OSD Office of Net Assessment, July 27, 1993. It was hoped that the precision of "smart" bombs would also bring low civilian casualties. Marshall himself claimed "only the bad guys get hurt." The claim proved only partly true. Around 10,000 civilians were killed in Afghanistan, probably more in Iraq.

This is a lot of corpses, though low by most historical conquest comparisons.

14   This is what Michael Ignatieff called "empire lite," in his *Empire Lite: Nation Building in Bosnia, Kosovo, Afghanistan* (London: Minerva, 2003).

15   Phyllis Bennis, *Calling the Shots: How Washington Dominates Today's UN* (New York: Interlink Publishing, 1996).

16   M. Hasan, *John Company to the Republic* (New Delhi: Roli Books, 2001), pp. 107–8, 120; P. S. Gupta and A. Deshpande, eds, *The British Raj and its Indian Armed Forces, 1857–1939* (New Delhi: Oxford University Press, 2002), pp. x, xx, 8; T. A. Heathcote, *The Military in British India* (Manchester: Manchester University Press, 1995), pp. 117, 127; T. Royle, *The Last Days of the Raj* (London: Michael Joseph, 1989), p. 34; L. H. Gann and P. Duignan, *Colonialism in Africa, 1870–1960* (Cambridge: Cambridge University Press, 1977), vol. 2, pp. 5–8, 316; Michael Crowder, *West Africa Under Colonial Rule* (London: Hutchinson, 1968), and *Colonial West Africa* (London: Frank Cass, 1978).

17   Conservative critics of the new imperialism agree. See Gary T. Dempsey, "Old Folly in a New Guise: Nation Building to Combat Terrorism," *Policy Analysis*, 429 (March 21, 2002).

18   Suzanne Kapner, "Pax Americana? Not in World TV Market," *The Straits Times*, Singapore (January 3, 2003); "Faiblit la domination de l'Internet de la part des US" (June 8, 2000), at http://fr.gsmbox .com/news/mobile_news/all/2156.gsmbox.

19   The Pew Global Attitudes Project, *What the World Thinks in 2002* (Washington, DC: The Pew Research Center for the People and the Press, 2002), and Pew Global Attitudes Project, *2002 & Views of a Changing World* (2003), both found at www.astridonline.it/ Cartella-p/What-the-W/; cf. also The German Marshall Fund/ Council on Foreign Relations poll, www.worldviews.org/; "How the Japanese, South Koreans and Chinese View the Post 9-11 World and US Military Action," *The Harris Poll*, 63 (December 26, 2001).

20   "Strategic Energy Policy Challenges for the 21st Century," *Report of an Independent Task Force*, at www.rice.edu/energy/publications/ docs/TaskForceReport_Final.pdf.

21   Talon News (October 24, 2003), "Text of Rumsfeld Memo to Senior Pentagon Officials," at www.gopusa.com/news/2003/october/ 1024_memo_textp.shtml.

3

Liberal Hegemony or Empire? American Power in the Age of Unipolarity

G. John Ikenberry

Introduction

American global power – military, economic, technological, cultural, political – is one of the great realities of our age. Never before has one country been so powerful and unrivaled. The United States began the 1990s as the world's only superpower and its advantages continued to grow through the decade. After the Cold War, the United States reduced its military spending at a slower rate than other countries and its economy grew at a faster pace. The globalization of the world economy has reinforced American economic and political dominance. Russia's economy collapsed after the Cold War and Japan has experienced a decade of malaise. Western Europe is turned inward and China is still a developing country undergoing transformation. No ideological challengers are in sight. More recently, in response to terrorist attacks, the United States has embarked on a massive military buildup, articulated an ambitious doctrine of preemption and expansive global security objectives, and invaded Afghanistan and Iraq to confront new-age threats. American power advantages are multidimensional, unprecedented, and unlikely to disappear any time soon.

The world has taken notice of these developments. Indeed, the post–Cold War rise of American power – what might be called the rise of American "unipolarity" – has unsettled world politics. Governments everywhere are worried about the uncertainties and insecurities that appear to flow from such extreme and unprecedented disparities of power. The shifting global security environment – triggered by the terrorist attacks of September 11, 2001 – has also conspired to upset old relationships and expectations. America's recent military interventions in the Middle East have put American power on display and raised far-reaching questions about the use of force, alliances, weapons of mass destruction, sovereignty, and interventionism. The Bush administration's willingness to act unilaterally – and its seeming disregard for rules and norms of the international community – raise the specter of an emerging unipolar era where the United States unbinds itself from its own postwar order and rules the world by force and fear.

The world is in the midst of a great geopolitical adjustment process. Governments are trying to figure out how an American-centered unipolar order will operate. How will the United States use its power? Will a unipolar world be built around rules and institutions or the unilateral exercise of American power? This global worry about how a unipolar world will operate – in which the most basic questions about the character of world politics are at stake, namely, who benefits and who commands – is the not-so-hidden subtext of all the recent controversies in America's relations with the rest of the world.

The rise of American unipolarity provokes basic questions about the character of international order. Four questions are most important. First, what is the character of United States domination? If it has always been a mix of force and consent, is it shifting increasingly toward force? Second, what are the restraints on American power – if there are any? That is, what disciplines unipolar power after the disappearance of countervailing Soviet power? Third, how tied is the United States to international rules and institutions? Put differently, does unipolarity "select" for unilateralism? Does unipolarity create incentives and opportunities for the United States to increasingly break out of multilateral rules and institutions? Finally, how stable is a unipolar world? Is bal-

ancing, resistance, and breakdown inevitable? Will the world fight
back and bring down unipolar order?

Implicit in these queries is the great political question of our
age. Is unipolarity consistent with rule-based international order?
Around the world a variation of this question – triggered by the
Bush administration's unilateral words and deeds – is being asked.
Has the United States made a fundamental shift away from its
postwar orientation? A long list of rejected treaties and agreements – such as the International Criminal Court, the Kyoto
Protocol, and a variety of arms control accords – suggests this
possibility.[1] One neoconservative pundit has described – and
celebrated – this shift as the "new unilateralism."[2] Richard
Holbrooke, former American ambassador to the United Nations,
charged that the Bush administration threatens to "make a radical
break with fifty-five years of a bipartisan tradition that sought
international agreements and regimes to benefit all."[3]

Governments and people around the world worry that the
United States is "out of control." The rise of terrorism has made
the United States feel more vulnerable – and it has responded by
mobilizing its military power and searching out new enemies and
threats. Divided from the world, the United States is now at war
while most other countries are still at peace. Likewise, the rise of
unipolarity has given the United States the opportunity to disentangle itself from the constraints of postwar commitments and
obligations. The United States needs the world – partners, rules,
alliances, institutions – less than other states do, and so it can
recapture its sovereignty and freedom of action. Capturing the
view of many unipolar worriers, one author has called the United
States a "rogue nation."[4]

Indeed, the United States appears poised between two logics of
global order. One logic is American hegemonic order with "liberal"
characteristics. This is order built around multilateralism, alliance
partnership, strategic restraint, cooperative security, and institutional and rule-based relationships. This is the order that the
United States and its partners built after World War II and which
has come to dominate the global system for half a century – sur-
viving the end of the Cold War and other upheavals.[5] The other
logic is American hegemonic order with "imperial" characteristics.

This is order built about American unilateralism, coercive domination, and reduced commitment to shared rules of the game. In this order, American power is the provider, protector, arbiter, and final word in international order.[6]

The view that America is making a grand historic turn toward imperial rule is reflected in a growing body of scholarship that evokes images of empire. "No one can deny the extent of the American informal empire," argues Niall Ferguson, who likens today's imperium to its British precursor. "Even recent American foreign policy recalls the gunboat diplomacy of the British Empire in its Victorian heyday, when a little trouble on the periphery could be dealt with by a short, sharp 'surgical strike.'"[7] The new theorists of empire argue that multilateralism and the rule of law will give way to American power exercised more directly. It is a vision in which sovereignty becomes more absolute for America even as it becomes more conditional for countries that challenge Washington's standards of external and internal behavior.[8]

The vision of coercive-unilateral American power inspires other theorists to argue that unipolarity will eventually generate counterbalancing resistance. Other states will not want to live in a world of imperial American power with its constant risks of domination and exploitation – and so balance of power politics will inevitably emerge. Because unipolarity is prone toward the rule of power rather than the rule of law, states will respond with the only strategy available to restrain and limit unipolar power, namely counterbalancing power.[9] Unipolarity will go the way of all great historical projects of geopolitical domination. The United States has too much power for its own good.[10] The rise of the European Union is driven, at least in part, by an effort to amass power so as to resist the vagaries and humiliations of a too powerful and increasingly unpredictable America.[11] The rest of the world will pull back and find alternative centers of power to resist unipolar dangers.

I argue otherwise. Unipolarity is actually quite consistent with multilateral, rule-based order. At the very least, powerful – even unipolar – states have deep and enduring incentives to construct and operate in a world of rules and institutions. The United States will act unilaterally in many areas – as it has in the past. But it is not destined to untangle itself from the postwar order and reorganize itself as a global imperial state. The best image of what is happening today is not an American rejection of rule-based order in favor of neo-imperial rule – even though many right-wing officials and pundits in Washington do indeed wish to end America's postwar commitment to multilateral order. A better image of what is happening today is a rising America trying to renegotiate the existing rule-based order. The United States is more powerful, so it wants a better deal. It also faces a transformed international environment, so it wants a different deal. But at the end of this sequence of crisis and institutional bargaining, the resulting international order will still be organized around agreed rules and institutions – but adjusted to the new realities. The United States is not abandoning its commitment to multilateral and rule-based order and the Western order is not falling apart. The postwar order is going through a crisis of renegotiation.

In what follows, I advance the thesis that the United States' unipolar order is relatively stable. Indeed, it is best to see it as a durable, complex, and distinctive transcontinental political formation. It is a political formation – built around capitalism, democracy, and security community among the advanced industrial countries – that is bigger than the United States itself. The political order was given shape by the United States over the decades – as it still is. But it is also an order that has structures and features in which the United States itself is embedded. In this sense, the United States must adjust and accommodate itself to this order and not simply run it as an imperial state.[12] American unipolar power is a dominant reality of this order but that power is expressed within and through the institutions, markets, politics, and community of this larger order. American presidents do not always act to restrain and bind power but the larger system – at least over the long haul – biases power in that direction.

The genius of today's unipolar order is that it is based on both power and restraint. On the one hand, American power is sufficiently benign, complex, and institutionalized not to trigger a counterbalancing coalition. On the other, American power advantages are sufficiently robust, multidimensional, and rooted in global structures of modernity to last for decades. At the worst,

the United States–centered international order of today is entering a new era with rising conflict among states that essentially are
incapable or unwilling to go to war against each other. The United
States and the other democratic great powers may not be as united
or harmonious as they were during the Cold War, when an external threat created unusual amounts of cohesion. But there is a
foundation of democracy, capitalism, and security community on
which today's differences rest.[13]

The first section of the paper explores the complex ways that
American power is manifest and experienced around the world
today. The United States is powerful but – despite the best efforts
of the Bush administration – it is not neo-imperial. The second
section examines the four major facets of American power. Again,
the conclusion is drawn that American power is robust but not
neo-imperial. Finally, the last section looks at the three major
sources or incentives that give the United States reasons – despite
its unipolar power – to commit itself to at least a loose form of
rule-based order.

The Uniqueness of American Power

America confronts the world as a complex creature. During the
last century, the United States has shown the world many different faces – it is to various degrees and in different mixtures at different moments unilateral, interventionist, isolationist, militarist,
hegemonic, nationalist, and unrivaled champion of democracy and
international law. The world has, in return, complex views of
American power. It worries about American excesses – but also
the absences of US power. The United States can be both too
pushy and too ready to go home. The United States provides both
dangers and opportunities for other states. Peoples in countries
around the world can simultaneously be drawn to American culture, political ideals, or its civil society and hate its leaders or
policies. American power – as manifested and experienced – is
anything but simple.[14]

In characterizing American power, it is useful to make five
general observations. First, it is important to note that despite the

rise of American unipolar power, the other major states are not making systematic choices to pull away from and balance against the United States. This is interesting. History suggests that states do not like to live in a world of a single dominant state. Balancing is a deeply rooted reaction to concentrated state power.[15] Charles V, Louis XIV, Napoleon I, and post-Bismarck Germany – all these hegemonic aspirants were eventually brought down by coalitions of states that were determined to rebalance the distribution of power.[16] Yet this sort of dynamic has not emerged. Despite the collapse of the Soviet Union and huge shifts in the distribution of power in favor of the United States, other states have not made moves toward geopolitical balance. United States relations with Western Europe and Japan after the Cold War have remained relatively stable. Deep shifts have not surfaced. The advanced democratic countries have reaffirmed their alliance ties, contained political conflict, expanded trade and investment across the continents, and avoided a return to strategic rivalry. Indeed, despite the crisis in 2002–3 over America's invasion of Iraq, Western Europe and Japan have not articulated visions of world order based on geopolitical balancing against the United States. France has been the most resistant to American unipolar power, but it has not attempted to organize a counterbalancing coalition based on independent and opposing military power.[17]

Even more surprisingly, rather than try to balance against United States power, China and Russia have moved closer to the United States. Russia is now in a near permanent alliance with the United States, integrated into the Western security framework. Remarkably, China has also dropped its rhetoric of anti-American "hegemonism" and worked with the United States in the fight against terrorism and the diplomatic engagement of North Korea. As Michael Mastanduno has argued:

> Rather than edging away from the United States, much less balancing against it, Europe and Japan have been determined to maintain the pattern of engagement that characterized the Cold War. Neither China nor Russia, despite having differences with the United States, has sought to organize a balancing coalition against it. Rather than edging away, much less balancing against it, the

other great powers have maintained a pattern of engagement with the United States. Indeed, the main security concern in Europe and Asia is not how to distance from an all-too-powerful United States, but how to prevent the United States from drifting away.[18]

Interestingly, the end of the Cold War has not eliminated the cohesion among the advanced industrial democracies. In both economic and military spheres, the United States leads its nearest rivals by a larger margin than has any other leading state in the last three centuries. Yet despite this concentration of American power, there is very little evidence that other states are actively seeking to balance against it or organize a counter-hegemonic coalition. This is a puzzle that must be answered: in a decade of sharp shifts in the distribution of power, why has there been so much stability and persistence of order among the major states?[19]

Second, the United States is a unique sort of global superpower. That is, it has a distinctive cluster of capabilities, institutions, attractions, and impulses. Indeed, American power is manifest in complex and paradoxical ways. For example, during the twentieth century, the United States was the greatest champion of rule-based order. It pushed onto the global stage a long list of international institutions and rules – the League of Nations, the United Nations, GATT, human rights norms, and so forth. But the United States has also been unusually ambivalent about actually operating itself within legal and institutional constraints. Moreover, the United States has used military force more than any other state in the last 50 years (with and without UN or NATO backing). Yet it also has an anti-imperial political culture and a strong isolationist tradition.[20]

The point here is that it is difficult for other countries to simply decide that American power is manifest in any one way. American power is sometimes menacing but at other times it helps provide global public goods and at other times it turns inward. American power is sufficiently complex and multifaceted that it is difficult for countries to simply decide to counter or work against United States power. American power is complex and because of this there are reasons for other states to have complex views of and strategies for dealing with the United States.

Third, countries and peoples "experience" American unipolar power in different ways. A threat to some is an opportunity to others. This is true across states – some states find American power more useful and easy to accommodate than others. For example, Japan finds America's security role in East Asia more useful to it than France finds America's security role in Europe. Likewise, people in particular states will see American power differently. In most states there is a range of views, and these views can be directed at American policy or more generally at America as a global power.[21]

Fourth, in this regard, it is useful to distinguish at least three levels or types of American power that are generating reactions around the world. At the most basic level, American power is manifest as the underwriter of American capitalism and globalization. This is where America gets implicated in the protests over the WTO and the IMF. In effect, the global spread of modern Western systems of politics and economics is a process in which power is being exercised. Power is manifest in two ways. One is "power through integration" – that is, power is manifest through the spread of capitalism and democracy which displaces local and non-Western social and political structures. As more and more parts of the world are absorbed into this American-dominated order, weak and vulnerable societies lose aspects of their autonomy and distinctiveness. The structures of global order act on them. The other way is "power through subordination" – that is, power is manifest as these newly integrated societies find themselves increasingly shaped and constrained by the more powerful societies at the core of the system, particularly the United States. The spread of modern, Western order creates new forms of superordinate and subordinate relations.[22]

At another level, American power is manifest as the leader of a global political and military alliance system. This is power that is evident as the United States builds on its postwar order making efforts – dating back to the 1940s – and extends and defends it today. Americans tend to see their country's global role as enlightened leadership, providing markets and security protection to Europe and East Asia in exchange for cooperation and partnership from countries in these regions. But peoples and governments in these regions can see the presence of American military and political power as intrusive and domineering. The institutional expression of American power is relatively stable over the postwar era, anchored in security and economic partnerships with key states in all geographical regions. But the circumstances in which America's extended order is perceived and experienced does change. Obviously, the end of the Cold War has altered the character of the threats that Europeans and Asians encounter, and this alters the way the United States is seen and appreciated as a security provider. Political change inside partner countries – and the turnover of generations of leaders – also alters the way American power is perceived.

It is at this level of American power, for example, that people in nations such as South Korea or Germany seek to push the United States out of their country. Some people attack or oppose the United States because it is the alliance partner that is supported by their own government. American power is challenged because that power – in some countries such as Pakistan or Saudi Arabia – helps perpetuate unwanted regimes.[23]

A final level of American power is manifest in specific policies or issues. For example, some people – such as in South Korea – oppose the United States because of specific Status of Forces Agreements in their country which protect American soldiers from local justice. Others oppose the United States because of its decisions on the use of force, such as in the recent invasion of Iraq. Governments and peoples can oppose the United States because of its new doctrine of preemption. This manifestation of American power – specific policies of specific leaders – is in constant motion. If you do not like American policy today, be patient – times will change. Germany's Chancellor Schroeder and French President Chirac may have unresolvable differences with American President Bush, but these elected leaders pass from the stage on a regular basis, and so too do views of United States power change.

Fifth, most of the great powers' responses to American unipolarity seem to be falling between the extremes of balancing and bandwagoning. States can resist without balancing and they can engage without simply acquiescing. During the Iraq War, British

Prime Minister Tony Blair pursued a strategy of getting as close as possible to the Bush administration. The strategy was to be so close to and supportive of the American exercise of power that Britain would ultimately get some voice in how policy unfolded. French President Chirac pursued a different policy, attempting to build an opposing political coalition to the Bush administration's Iraq policy. Both were attempting to deal with a difficult reality: the United States was powerful enough to go on its own. How to get some leverage over American exercise of power was the challenge. The two leaders chose different strategies. In the aftermath of the war, the effectiveness of the two strategies is being debated across Europe. How this debate unfolds will say a lot about future resort to the strategies. Again, it is useful to see the present moment as one where governments are making judgements, experimenting with strategies, learning lessons, and adapting their behavior.

Four Facets of American Power

American power advantages are multidimensional. In particular, four facets of American power reinforce unipolarity and undercut incentives to resist or balance against the United States. These facets of power are: traditional power assets; geography and historical timing; democracy and institutional restraints; and modernization and civic identity. Together these multiple dimensions of American power suggest that unipolarity is likely to persist and that the other major states are likely to continue to have incentives to engage and work with the United States – even as they devise new strategies to cope with unipolarity.[24]

Traditional power assets

The first facet of American power is its traditional power assets – material capabilities that allow it to pursue its objective and get other states to go along with it.[25] One aspect of material capabilities is the sheer size of the American military establishment. As

mentioned earlier, American military expenditures are greater
than those of the next 14 countries combined – and if current
trends continue, the United States' military expenditure will be
equal to the rest of the world combined by 2007. The advanced
technological character of much of this military power makes this
power disparity even greater.

This mass of military power makes it difficult if not impossible
for a group of states to develop capabilities that could balance or
counter that of the United States. But other considerations further
increase the difficulties of organizing a counterbalancing coalition.
First, there are collective action problems. States might like to see
the formation of a counter-unipolar coalition but they would
prefer other states to do the work of organizing it and covering
its costs. This is the problem of "buck passing" – the collective
action problem that makes it less likely that a coalition will form.
There is also the problem of regional blocking problems. If
particular great powers do decide to amass greater military power
to challenge the United States, other major states in their region
are likely to be threatened by this move and challenge it. For
example, if Japan were to undertake military mobilization to
counter the United States, it would find a hostile East Asian neigh-
borhood awaiting it. These considerations make counterbalancing
unlikely.[26]

Other material power assets also work to America's advantage
– namely, security protection, markets, and nuclear weapons.
Alliance security protection that the United States has the capacity to extend to states in all four corners of the world provides
a positive incentive to cooperate with the United States. This
incentive is of two sorts. One is simply that American security
protection reduces the resources that these countries would otherwise need to generate to cover their own protection. It is a cost-
effective way to deal with the elemental problem of national
security. If it means working with the United States and not offering opposition to it, the forgoing of this option of opposition is a
cost that is more than compensated for by the value of the security protection itself. The second benefit of security protection, at
least for some states, is that it means that these states won't need
to face the regional challenges that might come if they provided
for their own security. Germany and Japan are the best examples

of this. By positioning themselves under the American security umbrella, Germany and Japan were able to reassure their worried neighbors that they would not become future security threats to their respective regions. The United States is able to provide it to so many countries because it has the economic and military capabilities to do so on a worldwide basis. Indeed, it might well be that economies of scale exist for a versatile and high-tech military power such as the United States.

Another aspect of American material power is its large domestic market. Both Europeans and East Asians depend mightily on access to the American market. Of course, the United States relies heavily on both regions for its own economic prosperity. But the simple point here is that East Asia and Western Europe have incentives not to resist American unipolarity in such a way as to break apart the open markets that cut across the Pacific and Atlantic.

American unipolarity is also sustained by nuclear weapons. Even if the other major powers wanted to overturn the existing order, the mechanism of great-power war is no longer available. As Robert Gilpin has noted, great-power war is precisely the mechanism of change that has been used throughout history to redraw the international order. Rising states depose the reigning – but declining – state and impose a new order.[27] But nuclear weapons make this historical dynamic profoundly problematic. On the one hand, American power is rendered more tolerable because in the age of nuclear deterrence American military power cannot now be used for conquest against other great powers. Deterrence replaces alliance counterbalancing. On the other hand, the status quo international order led by the United States is rendered less easily replaceable. War-driven change is removed as an historical process, and the United States was lucky enough to be on top when this happened.

Geography and historical setting

The geographic setting and historical timing of America's rise to power have also shaped the way American primacy has been manifest. The United States is the only great power that is not neighbored by other great powers. This geographical remoteness made the power ascent of the United States less threatening to the rest of the world and it reinforced the disinclination of American leaders to directly dominate or manage great-power relations. In the twentieth century, the United States became the world's preeminent power but the location and historical entry point of that power helped shape how this arrival was greeted.

When the United States was drawn into European power struggles, it did so primarily as an offshore balancer.[28] This was an echo of Britain's continental strategy, which for several centuries was based on aloofness from European power struggles, with intervention at critical moments to tip and restore the balance among the other states. This offshore balancing role was played out by the United States in the two world wars. America entered each war relatively late and tipped the balance in favor of the allies. After World War II, the United States emerged as an equally important presence in Europe, Asia, and the Middle East as an offshore military force that each region found useful in solving its local security dilemmas. In Europe, the reintegration of West Germany into the West was only possible with the American security commitment. The Franco-German settlement was explicitly and necessarily embedded in an American-guaranteed Atlantic settlement. In Joseph Joffe's apt phrase, the United States became "Europe's pacifier."[29] In East Asia, the American security pact with Japan also solved regional security dilemmas by creating restraints on the resurgence of Japanese military power. In the Middle East a similar dynamic drew the United States into an active role in mediating between Israel and the Arab states. In each region, American power is seen less as a source of domination and more as a useful tool.[30]

Because the United States is geographically remote, abandonment rather than domination has been seen as the greater risk by many states. As a result, the United States has found itself constantly courted by governments in Europe, Asia, and elsewhere. When Winston Churchill advanced ideas about postwar order he was concerned above all to find a way to tie the United States to Europe.[31] As Geir Lundestad has observed, the expanding American political order in the half-century after World War II has been in important respects an "empire by invitation."[32] The remarkable global reach of American postwar hegemony has been at least in part driven by the efforts of European and Asian governments to harness American power, render that power more predictable, and use it to overcome their own regional insecurities. The result has been a durable system of America-centered economic and security partnerships.

Finally, the historical timing of America's rise in power also left a mark. The United States came relatively late to the great power arena, after the colonial and imperial eras had run their course. This meant that the pursuit of America's strategic interests was not primarily based on territorial control but on championing more principled ways of organizing great-power relations. As a late-developing great power the United States needed openness and access to the regions of the world rather than recognition of its territorial claims. The American issuance of its Open Door policy toward China reflected this orientation. American officials were never fully consistent in wielding such principled claims about order and they were often a source of conflict with the other major states. But the overall effect of this alignment of American geostrategic interests with enlightened normative principles of order reinforced the image of the United States as a relatively non-coercive and nonimperial hegemonic power.

Democracy and institutional restraints

The American unipolar order is also organized around democratic polities and a complex web of intergovernmental institutions, and these features of the American system alter and mute the way in which hegemonic power is manifest. One version of this argument is the democratic peace thesis: open democratic polities are less able or willing to use power in an arbitrary and indiscriminate manner against other democracies.[33] The calculations of smaller and weaker states as they confront a democratic hegemon are altered. Fundamentally, power asymmetries are less threatening or destabilizing when they exist between democracies. American power is "institutionalized" – not entirely, of course, but more so than in the case of previous world-dominating states. This institutionalization of hegemonic strategy serves the interest of the United States by making its power more legitimate, expansive, and durable. But the price is that some restraints are indeed placed on the exercise of power.[34]

In this view, three elements matter most in making American power more stable, engaged, and restrained. First, America's mature political institutions organized around the rule of law have made it a relatively predictable and cooperative hegemon. The pluralistic and regularized way in which American foreign and security policy is made reduces surprises and allows other states to build long-term, mutually beneficial relations. The governmental separation of powers creates a shared decision-making system that opens up the process and reduces the ability of any one leader to make abrupt or aggressive moves toward other states. An active press and competitive party system also provide a service to outside states by generating information about United States policy and determining its seriousness of purpose. The messiness of democracy can frustrate American diplomats and confuse foreign observers. But over the long term, democratic institutions produce more consistent and credible policies than autocratic or authoritarian states.[35]

This open and decentralized political process works in a second way to reduce foreign worries about American power. It creates what might be called "voice opportunities" – it offers opportunities for political access and, with it, the means for foreign governments and groups to influence the way Washington's power is exercised. Foreign governments and corporations may not have elected officials in Washington but they do have representatives.[36] Looked at from the perspective of the stable functioning of America's unipolar order, this is one of the most functional aspects of the United States as a global power. By providing other states with opportunities to play the game in Washington, the United States draws them into active, ongoing partnerships that serve its long-term strategic interests.

A final element of the unipolar order that reduces the worry about power asymmetries is the web of institutions that mark the postwar order. After World War II, the United States launched history's most ambitious era of institution building. The UN, IMF, World Bank, NATO, GATT, and other institutions that emerged provided the most rule-based structure for political and economic relations in history. The United States was deeply ambivalent about making permanent security commitments to other countries or allowing its political and economic policies to be dictated by intergovernmental bodies. The Soviet threat was critical in overcoming these doubts. Networks and political relationships were built that – paradoxically – both made American power more far-reaching and durable but also more predictable and malleable.[37]

Modernization and civic nationalism

American power has been rendered more acceptable to the rest of the world because the United States "project" is congruent with the deeper forces of modernization. The point here is not that the United States has pushed other states to embrace its goals and purposes but that all states are operating within a transforming global system – driven by modernization, industrialization, and social mobilization. The synchronicity between the rise of the United States as a liberal global power and the system-wide imperatives of modernization creates a sort of functional "fit" between the United States and the wider world order. If the United States were attempting to project state socialist economic ideas or autocratic political values, its fit with the deep forces of modernization would be poor. Its purposes would be resisted around the world and trigger resistance to American power. But the deep congruence between the American model and the functional demands of modernization both boost the power of the United States and make its relationship with the rest of the world more harmonious.

Industrialization is a constantly evolving process and the social and political characteristics within countries that it encourages and rewards – and that promote or impede industrial advancement – change over time and as countries move through developmental stages. In this sense, the fit between a polity and modernization is never absolute or permanent.[38] Industrialism in advanced societies tends to feature highly educated workforces, rapid flows of information, and progressively more specialized and complex systems of social and industrial organization. These features of industrial society – sometimes called "late industrialism" – tend to foster a citizenry that is heterogenous, well educated, and difficult to coerce.[39] From this perspective it is possible to see why various state socialist and authoritarian countries – including the Soviet Union – ran into trouble as the twentieth century proceeded. The old command order impeded industrial modernization while, at the same time, industrial modernization undercut the old command order. In contrast, the American polity has tended to have a relatively good fit with the demands and opportunities of industrial modernization. European and Asian forms of capitalist democracy have also exhibited features that seem in various ways to be quite congruent with the leading edge of advanced industrial development. The success of the American model is partly due to the fact that it used its postwar power to build an international order that worked to the benefit of the American style of industrial capitalism. But the success of the American model – and the enhanced global influence and appeal that the United States has experienced in recent decades – is also due to the deep congruence between the logic of modernization and the American system.

The functionality between the United States polity and wider evolutionary developments in the international system can also be traced to the American political identity, which is rooted in civic nationalism and multiculturalism. The basic distinction between civil and ethnic nationalism is useful in locating this feature. Civic nationalism is group identity that is composed of commitments to the nation's political creed. Race, religion, gender, language, or ethnicity are not relevant in defining a citizen's rights and inclusion within the polity. Shared belief in the country's principles and values embedded in the rule of law is the organizing basis for political order, and citizens are understood to be equal and rights-bearing individuals. Ethnic nationalism, in contrast, maintains that individuals' rights and participation within the polity are inherited – based on ethnic or racial ties.[40]

Because civic nationalism is shared with other Western states it tends to be a source of cohesion and cooperation. Throughout the industrial democratic world, the dominant form of political identity is based on a set of abstract and juridical rights and responsibilities, which coexist with private ethnic and religious associations. Just as warring states and nationalism tend to reinforce each other, so too do Western civic identity and cooperative political relations. Political order – domestic and international – is strengthened when there exists a substantial sense of community and shared identity. It matters that the leaders of today's advanced industrial states are not seeking to legitimate their power by making racial or imperialist appeals. Civic nationalism, rooted in shared commitment to democracy and the rule of law, provides a widely embraced identity across most of the American hegemonic order. At the same time, potentially divisive identity conflicts – rooted in antagonistic ethnic or religious or class divisions – are dampened by relegating them to secondary status within civil society.

Unipolar Power and Multilateralism

Has the rise of American unipolar power in the 1990s reduced its incentives for operating in a multilateral, rule-based order? In this view, the United States has become so powerful that it does not need to sacrifice its autonomy and freedom of action within multilateral agreements. With the end of the Cold War and the absence of serious geopolitical challengers, the United States is able to act alone without serious costs.

Multilateralism can be a tool or expedient in some circumstances but states will not want to be tangled up in institutions and rules and they will avoid or shed entanglements when they can. Power disparities make it easier for the United States to walk away from potential international agreements. Across the spectrum of economic, security, environmental, and other policy issues, the sheer size and power advantages of the United States make it easier to resist multilateral restraints. That is, the costs of non-agreement are lower for the United States than for other states – which gives it bargaining advantages if it wants them but also a greater ability to live without agreement without suffering consequences.

The shifting power differentials have also created new divergent interests between the United States and the rest of the world, which further reduces possibilities for multilateral cooperation. For example, the sheer size of the American economy – and a decade of growth unmatched by Europe, Japan, or the other advanced countries – means that United States obligations under the Kyoto Protocol would be vastly greater than those of other states. In the security realm, the United States has global interests and security threats that no other state has. Its troops are more likely to be dispatched to distant battlefields than those of the other major states – which means that it is more exposed to the legal liabilities of the ICC (International Criminal Court) than others. The United States must worry about threats to its interests in all the major regions of the world. American unipolar power makes it a unique target for terrorism. It is not surprising that Europeans and Asians make different threat assessments about terrorism and rogue states seeking weapons of mass destruction than American officials do. If multilateralism entails working within agreed rules and institutions for the use of force, this growing divergence will make such multilateral agreements less easy to achieve – and less desirable in the view of the United States.

Yet the United States is not structurally destined to disentangle itself from multilateral order and go it alone. Indeed, there continue to be deep underlying incentives for the United States to support multilateralism and rule-based order – incentives that in many ways are in fact increasing. These sources of multilateralism stem from the functional demands of interdependence, the long-term power calculations of power management, and American political tradition and identity.[41]

Economic interdependence and multilateralism

American support for multilateralism is likely to be sustained – even in the face of resistance and ideological challenges to multilateralism within the Bush administration – in part because of a simple logic: as global economic interdependence grows, the need for multilateral coordination of policies also increases. The more economically interconnected that states become the more dependent they are for the realization of their objectives on the actions of other states. "As interdependence rises," Robert Keohane argues, "the opportunity costs of not co-ordinating policy increase, compared with the costs of sacrificing autonomy as a consequence of making binding agreements."[42] Rising economic interdependence is one of the great hallmarks of the contemporary international system. Over the postwar era, states have actively and consistently sought to open markets and reap the economic, social, and technological gains that derive from integration into the world economy. If this remains true in the years ahead, it is easy to predict that the demands for multilateral agreements – even and perhaps especially by the United States – will increase and not decrease.[43]

The American postwar commitment to a system of multilateral economic rules and institutions can be understood in this way. As the world's dominant state, the United States championed GATT – and the Bretton Woods institutions – as a way of locking in other countries to an open world economy that would ensure massive economic gains for itself. But to get these states to organize their postwar domestic orders around an open world economy – and accept the political risks and vulnerabilities associated with openness – the United States had to signal that it too would play by the rules and not exploit and abandon these weaker countries. The postwar multilateral institutions facilitated this necessary step. As the world economy and trading system has expanded over the decades, this logic has continued. This is reflected in the WTO which replaced the GATT in 1995 and embodies an expansive array of legal-institutional rules and mechanisms. In effect, the United States demands an expanding and ever more complex international economic environment, but to get other states to support it the United States must itself become more embedded in this system of rules and institutions. Accordingly, it is not surprising that the Bush administration has succeeded in gaining "fast track" authority from Congress and led the launch of a new multilateral trade round.

American hegemony and multilateralism

American support for multilateralism can also stem from a grand strategic interest in preserving power and creating a stable and legitimate international order. The support for multilateralism is a way to signal restraint and commitment to other states, thereby encouraging the acquiescence and cooperation of weaker states.[44] This has been a strategy that the United States has pursued to a greater or lesser degree across the twentieth century – and it explains the remarkably durable and legitimate character of the existing international order. From this perspective, multilateralism – and the search for rule-based agreements – should increase rather than decrease with the rise of American unipolarity. It predicts that the existing multilateral order, which itself reflects an older multilateral bargain between the United States and the outside world, should rein in the Bush administration – and it suggests that the current administration should respond to general power management incentives and limit its tilt toward unilateralism.[45]

This theoretical perspective begins by looking at the choices that dominant states face when they are in a position to shape the fundamental character of the international order. A state that wins a war or through some other turn of events finds itself in a dominant global position faces a choice: it can use its power to bargain and coerce other states in struggles over the distribution of gains or, knowing its power position will someday decline and that there are costs to enforcing its way within the order, it can move toward a more rule-based, institutionalized order in exchange for the acquiescence and compliant participation of weaker states. In seeking a more rule-based order, the leading state is agreeing to engage in strategy restraint – it is acknowledging that there will be limits on the way in which it can exercise its power. Such an order, in effect, has "constitutional" characteristics. Limits are set on what a state within the order can do with its power advantages. Just as in constitutional polities, the implications of "winning" in politics are reduced. Weaker states realize that the implications of their inferior position are limited and perhaps temporary – to operate within the order despite their disadvantages is not to risk everything nor will it give the dominant state a permanent advantage. Both powerful and weak states agree to operate within the same order despite radical asymmetries in the distribution of power.[46]

Multilateralism becomes a mechanism by which a dominant state can reach a bargain with weaker states over the character of international order. The dominant state reduces its "enforcement costs" and it succeeds in establishing an order where weaker states will participate willingly – rather than resist or balance against the leading power.[47] It accepts some restrictions on how it can use its power; the rules and institutions that are created serve as an "investment" in the longer-run preservation of its power advantages. Weaker states agree to the order's rules and institutions and in return they are assured that the worst excesses of the leading state – manifest as arbitrary and indiscriminate abuses of state power – will be avoided, and they gain institutional opportunities to work and help influence the leading state.[48]

Political identity and multilateralism

A final source of American multilateralism emerges from the polity itself. The United States has a distinctive self-understanding about the nature of its own political order, and this has implications for how it thinks about international political order. To be sure, there are multiple political traditions in the United States that reflect divergent and often competing ideas about how the United States should relate to the rest of the world. These traditions variously counsel isolationism and activism, realism and idealism, aloofness and engagement in the conduct of American foreign affairs. But behind these political-intellectual traditions are deeper aspects of the American political identity that inform the way the United States seeks to build order in the larger global system. The Enlightenment origins of the American founding have given the United States an identity that sees its principles of politics as being of universal significance and scope. The republican–democratic tradition that enshrines the rule of law reflects an enduring American view that polities – domestic or international

– are best organized around rules and principles of order. America's tradition of civil nationalism also reinforces this notion that the rule of law is the source of legitimacy and political inclusion. This tradition provides a background support for a multilaterally oriented foreign policy.

Of course American leaders can campaign against multilateral treaties and institutions and win votes. But this has been true across the last century, manifest most dramatically with the rejection of the League of Nations treaty in 1919 but also reflected in other defeats, such as the International Trade Organization after World War II. When President Bush went to the United Nations to rally support for his hardline approach to Iraq, he did not articulate a central role for the world body in promoting international security and peace. He told the General Assembly: "We will work with the U.N. Security Council for the necessary resolutions." But he also made clear: "The purposes of the United States should not be doubted. The Security Council resolutions will be enforced . . . or action will be unavoidable." In contrast, just twelve years earlier, when the elder President Bush appeared before the General Assembly to press his case for resisting Iraq's invasion of Kuwait, he offered a "vision of a new partnership of nations . . . a partnership based on consultations, cooperation and collective action, especially through international and regional organizations, a partnership united by principle and the rule of law and supported by an equitable sharing of both cost and commitment." It would appear that quite divergent visions of American foreign policy can be articulated by different presidents – each resonating in its own way with ideas and beliefs within the American polity. If this is true, it means that American presidents do have political and intellectual space to shape policy – and that they are not captives of a unilateralist-minded public.

Conclusion

In evaluating the emerging great power reactions to unipolarity, the first question that must be asked is: what precisely are the threats that concentrated American power present to the other major states? The fact that the United States does not seek territorial conquest or direct domination of the other states – either because it has no incentives to do so or because nuclear weapons and other factors make it very costly or impossible – sets the parameters for thinking about the reactions to unipolarity.

As noted at the beginning, it can be argued that the greater the willingness of the United States to exercise its power through multilateral, rule-based mechanisms and institutions the less the likelihood of systematic great power resistance to American unipolar power. This hypothesis brings us back to the question posed earlier: to what extent does unipolarity create incentives and pressures for the United States to reduce its willingness to operate in multilateral, rule-based ways? Does the distribution of power increasingly "select" for unilateralism in American foreign policy? Is the United States doomed to act unilaterally and exercise its power in increasingly arbitrary and indiscriminate ways or to act in a coercive and imperial manner? To answer these questions is to determine whether great power reactions to American unipolarity will move in the direction of resistance and loosening of ties or in the direction of engagement and bandwagoning.

There are at least three sources of rule-based multilateralism in American foreign policy that serve as counterpressures to unipolar unilateralism. One is simply the functional demands of cooperation in the face of growing economic interdependence. American support for multilateralism can also stem from a grand strategic interest in preserving power and creating a stable and legitimate international order. A final source of American multilateralism emerges from the United States polity itself. The United States has a distinctive self-understanding about the nature of its own political order – and this has implications for how it thinks about international political order.

These considerations allow us to specify a variety of mechanisms that reinforce restraint in the exercise of American unipolar power. One restraint mechanism is simply the by-product of functional bargaining with other states. The United States may be preeminent but it is not omnipotent. It needs other states, and so the United States and the other major states will seek bargains that allow them to achieve mutual gains. Another restraint is a by-product of the sensitivity of the United States to its international legitimacy. The United States has a great incentive for other states to willingly accept America's preeminent position rather than resist it. It is not in America's interest to be the lead state in a coercive order built around the exercise of naked power. The decision by the Bush administration to go back to the UN Security Council to get support for its confrontation with Iraq shows how even an administration that is skeptical of the UN understands the benefits that ensue from the legitimate use of force. A third mechanism of restraint comes from the intergovernmental pulling and hauling which is facilitated by democracy and global institutions. Even a unipolar state is embedded in a larger structure of ongoing political relations and interactions.

A final mechanism of restraint resides in the deeper processes of modernization. States are not simply interacting power packages, they are also societies undergoing long-term transformations driven by the forces of industrialization and modernization. In this regard, the functionality between the United States and the wider evolutionary developments in the international system will be critical in determining the degree of congruence and incongruence between it and the other major states. To the extent that the United States continues to be at the leading edge of modernization, the other major states will ultimately find reasons to work with and engage the United States. If the United States falls off the cutting edge of modernization and becomes a huge backwater that seeks only to protect its existing gains, great power conflicts will likely re-emerge. American unipolar power built on a twenty-first-century version of the "iron and rye" coalition will have a different foreign policy and global presence than one built on leading edge, internationally oriented socioeconomic interests and coalitions. Which is another way of saying that the world reacts not just to American power but also to its purpose and functionality within the larger system.

Notes

1   For surveys of recent American unilateralism, see Stewart Patrick and Shepard Forman, eds, *Multilateralism and U.S. Foreign Policy:*

Ambivalent Engagement (Boulder, CO: Lynne Rienner Publishers, 2002); David M. Malone and Yuen Foong Khong, eds, *Unilateralism and U.S. Foreign Policy: International Perspectives* (Boulder, CO: Lynne Rienner Publishers, 2003); and Nicole Deller, Arjun Makhijani, and John Burroughs, eds, *Rule of Power or Rule of Law? An Assessment of U.S. Policies and Actions Regarding Security-Related Treaties* (New York: Apex Press, 2003).

2   Charles Krauthammer, "The New Unilateralism," *The Washington Post* (8 June 2001), p. A29.

3   Quoted in Todd S. Purdum, "Embattled, Scrutinized, Powell Soldiers On," *The New York Times* (July 25, 2002), p. 1.

4   Clyde Prestowitz, *Rogue Nation: American Unilateralism and the Failure of Good Intentions* (New York: Basic Books, 2003).

5   I have sketched this logic of order in various writings, including Ikenberry, *After Victory: Institutions, Strategic Restraint, and the Rebuilding of Order After Major War* (Princeton: Princeton University Press, 2001).

6   Ikenberry, "America's Imperial Ambition," *Foreign Affairs*, 81, 5 (September–October 2002), pp. 44–60.

7   Niall Ferguson, *Empire: The Rise and Demise of the British World Order and the Lessons for Global Power* (New York: Basic Books), p. 368.

8   See Andrew J. Bacevich, *American Empire: The Realities and Consequences of U.S. Diplomacy* (Cambridge, MA: Harvard University Press, 2002); Robert Kaplan, "Supremacy by Stealth," *Atlantic Monthly* (July–August 2003), pp. 65–84; Jack Snyder, "Imperial Temptation," *National Interest* (Spring 2003); Stephen Rosen, "An Empire, If You Can Keep It," *National Interest* (Spring 2003); "An American Empire?" Special Issue of *The Wilson Quarterly* (Summer 2002); and Andrew J. Bacevich, ed., *The Imperial Tense: Prospects and Problems of American Empire* (Chicago, IL: Ivan R. Dee, 2003).

9   This argument is developed most systematically by Kenneth N. Waltz. See Waltz, "Structural Realism after the Cold War," *International Security*, 25, 1 (Summer 2000), pp. 5–41. For an exploration of this thesis, see Ikenberry, ed., *America Unrivaled: The Future of the Balance of Power* (Ithaca, NY: Cornell University Press, 2002).

10   See Timothy Garton Ash, "The Peril of Too Much Power," *The New York Times* (9 April 2002).

11   See Charles A. Kupchan, *The End of the American Era: U.S. Foreign Policy and the Geopolitics of the Twenty-First Century* (New York: Alfred A. Knopf, 2002).

12 If I am right, the Bush administration's unilateral and neo-imperial policy extremes will be found – even by their supporters – to be politically unsustainable and functionally incompatible with America's own postwar multilateral order. American policy will change and adapt as much or more than the larger international order will change and adapt to neo-imperial thinking in Washington.

13 I develop earlier versions of this argument in Ikenberry, "American Power and the Empire of Democratic Capitalism," *Review of International Studies* (December–January 2001–2); and "America's Liberal Hegemony," *Current History* (January 1999).

14 For a collection of essays that survey European views of the United States, see R. Laurence Moore and Maurizio Vaudagna, eds, *The American Century in Europe* (Ithaca, NY: Cornell University Press, 2003).

15 See Kenneth N. Waltz, *Theory of International Politics* (Reading, MA: Addison-Wesley, 1979). For discussions of balancing under conditions of unipolarity, see Ikenberry, ed., *America Unrivaled*; Michael Mastanduno and Ethan Kapstein, eds, *Unipolar Politics: Realism and State Strategies after the Cold War* (New York: Columbia University Press, 1999).

16 See Paul Kennedy, *The Rise and Fall of the Great Powers: Economic Change and Military Conflict from 1500 to 2000* (New York: Random House, 1987); and William R. Thompson, ed., *Great Power Rivalries* (Columbia: University of South Carolina Press, 1999).

17 Ikenberry, "The Myth of Post–Cold War Chaos," *Foreign Affairs* (May–June 1996).

18 Michael Mastanduno, "Preserving the Unipolar Moment: Realist Theories and U.S. Grand Strategy after the Cold War," *International Security*, 21, 4 (Spring 1997), pp. 49–88.

19 This puzzle is posed in Ikenberry, *After Victory*, chapter 1.

20 On American ambivalence about multilateralism, see Joseph Nye, *The Paradox of American Power: Why the World's Only Superpower Can't Go It Alone* (New York: Oxford University Press, 2002); Edward C. Luck, *Mixed Messages: American Politics and International Organization, 1919–1999* (Washington, DC: The Brookings Institution, 1999); John Gerard Ruggie, *Winning the Peace: America and World Order in the New Era* (New York: Columbia University Press, 1996).

21 For a recent survey of views of the United States, see The Pew Global Attitudes Project, "Views of a Changing World 2003:

War with Iraq Further Divides Global Publics," (June 3, 2003). The full report is available at http://people-press.org/reports/display.php3?ReportID=185; and see German Marshall Fund of the United States, "Europeans See the World as Americans Do, But Critical of U.S. Foreign Policy," press release (September 4, 2002).

22 This form of power has been described most recently in Michael Hardt and Antonio Negri, *Empire* (Cambridge, MA: Harvard University Press, 2000). In a sweeping neo-Marxist vision of world order, the authors argue that globalization is not eroding sovereignty but transforming it into a system of diffuse national and supranational institutions – in other words, a new "empire."

23 The most evocative view of American hegemony that emphasizes its coercive and exploitive character is Chalmers Johnson, *Blowback: The Costs and Consequences of American Empire* (New York: Metropolitan Books, 2000).

24 This section draws on Ikenberry, "American Unipolarity: The Sources of Persistence and Decline," in Ikenberry, ed., *America Unrivaled*, pp. 287–99.

25 This dimension of American predominance is stressed by Robert Gilpin in his work on power and international order. See Gilpin, *War and Change in World Politics* (New York: Cambridge University Press, 1981).

26 This is argued in William Wohlforth, "The Stability of a Unipolar World," *International Security* (Summer 1999).

27 Gilpin, *War and Change.*

28 On the notion of offshore balancing, see Christopher Layne, "From Preponderance to Offshore Balancing," *International Security*, 22, 1 (Summer 1997).

29 Josef Joffe, "Europe's American Pacifier," *Foreign Policy*, 54 (Spring 1984); see also Robert Art, "Why Western Europe Needs the United States and NATO," *Political Science Quarterly*, 111 (1996), pp. 1–39.

30 For a discussion of the relationship between geographical proximity and threats, see Stephen M. Walt, *The Origins of Alliances* (Ithaca, NY: Cornell University Press, 1987); and John Mearsheimer, *The Tragedy of Great Power Politics* (New York: Norton, 2001).

31 See Ikenberry, *After Victory*, chapter 6.

32 Geir Lundestad, "Empire by Invitation? The United States and Western Europe, 1945–1952," *The Journal of Peace Research*, 23 (September 1986), pp. 263–77.

33 See Bruce Russett and John Oneal, *Triangulating Peace: Democracy, Interdependence, and International Organizations* (New York: Norton, 2001).

34 This is the argument of Ikenberry, *After Victory*.

35 For an important statement of the "contracting advantages" of democratic states, see Charles Lipson, *Reliable Partners: How Democracies Have Made a Separate Peace* (Princeton, NJ: Princeton University Press, 2003).

36 For a discussion of "voice opportunities," see Joseph M. Grieco, "State Interests and Institutional Rule Trajectory: A Neorealist Interpretation of the Maastricht Treaty and European Economic and Monetary Union," *Security Studies*, 5, 3 (Spring 1996). The classic formulation of this logic is Albert Hirschman, *Exit, Voice, and Loyalty – Responses to Decline in Firms, Organizations, and States* (Cambridge, MA: Harvard University Press, 1970).

37 On the logic of security binding, see Paul Schroeder, "Alliances, 1815–1945: Weapons of Power and Tools of Management," in Klaus Knorr, ed., *Historical Dimensions of National Security Problems* (Lawrence, KS: University of Kansas Press, 1975), pp. 227–62. For more recent formulations, see Daniel Deudney and G. John Ikenberry, "The Sources and Character of Liberal International Order," *Review of International Studies*, 25, 2 (1999), pp. 179–96.

38 For discussions of industrial society arguments, see Raymond Aron, *The Industrial Society: Three Essays on Ideology and Development* (New York: Clarion Books, 1996); Leon Lindberg, ed., *Politics and the Future of Industrial Society* (New York: David McKay, 1976); and Clark Kerr, *The Future of Industrial Societies: Convergence or Continuing Diversity?* (Cambridge, MA: Harvard University Press, 1983).

39 See Daniel Bell, *The Coming of Post-Industrial Society* (New York: Basic Books, 1973).

40 This distinction is made by Anthony D. Smith, *The Ethnic Origins of Nations* (Oxford: Blackwell, 1986).

41 This section draws on Ikenberry, "Is American Multilateralism in Decline?" *Perspectives on Politics*, 1, 3 (Fall 2003).

42 Robert Keohane, "Multilateralism: An Agenda for Research," *International Journal*, 45, 4 (1990), p. 742.

43 A general version of this argument is developed in Nye, *The Paradox of American Power*.

44 This argument is developed in Ikenberry, *After Victory*.

45 The larger literature on hegemonic stability theory argues that the presence of a single powerful state is conducive to multilateral

regime creation. The hegemonic state – by virtue of its power – is able to act on its long-term interests rather than struggle over short-term distributional gains. This allows it to identify its own national interest with the openness and stability of the larger global system. The classic statement of this thesis is Robert Gilpin, *War and Change in World Politics* (New York: Cambridge University Press, 1981). In Robert Keohane's formulation, the theory holds that "hegemonic structures of power, dominated by a single country, are most conducive to the development of strong international regimes whose rules are relatively precise and well obeyed." Such states have the capacity to maintain regimes that they favor through the use of coercion or positive sanctions. The hegemonic state gains the ability to shape and dominate the international order, while providing a flow of benefits to smaller states that is sufficient to persuade them to acquiesce. Keohane, "The Theory of Hegemonic Stability and Changes in International Economic Regimes, 1967–1977," in Ole R. Holsti, Randolph M. Siverson, and Alexander L. George, eds, *Change in the International System* (Boulder, CO: Westview Press, 1980), pp. 131–62.

46 For a discussion of constitutional logic and international relations, see Ikenberry, "Constitutional Politics in International Relations," *European Journal of International Relations*, 4, 2 (1998), pp. 147–78.

47 For sophisticated arguments along these lines, see Lisa L. Martin, "The Rational State Choice of Multilateralism," in John Gerard Ruggie, ed., *Multilateralism Matters*, pp. 91–121; and David Lake, *Entangling Relations: America in its Century* (Princeton, NJ: Princeton University Press, 1999).

48 Ikenberry, *After Victory*, chapter 3.

4

Hard Power, Soft Power, and "The War on Terrorism"

Joseph S. Nye, Jr

The United States is the most powerful nation on earth. Its stature in the world arena is more dominant, perhaps, than any other since the Roman Empire. But like Rome, the US is not invincible. Rome did not succumb to the rise of another empire, but to the onslaught of waves of barbarians. Modern transnational terrorists are the new barbarians. As America gets deeper into a struggle against terrorism, it becomes increasingly apparent that there are many things outside of US control. It cannot alone hunt down every suspected Al-Qaeda leader hiding in remote regions of the globe. Nor can it launch a war whenever it wishes without alienating other countries and losing the cooperation it needs for winning the peace.

The four-week war in Iraq was a dazzling display of America's hard military power that removed a dangerous dictator, but it did not solve the problem of terrorism. It was also costly in terms of America's soft power to attract others. In the aftermath of the war, polling by the Pew Research Center showed a dramatic decline in the popularity of the United States even in countries like Spain and Italy whose governments had supported the war.

And the standing of the US plummeted in Islamic countries from Morocco through Turkey to Indonesia. Yet the US will need the help of such countries in the long term to track the flow of terrorists, tainted money, and dangerous weapons everywhere in the world. In the words of London's *Financial Times*, "to win the peace, therefore, the US will have to show as much skill in exercising soft power as it has in using hard power to win the war."[1]

At the 2003 World Economic Forum in Davos, George Carey, former Archbishop of Canterbury, stood up and asked Secretary of State Colin Powell why the United States seemed to focus only on its hard power rather than its soft power. Secretary Powell correctly replied that the United States needed hard power to win World War II but it followed up with the Marshall Plan and support for democracy. The Marshall Plan was a source of both hard and soft power, providing economic inducements as well as making America more attractive. And, of course, the attraction of American ideas and values was crucial to the US victory in the Cold War. The Soviet Union was still attractive in many parts of Western Europe after World War II, but it squandered its soft power with repressive policies at home and its invasions of Hungary and Czechoslovakia. As in the Cold War, success in the war on terrorism will require patience and the use of soft power. Military containment was only part of the answer. Internal transformation of the Soviet bloc was equally important.

Some hard-line skeptics say that whatever the merits of soft power, it has little role to play in the current war on terrorism. Osama bin Laden and his followers are repelled, not attracted, by American culture, values, and policies. Military power was essential in defeating the Taliban government in Afghanistan, and soft power will never convert fanatics. True, but the skeptics mistake half the answer for the whole answer.

Look again at Afghanistan. Precision bombing and special forces defeated the Taliban government, but US forces wrapped up less than a quarter of Al-Qaeda, a transnational network with cells in 60 countries. The United States cannot bomb Al-Qaeda cells in Hamburg, Kuala Lumpur, or Detroit. Success against them depends on close civilian cooperation, whether sharing intelligence, coordinating police work across borders, or tracing global financial flows. America's partners work with it partly out of self-interest, but the inherent attractiveness of US policies can and does influence their degree of cooperation.

Equally important is the fact that the current struggle against Islamic terrorism is not a clash of civilizations but a contest whose outcome is closely tied to a civil war between moderates and extremists within Islamic civilization. The United States is not alone as a target of the extremists who have already attacked European, Australian, and moderate Muslim targets. The extreme Islamists pose a threat to all postmodern urban democracies. Democracy will win only if moderate Muslims win, and the ability to attract the moderates is critical to victory. The US and its allies will need to adopt policies that appeal to moderates, and use public diplomacy more effectively to explain common interests. In other words, the world's only superpower will have to learn better to use its soft power.

Some non-Americans might ask whether it is good for other countries that American power should prevail, whether hard or soft. There is both a positive and a normative dimension to the answer. In practical terms, the United States is so far ahead in military power and expenditure that it is very unlikely that any other country or group of countries will be able to challenge it in the next decades. Hopes for a classical balance of power or military multipolarity are unlikely to be fulfilled. But even though multipolarity is not likely, multilateralism is still possible. Polls show that the majority of Americans support the UN and co-operation with other countries. Americans and others share an interest in policies that place more emphasis on soft power. Multilateral legitimacy is part of the soft power. Preventive attacks against terrorist targets that have multilateral support – as in Afghanistan – are less dangerous precedents for the normative world order than those deficient in such support – as was the case in Iraq. At the same time, an American superpower that works with others can contribute to the global public good of stability, especially in the war against transnational terrorist threats. Thus how the world's only superpower shapes its policies is in the interest of all.

Dimensions of Power

The dictionary tells us that power is the ability to do things and control others. Simply put, power is the ability to get the outcomes you want, and to affect the behavior of others to make this happen. Some analysts define power purely in terms of behavior. You experience it when you can make others do what they would otherwise not do.[2] But when we measure power in terms of the changed behavior of others, we have first to know their preferences. Otherwise we may be as mistaken about our power as Brer Fox who thought he was hurting Brer Rabbit by throwing him into the briar patch. Yet knowing in advance how others would behave in the absence of our efforts is often difficult.

Because the ability to control others and obtain the outcomes one wants is associated with the possession of certain resources, political leaders often resort to a shorthand and simply define power as possession of resources. For example, we consider a country powerful if it has a relatively large population, territory, natural resources, economic strength, military force, and social stability. The virtue of this definition is that it makes power appear more concrete, measurable, and predictable. Power in this sense is like holding the high cards in the international poker game.

If you show the highest cards in a poker game, others are likely to fold their hands rather than challenge you. Of course, if you play your hand poorly, or fall victim to bluff and deception, you can still lose. Having the resources of power does not guarantee that you will always get the outcome you want. For example, in terms of resources, the United States was the largest power after World War I, but it failed to prevent Pearl Harbor. And America was the world's only superpower in 2001, but it failed to prevent September 11. Converting resources into realized power requires well-designed policy and skillful leadership. Yet policies are often inadequate and leaders frequently misjudge. Some wars are started by their eventual losers – witness Japan in 1941 or Saddam Hussein in 1990. Power measured in terms of resources is a useful but imperfect shorthand. But as a first approximation in any game, it helps to start by figuring out who is holding the high cards.

Power and Military Force

Another measurement problem is determining which resources
provide the best basis for power behavior in any particular
context. In earlier periods, power resources were easier to judge.
A. J. P Taylor argued that traditionally the test of a great power
in international politics was its "strength for war."[3] War was the
ultimate game in which the cards of international politics were
played, and estimates of relative power were proven. Over the
centuries, as technologies evolved, the sources of power have
changed. In the agrarian economies of seventeenth- and eigh-
teenth-century Europe, population was a critical power resource
because it provided a base for taxes and the recruitment of
infantry (who were mostly mercenaries), and this combination of
men and money gave the edge to France.

The nineteenth century saw the growing importance of indus-
try that benefited first Britain, and later Germany, which used efficient administration and railways to transport armies for quick
victories on the Continent (though Russia had a larger population
and army). The growth of the rail system in Western Russia at the
beginning of the twentieth century was one of the reasons that
Germany feared rising Russian military power and took the risks
it did in 1914. By the middle of the twentieth century, science
and technology added a new dimension to military power
resources. With the advent of the nuclear age, the United States
and the Soviet Union possessed not only industrial might, but
nuclear arsenals and intercontinental missiles. The age of the
superpowers had begun. Subsequently, the leading role of the
United States in the information revolution late in the century
allowed it to create a revolution in military affairs. The ability to
use information technology to create precision weapons, real-time
intelligence, broad surveillance of regional battlefields, and
improved command and control allowed the United States to
surge ahead as the world's only military superpower.

But the progress of science and technology had contradictory
effects on military power over the past century. On the one hand,
it made the United States the world's only superpower with
unmatched military might, but at the same time, it gradually

increased the political and social costs of using military force and conquest. Paradoxically, nuclear weapons proved so awesome and destructive that they became muscle-bound – too costly to use except, theoretically, in the most extreme circumstances.[4] A second important change was the way that modern communications technology fomented the rise and spread of nationalism, which made it more difficult for empires to rule over socially awakened populations. In the nineteenth century, Britain ruled a quarter of the globe with a tiny fraction of the world's population. In an age of widespread nationalism, colonial rule became expensive. Formal empires with direct rule over subject populations, such as Europe exercised during the nineteenth and twentieth centuries, are simply too costly in the twenty-first century.

In addition to nuclear and communications technology, societal change inside great powers has also raised the costs of using military power. Postindustrial societies are focused on welfare rather than glory, and they dislike high casualties. This does not mean that they will not use force, even when casualties are expected – witness Britain, France, and the United States in the 1991 Gulf War, and Britain and the United States in the 2003 Gulf War. But the absence of a warrior ethic in modern democracies means that the use of force requires an elaborate moral justification to ensure popular support (except in cases where survival is at stake).

Roughly speaking there are three types of countries in the world today: poor, weak, pre-industrial states, which are often the chaotic remnants of collapsed empires; modernizing industrial states like India or China; and the postindustrial societies that prevail in Europe, North America, and Japan. The use of force is common in the first type of country where predatory warlords and ethnic entrepreneurs use force for plunder and profit. Interstate war is less accepted in the second and third types of state. In the words of British diplomat Robert Cooper, "a large number of the most powerful states no longer want to fight or to conquer."[5]

War remains possible, but much less acceptable than a century, or even a half-century ago.[6] Robert Kagan correctly points out that these social changes have affected Europe more than the United States.[7] But his too clever phrase that Americans are from Mars and Europeans from Venus oversimplifies the differences. Public opinion in the "old European" countries of France and Germany supported the use of force against Iraq in 1991, and both countries joined in the use of force in Kosovo in 1999 despite the absence of a UN resolution. In both cases, they believed the use of force to be legitimate. The success of the European Union in creating an island of peace in place of the three Franco-German wars that ravaged the continent may predispose Europeans toward peaceful solutions to conflict, but not all Europeans deny the harsh realities that exist in many other parts of the world.

Moreover, in a global economy, both Europe and the United States must consider how the use of force might jeopardize their economic objectives. In 1853, the American Admiral Matthew Perry could threaten to bombard Japan if it did not open its ports to trade, but it is hard to imagine that the United States today could effectively threaten force to open Japanese markets. Nor can one imagine the United States using force to resolve disputes with Canada or Europe. Unlike earlier periods, islands of peace where the use of force is no longer an option in relations among states have come to characterize relations among most modern democracies, and not just in Europe. In their relations with each other, all advanced democracies are from Venus.

Even nondemocratic countries that feel fewer popular moral constraints on the use of force have to consider its effects on their economic objectives. As Thomas Friedman has put it, countries today are disciplined by an "electronic herd" of investors who control their access to capital in a globalized economy.[8] "In the past, it was cheaper to seize another state's territory by force than to develop the sophisticated economic and trading apparatus needed to derive benefit from commercial exchange with it."[9] Imperial Japan used the former approach when it created the Greater East Asia Co-Prosperity Sphere in the 1930s, but Japan's post-World War II role as a trading state turned out to be far more successful, leading it to become the second-largest national economy in the world. It is difficult to imagine a scenario in which Japan would try, or succeed, in colonizing its neighbors today.

None of this is to suggest that the hard power of military force plays no role in international politics today. On the contrary, the information revolution has yet to transform most of the world, and many states are unconstrained by democratic societal forces. Civil wars are rife in many parts of the world where collapsed empires left power vacuums. Even more important is the way in which the democratization of technology is leading to the privatization of war. On the one hand, technological and social changes are making war more costly for modern democracies. But at the same time, technology is putting new means of destruction into the hands of pathological groups and individuals.

Terrorism and the Privatization of War

Terrorism is not new, nor is it a single enemy. It is a long-standing method of conflict frequently defined as deliberate attack on the innocent with the objective of spreading fear and intimidation. Already a century ago, the novelist Joseph Conrad had drawn an indelible portrait of the terrorist mind, and terrorism was a familiar phenomenon in the twentieth century. Whether homegrown or transnational, it was a staple of conflicts throughout the Middle East, in Northern Ireland, Spain, Sri Lanka, Kashmir, South Africa, and elsewhere. It occurred on every continent except Antarctica and affected nearly every country. September 11, 2001, was a dramatic escalation of an age-old phenomenon. Yet two developments have made terrorism more lethal and more difficult to manage in the twenty-first century.

One set of trends grows out of progress in science and technology. First, there is the complex, highly technological nature of modern civilization's basic systems. As a committee of the National Academy of Sciences pointed out, market forces and openness have combined to increase the efficiency of many of our vital systems – such as those that provide transportation, information, energy, and health care. But ironically such systems become more vulnerable and fragile as they become more complex and efficient. The result is that progress makes our infrastructures "vulnerable to local disruptions which could lead to widespread or catastrophic failures."[10]

At the same time, progress is "democratizing technology," making the instruments of mass destruction smaller, cheaper, and more readily available to a far wider range of individuals and groups. Where bombs and timers were once heavy and expensive, plastic explosives and digital timers are light and cheap. The costs of hijacking an airplane are sometimes little more than the price of a ticket.

Finally, the success of the information revolution is providing inexpensive means of communication and organization that allow groups once restricted to local and national police jurisdictions to become global in scope. Thirty years ago, instantaneous global communication was sufficiently expensive that it was restricted to large entities with huge budgets like governments, multinational corporations, or the Catholic Church. Today the Internet makes global communication virtually free for anyone with access to a modem.[11] Similarly, the Internet has reduced the costs of searching for information and making contacts related to instruments of widescale destruction.

The second set of trends reflects changes in the motivation and organization of terrorist groups. Terrorists in the mid-twentieth century tended to have relatively well-defined political objectives, which were often ill-served by mass destruction. They were said to want many people watching rather than many people killed. Such terrorists were often supported and covertly controlled by governments. Toward the end of the century, radical groups grew on the fringes of several religions. Most numerous were the tens of thousands of young Muslim men who went to fight against the Soviet occupation of Afghanistan. There they were trained in a wide range of techniques and many were recruited to organizations with an extreme view of the religious obligation of jihad. As Walter Laqueur has observed, "traditional terrorists, whether left-wing, right-wing, or nationalist-separatists, were not greatly drawn to these opportunities for greater destruction. . . . Terrorism has become more brutal and indiscriminate since then."[12] This is reinforced when motivations change from specific political to unlimited or retributive objectives reinforced by promises of rewards in another world. Organization has also changed. For example, Al-Qaeda's network of tens of thousands of people in loosely affiliated cells in some 60 countries gives it a scale well beyond anything seen before. But even small networks can be more difficult to penetrate than the hierarchical quasi-military organizations of the past.

Both trends – technological and ideological – have created a new set of conditions that have increased the lethality and the difficulty of managing terrorism today. Because of September 11 and the unprecedented scale of Al-Qaeda, the current focus is properly on terrorism associated with Islamic extremists. But it would be a mistake to limit our attention or responses to Islamic terrorists, for that would ignore the wider effects of the democratization of technology and the broader set of challenges that must be met. Technological progress is putting into the hands of deviant groups and individuals destructive capabilities that were once limited primarily to governments and armies. Every large group of people has some members who deviate from the norm, and some are bent on destruction. It is worth remembering that the worst case of terrorism in the United States before September 11 was that of Timothy McVeigh, a purely homegrown anti-government fanatic. Similarly, the Aum Shinrykio cult that spread sarin in the Tokyo subway system in 1995 had nothing to do with Islam. Even if the current wave of Islamic terrorism turns out to be generational or cyclical like terrorist waves in the past, we will still have to confront the long-term secular dangers arising out of the democratization of technology.

Lethality has been increasing. In the 1970s, Palestinians attacked Israeli athletes at the Munich Olympics, and Red Brigade killings galvanized world attention and cost dozens of lives. In the 1980s, Sikh extremists bombed an Air India flight and killed over 300 people. September 11, 2001, cost several thousand lives – and all of this escalation occurred without using weapons of mass destruction. If one extrapolates this lethality trend and imagines a deviant group in some society gaining access to biological or nuclear materials within the coming decade, it is possible to imagine terrorists being able to destroy millions of lives.

To kill so many people in the twentieth century, a destructive individual like Hitler or Stalin required the apparatus of a totalitarian government. Unfortunately, it is now all too easy to envisage extremist groups and individuals killing millions without the instruments of governments. This is truly the "privatization of war" and a dramatic change in world politics. Moreover, this next step in the escalation of terrorism would have profound effects on the nature of modern urban civilization. What would happen to people's willingness to locate in cities, to real estate prices, to museums and theatres, if instead of destroying two office buildings, a future attack destroyed the lower half of Manhattan, the City of London, or the Left Bank of Paris?

The new terrorism is not like the 1970s terrorism of the IRA, ETA, or the Red Brigades. Nor is the vulnerability limited to any one society. A "business as usual" attitude toward curbing terrorism is not enough. The role of force in world politics is not over, but its nature has changed in the twenty-first century. The Bush administration was correct in altering America's national security strategy to focus on terrorism and weapons of mass destruction after September 11, 2001. But the question remains whether the means have focused too heavily on hard power and not taken enough account of soft power.

Soft Power

Military power and economic power are both examples of "hard" command power that can be used to get others to change their position. Hard power can rest on inducements ("carrots") or threats ("sticks"). But there is also an indirect way to get what you want that could be called the second face of power. A country may obtain the outcomes it wants in world politics because other countries want to follow it, admiring its values, emulating its example, aspiring to its level of prosperity and openness. In this sense, it is just as important to set the agenda and attract others in world politics as it is to force them to change through the threat or use of military or economic weapons. This aspect of power – getting others to want what you want – is "soft" power.[13] It co-opts people rather than coerces them.

Soft power rests on the ability to set the political agenda in a way that shapes the preferences of others. At the personal level, wise parents know that if they have brought up their children with the right beliefs and values, their power will be greater and will last longer than if they have relied only on spankings, allowances, or taking away the car keys. Similarly, political leaders and thinkers such as Antonio Gramsci have long understood the power that comes from setting the agenda and determining the framework of a debate. The ability to establish preferences tends to be associated with intangible power resources such as an attractive culture, political values and institutions, and policies that are seen as legitimate or having moral authority. If I can get you to want to do what I want, then I do not have to force you to do what you do *not* want. If the United States represents values that others want to follow, it will cost us less to lead.

Soft power is not merely the same as influence, though it is one source of influence. After all, influence can also rest on threats or rewards. And soft power is more than persuasion or the ability to move people by argument. It is also the ability to entice and attract. And attraction often leads to acquiescence or imitation. Simply put, soft power is attractive power.

Soft power arises in large part from the values a country expresses in its culture, in the domestic policies it follows, and in the way it handles itself internationally. The government sometimes finds it difficult to control and to employ soft power, but that does not diminish its importance. It was a French foreign minister who observed that Americans are powerful because they can "inspire the dreams and desires of others, thanks to the mastery of global images through film and television and because, for these same reasons, large numbers of students from other countries come to the United States to finish their studies."[14]

Sometimes the same power resources can affect the entire spectrum of behavior from coercion to attraction.[15] A country that suffers economic and military decline is likely to lose its ability to shape the international agenda as well as its attractiveness. And some countries may be attracted to others with hard power by the myth of invincibility or inevitability. Both Hitler and Stalin tried to develop such myths. Hard power can also be used to establish empires and institutions that set the agenda for smaller states – witness Soviet rule over the countries of Eastern Europe.

But soft power is not simply the reflection of hard power. The Vatican did not lose its soft power when it lost the Papal States in Italy in the nineteenth century. Conversely, the Soviet Union lost much of its soft power after it invaded Hungary and Czechoslovakia, even though its hard power measured in economic and military resources continued to grow. Imperious policies that utilized Soviet hard power actually undercut its soft power. In contrast, some countries such as Canada, the Netherlands, and the Scandinavian states have political clout that is greater than their military and economic weight, because of the incorporation of attractive causes such as economic aid or peacemaking into their definitions of their national interest.

Britain in the nineteenth century and America in the second half of the twentieth century enhanced their power by creating liberal international economic rules and institutions that were consistent with the liberal and democratic structures of British and American capitalism – free trade and the gold standard in the case of Britain; the International Monetary Fund, World Trade Organization, and other institutions in the case of the United States. If a country can make its power legitimate in the eyes of others, it will encounter less resistance to its wishes. If its culture and ideology are attractive, others more willingly follow. If it can establish international rules that are consistent with its society, it will be less likely to have to change. If it can help support institutions that encourage other countries to channel or limit their activities in ways it prefers, it may not need as many costly carrots and sticks.

In short, the universality of a country's culture and its ability to establish a set of favorable rules and institutions that govern areas of international activity are critical sources of power. The values of democracy, personal freedom, upward mobility, and openness that are often expressed in American popular culture, higher education, and foreign policy contribute to American power. The German editor Josef Joffe has argued that America's soft power is even greater than its economic and military assets. "U.S. culture, low-brow or high, radiates outward with an intensity last seen in the days of the Roman Empire – but with a novel twist. Rome's and Soviet Russia's cultural sway stopped exactly at their military borders. America's soft power, though, rules over an empire on which the sun never sets."[16]

The soft power of a country rests primarily on three sources: its culture (in places where it is attractive to others), its political values such as democracy and human rights (when it lives up to them), and its policies (when they are seen as legitimate because they are framed with some humility and awareness of others' interests). Sometimes people treat soft power simply as cultural power. They make the mistake of equating soft power with the cultural resources that sometimes help produce it. They confuse the cultural resources with the behavior of attraction. For example, the historian Niall Ferguson described soft power as "nontraditional forces such as cultural and commercial goods" and then dismissed it on the grounds "that it's, well, soft."[17] Of course, Coke and Big Macs do not necessarily attract people in the Islamic world to love the United States. And American films that make the United States attractive in China or Latin America may have the opposite effect and actually reduce our soft power in Saudi Arabia or Pakistan. Ferguson concluded that real power depends on "having credibility and legitimacy." But credibility and legitimacy are exactly a large part of the attraction that soft power is all about.

The values a government champions in its behavior at home (for example, democracy), in international institutions (consulting others), and in foreign policy (promoting peace and human rights) also affect the preferences of others. It can attract (or repel) others by the influence of its example. But soft power does not belong to the government in the same degree that hard power does. Some hard power assets (such as armed forces) are strictly governmental; others are inherently national (such as oil and gas reserves); and many can be transferred to collective control (such as industrial assets that can be mobilized in an emergency). In contrast, many soft power resources are separate from American government, and only partly responsive to its purposes. In the Vietnam era, for example, American popular culture worked at cross-purposes to government policy. Today, Hollywood movies that show scantily clad women with libertine attitudes, or fundamentalist Christian groups that castigate Islam as an evil religion are both (properly) outside the control of government in our liberal society, but they undercut government efforts to improve relations with Islamic nations.

Some skeptics object to using the term soft power in international politics because governments are not in full control of the attraction. But the fact that civil society is the origin of much of America's soft power does not deny its existence. In a liberal society, government cannot and should not control the culture. Indeed, the absence of policies of control can itself be a source of attraction. It is true that firms, universities, foundations, churches, and other nongovernmental groups develop soft power of their own which may reinforce or be at odds with official foreign policy goals. That is all the more reason for governments to make sure that their own actions and policies, which they do control, reinforce rather than undercut their soft power. All these private sources of soft power are likely to become increasingly important in the global information age of this new century.

At the same time, government will continue to matter, and policies can create or squander soft power. Domestic or foreign policies that appear hypocritical, arrogant, indifferent to the opinion of others, or based on a narrow approach to national interests can undermine soft power. For example, in the steep decline in the attractiveness of the United States as measured by polls taken after the Iraq War in 2003, people with unfavorable views for the most part said they were reacting to the administration and its policies rather than the United States generally. The publics in most nations continued to admire the United States for its technology, music, movies, and television. But large majorities in most countries said they disliked the growing influence of America in their country.[18]

The Iraq War is not the first policy that has made the United States unpopular. Three decades ago, many people around the world objected to America's war in Vietnam and the standing of the United States reflected the unpopularity of that policy. When the policy changed and the memories of the war receded, the United States recovered much of its lost soft power.

The initial effect of the Iraq War on opinion in the Islamic world was quite negative. In Pakistan, a former diplomat reported that "the US invasion of Iraq is a complete gift to the Islamic parties. People who would otherwise turn up their noses at them are now flocking to their banner."[19] Intelligence and law enforcement officials reported that Al-Qaeda and other terrorist groups intensified their recruitment on three continents by "tapping into rising anger about the American campaign for war in Iraq."[20] After the war, the Pew Center polls found a rise in support for bin Laden and a fall in the popularity of the United States even in friendly countries like Indonesia and Jordan.[21] It is still too soon to tell whether the hard power gains from the war in Iraq will in the long run exceed the soft power losses, or how permanent the latter will turn out to be, but the war provided a fascinating case study of the interaction of the two types of power.

Looking Ahead

Looking to the future, much will depend on the effectiveness of American policies in creating a better Iraq and moving forward with the Middle East peace process. In addition, much will depend on whether the exaggeration of intelligence evidence will have a permanent damaging effect on the credibility of the American government when it approaches other countries for help in the war on terrorism. Skeptics argue that because countries co-operate out of self-interest, the loss of soft power does not matter much. But the skeptics miss the point that cooperation is a matter of degree, and the degree is affected by attraction or repulsion. They also miss the point that the effects on non-state actors and recruitment to terrorist organizations do not depend on government attitudes alone. Hard and soft power are inextricably inter-twined in today's world, but the role of soft power is increasing.

Power in a global information age is becoming less tangible and less coercive, particularly among the advanced democracies, but most of the world does not consist of advanced democracies, and that limits the transformation of power. Much of Africa and the Middle East remains locked in preindustrial agricultural societies with weak institutions and authoritarian rulers. Other countries, such as China, India, and Brazil are industrial economies analogous to parts of the West in the mid-twentieth century.[22] In such a variegated world, all three sources of power – military, economic, and soft – remain relevant, although in different degrees in different relationships. However, if current economic and social trends continue, leadership in the information revolution and soft power will become more important in the mix.

After the collapse of the Soviet Union, some analysts described the resulting distribution of power in the world as unipolar; some as multipolar. Both were wrong because each referred to a different dimension of power that can no longer be assumed to be homogenized by military dominance. Unipolarity is misleading because it exaggerates the degree to which the United States is able to get the results it wants in some dimensions of world politics, but multipolarity is misleading because it implies several roughly equal countries.

Instead, power in a global information age is distributed among countries in a pattern that resembles a complex three-dimensional chess game. On the top chessboard of political-military issues, military power is largely unipolar. The US is the only country with both intercontinental nuclear weapons and large, state-of-the-art air, naval, and ground forces capable of global deployment. But on the middle chessboard of economic issues, power is distributed in a multipolar way, with the US, Europe, and Japan representing two-thirds of world product, and with China's dramatic growth likely to make it the fourth major player. On this economic board, the United States is not a hegemon, and often must bargain as an equal with Europe when it acts in a unified way.

The bottom chessboard is the realm of transnational relations that cross borders outside of government control. This realm includes actors as diverse as bankers electronically transferring sums larger than most national budgets at one extreme, and terrorists transferring weapons, or hackers disrupting Internet operations, at the other. On this bottom board, power is chaotically dispersed, and it makes no sense to speak of unipolarity, multipolarity, hegemony, or American empire. And it is on this transnational board that the largest part of the war on terrorism will be conducted. Those hard power realists who recommend a hegemonic American foreign policy based on traditional descriptions of American power are relying on woefully inadequate analysis. When you are in a three-dimensional game, you will lose if you focus only on the top board and fail to notice the other boards and the vertical connections among them.

Because of its leading edge in the information revolution and its past investment in military power the United States will likely remain the world's single most powerful country well into the twenty-first century. But as Josef Joffe has written, "unlike centuries past, when war was the great arbiter, today the most interesting types of power do not come out of the barrel of a gun. . . . Today there is a much bigger payoff in 'getting others to want what you want,' and that has to do with cultural attraction and ideology and agenda setting and economic incentives for cooperation."[23]

Both hard and soft power are relevant to getting desirable outcomes on all three chessboards, but many of the transnational issues such as climate change, the spread of infectious diseases, and international crime and terrorism cannot be resolved by military force alone. Representing the dark side of globalization, these issues are inherently multilateral and require cooperation for their solution. Thus soft power is particularly important in dealing with the issues that arise from the bottom chessboard of transnational relations. Unless the United States learns to see the war on terrorism in this broader analytical context, and to appreciate the crucial role of soft power, it will find victory elusive.

Notes

1   "A Famous Victory and a Tough Sequel," *Financial Times* (April 10, 2003), p. 12.
2   Robert Dahl, *Who Governs? Democracy and Power in an American City* (New Haven, CT: Yale University Press, 1961).
3   A. J. P. Taylor, *The Struggle for Mastery in Europe, 1848–1918* (Oxford: Oxford University Press, 1954), p. xxix.
4   Whether this would change with the proliferation of nuclear weapons to more states is hotly debated among theorists. Deterrence should work with most states, but the prospects of accident and loss of control would increase. For my views, see Joseph Nye, *Nuclear Ethics* (New York: Free Press, 1986).

5   Robert Cooper, *The Postmodern State and the World Order* (London: Demos, 2000), p. 22.

6   John Meuller, *Retreat from Doomsday: The Obsolescence of Major War* (New York: Basic Books, 1989).

7   Robert Kagan, *Of Paradise and Power* (New York: Alfred A. Knopf, 2003).

8   Thomas Friedman, *The Lexus and the Olive Tree: Understanding Globalization* (New York: Farrar Straus and Giroux, 1999), chapter 6.

9   Richard N. Rosecrance, *The Rise of the Trading State* (New York: Basic Books, 1986), pp. 16, 160.

10 National Research Council, *Making the Nation Safer* (Washington: National Academies Press, 2002), p. 25.

11 See Nye, *The Paradox of American Power* (Oxford: Oxford University Press, 2002), chapter 2, for details.

12 Walter Laqueur, "Left, Right and Beyond: The Changing Face of Terror," in James Hoge and Gideon Rose, *How Did This Happen?* (New York: Public Affairs Press, 2001), p. 74.

13 I first introduced this concept in *Bound to Lead: The Changing Nature of American Power* (New York: Basic Books, 1990), chapter 2. It builds on what Peter Bachrach and Morton Baratz called the "second face of power." See their "Decisions and Nondecisions: An Analytical Framework," *American Political Science Review* (September 1963), pp. 632–42.

14 Hubert Védrine, with Dominique Moisi, *France in an Age of Globalization* (Washington, DC: Brookings Institution Press, 2001), p. 3.

15 The distinction between hard and soft power is one of degree, both in the nature of the behavior and in the tangibility of the resources. Both are aspects of the ability to achieve one's purposes by affecting the behavior of others. Command power – the ability to change what others do – can rest on coercion or inducement. Co-optive power – the ability to shape what others want – can rest on the attractiveness of one's culture and ideology or the ability to manipulate the agenda of political choices in a manner that makes actors fail to express some preferences because they seem to be too unrealistic. The forms of behavior between command and co-optive power range along a continuum: Command power – coercion – inducement – agenda-setting – attraction – co-optive power. Soft power resources tend to be associated with co-optive power behavior, whereas hard power resources are usually associated with command behavior. But the relationship is imperfect. For example,

countries may be attracted to others with command power by myths of invincibility, and command power may sometimes be used to establish institutions that later become regarded as legitimate. But the general association is strong enough to allow the useful shorthand reference to hard and soft power.

16 Josef Joffe, "Who's Afraid of Mr. Big?" *The National Interest* (Summer 2001), p. 43.

17 Niall Ferguson, "Think Again: Power," *Foreign Policy* (January–February 2003).

18 The Pew Global Attitudes Project, *Views of a Changing World* (Washington, DC: The Pew Research Center for the People and the Press, June 2003), pp. 22–3.

19 "US Invasion Pushes Pakistani Elite Closer to Hardline Islam," *Financial Times* (March 28, 2003), p. 1.

20 Don Van Natta, Jr, and Desmond Butler, "Anger on Iraq Seen as New Qaeda Recruiting Tool," *New York Times* (March 16, 2003), p. 1.

21 Pew Center, *Views of a Changing World*.

22 See Cooper, *The Postmodern State*; and Daniel Bell, *The Coming of Post-Industrial Society: A Venture in Social Forecasting* (New York: Basic Books, 1999).

23 Josef Joffe, "America the Inescapable," *New York Times [Sunday] Magazine* (June 8, 1997), p. 38.

5

Power and Weakness*
Robert Kagan

It is time to stop pretending that Europeans and Americans share a common view of the world, or even that they occupy the same world. On the all-important question of power – the efficacy of power, the morality of power, the desirability of power – American and European perspectives are diverging. Europe is turning away from power, or to put it a little differently, it is moving beyond power into a self-contained world of laws and rules and transnational negotiation and cooperation. It is entering a post-historical paradise of peace and relative prosperity, the realization of Kant's "Perpetual Peace." The United States, meanwhile, remains mired in history, exercising power in the anarchic Hobbesian world where international laws and rules are unreliable and where true security and the defense and promotion of a liberal order still depend on the possession and use of military might. That is why on major strategic and international questions today, Americans are from Mars and Europeans are from Venus: they agree on little and understand one another less and less. And this state of affairs is not transitory – the product of one American election or one catastrophic event. The reasons for the transatlantic divide are deep, long in development, and likely to endure. When it comes to setting national priorities, determining threats, defining challenges, and fashioning and implementing foreign and defense policies, the United States and Europe have parted ways.

It is easier to see the contrast as an American living in Europe. Europeans are more conscious of the growing differences, perhaps because they fear them more. European intellectuals are nearly unanimous in the conviction that Americans and Europeans no longer share a common "strategic culture." The European caricature at its most extreme depicts an America dominated by a "culture of death," its warlike temperament the natural product of a violent society where every man has a gun and the death penalty reigns. But even those who do not make this crude link agree there are profound differences in the way the United States and Europe conduct foreign policy.

The United States, they argue, resorts to force more quickly and, compared with Europe, is less patient with diplomacy. Americans generally see the world divided between good and evil, between friends and enemies, while Europeans see a more complex picture. When confronting real or potential adversaries, Americans generally favor policies of coercion rather than persuasion, emphasizing punitive sanctions over inducements to better behavior, the stick over the carrot. Americans tend to seek finality in international affairs: they want problems solved, threats eliminated. And, of course, Americans increasingly tend toward unilateralism in international affairs. They are less inclined to act through international institutions such as the United Nations, less inclined to work cooperatively with other nations to pursue common goals, more skeptical about international law, and more willing to operate outside its strictures when they deem it necessary, or even merely useful.[1]

Europeans insist they approach problems with greater nuance and sophistication. They try to influence others through subtlety and indirection. They are more tolerant of failure, more patient when solutions don't come quickly. They generally favor peaceful responses to problems, preferring negotiation, diplomacy, and persuasion to coercion. They are quicker to appeal to international law, international conventions, and international opinion to adjudicate disputes. They try to use commercial and economic ties to bind nations together. They often emphasize process over result, believing that ultimately process can become substance.

This European dual portrait is a caricature, of course, with its share of exaggerations and oversimplifications. One cannot generalize about Europeans: Britons may have a more "American" view of power than many of their fellow Europeans on the continent. And there are differing perspectives within nations on both sides of the Atlantic. In the US, Democrats often seem more "European" than Republicans; Secretary of State Colin Powell may appear more "European" than Secretary of Defense Donald Rumsfeld. Many Americans, especially among the intellectual elite, are as uncomfortable with the "hard" quality of American foreign policy as any European; and some Europeans value power as much as any American.

Nevertheless, the caricatures do capture an essential truth: the United States and Europe are fundamentally different today. Powell and Rumsfeld have more in common than do Powell and Hubert Védrine or even Jack Straw. When it comes to the use of force, mainstream American Democrats have more in common with Republicans than they do with most European Socialists and Social Democrats. During the 1990s even American liberals were more willing to resort to force and were more Manichean in their perception of the world than most of their European counterparts. The Clinton administration bombed Iraq, as well as Afghanistan and Sudan. European governments, it is safe to say, would not have done so. Whether they would have bombed even Belgrade in 1999, had the US not forced their hand, is an interesting question.[2]

What is the source of these differing strategic perspectives? The question has received too little attention in recent years, either because foreign policy intellectuals and policymakers on both sides of the Atlantic have denied the existence of a genuine difference or because those who have pointed to the difference, especially in Europe, have been more interested in assailing the United States than in understanding why the United States acts as it does – or, for that matter, why Europe acts as it does. It is past time to move beyond the denial and the insults and to face the problem head-on.

Despite what many Europeans and some Americans believe, these differences in strategic culture do not spring naturally from the national characters of Americans and Europeans. After all, what Europeans now consider their more peaceful strategic culture is, historically speaking, quite new. It represents an evolution away from the very different strategic culture that dominated Europe for hundreds of years and at least until World War I. The European governments – and peoples – who enthusiastically launched themselves into that continental war believed in *Machtpolitik*. While the roots of the present European worldview, like the roots of the European Union itself, can be traced back to the Enlightenment, Europe's great-power politics for the past 300 years did not follow the visionary designs of the philosophes and the physiocrats.

As for the United States, there is nothing timeless about the present heavy reliance on force as a tool of international relations, nor about the tilt toward unilateralism and away from a devotion to international law. Americans are children of the Enlightenment, too, and in the early years of the republic were more faithful apostles of its creed. America's eighteenth- and early nineteenth-century statesmen sounded much like the European statesmen of today, extolling the virtues of commerce as the soothing balm of international strife and appealing to international law and international opinion over brute force. The young United States wielded power against weaker peoples on the North American continent, but when it came to dealing with the European giants, it claimed to abjure power and assailed as atavistic the power politics of the eighteenth- and nineteenth-century European empires.

Two centuries later, Americans and Europeans have traded places – and perspectives. Partly this is because in those 200 years, but especially in recent decades, the power equation has shifted dramatically: when the United States was weak, it practiced the strategies of indirection, the strategies of weakness; now that the United States is powerful, it behaves as powerful nations do. When the European great powers were strong, they believed in strength and martial glory. Now, they see the world through the eyes of weaker powers. These very different points of view, weak versus strong, have naturally produced differing strategic judgments, differing assessments of threats and of the proper means of addressing threats, and even differing calculations of interest.

But this is only part of the answer. For along with these natural consequences of the transatlantic power gap, there has also opened a broad ideological gap. Europe, because of its unique historical experience of the past half-century – culminating in the past decade with the creation of the European Union – has developed a set of ideals and principles regarding the utility and morality of power different from the ideals and principles of Americans, who have not shared that experience. If the strategic chasm between the United States and Europe appears greater than ever today, and grows still wider at a worrying pace, it is because these material and ideological differences reinforce one another. The divisive trend they together produce may be impossible to reverse.

The Power Gap: Perception and Reality

Europe has been militarily weak for a long time, but until fairly recently its weakness had been obscured. World War II all but destroyed European nations as global powers, and their postwar inability to project sufficient force overseas to maintain colonial empires in Asia, Africa, and the Middle East forced them to retreat on a massive scale after more than five centuries of imperial dominance – perhaps the most significant retrenchment of global influence in human history. For a half-century after World War II, however, this weakness was masked by the unique geopolitical circumstances of the Cold War. Dwarfed by the two superpowers on its flanks, a weakened Europe nevertheless served as the central strategic theater of the worldwide struggle between communism and democratic capitalism. Its sole but vital strategic mission was to defend its own territory against any Soviet offensive, at least until the Americans arrived. Although shorn of most traditional measures of great-power status, Europe remained the geopolitical pivot, and this, along with lingering habits of world leadership, allowed Europeans to retain international influence well beyond what their sheer military capabilities might have afforded.

Europe lost this strategic centrality after the Cold War ended, but it took a few more years for the lingering mirage of European global power to fade. During the 1990s, war in the Balkans kept both Europeans and Americans focused on the strategic importance of the continent and on the continuing relevance of NATO. The enlargement of NATO to include former Warsaw Pact nations and the consolidation of the Cold War victory kept Europe in the forefront of the strategic discussion.

Then there was the early promise of the "new Europe." By bonding together into a single political and economic unit – the historic accomplishment of the Maastricht treaty in 1992 – many hoped to recapture Europe's old greatness but in a new political form. "Europe" would be the next superpower, not only economically and politically, but also militarily. It would handle crises on the European continent, such as the ethnic conflicts in the Balkans, and it would re-emerge as a global player. In the 1990s Europeans could confidently assert that the power of a unified Europe would restore, finally, the global "multipolarity" that had been destroyed by the Cold War and its aftermath. And most Americans, with mixed emotions, agreed that superpower Europe was the future. Harvard University's Samuel P. Huntington predicted that the coalescing of the European Union would be "the single most important move" in a worldwide reaction against American hegemony and would produce a "truly multipolar" twenty-first century.[3]

But European pretensions and American apprehensions proved unfounded. The 1990s witnessed not the rise of a European superpower but the decline of Europe into relative weakness. The Balkan conflict at the beginning of the decade revealed European military incapacity and political disarray; the Kosovo conflict at the decade's end exposed a transatlantic gap in military technology and the ability to wage modern warfare that would only widen in subsequent years. Outside of Europe, the disparity by the close of the 1990s was even more starkly apparent as it became clear that the ability of European powers, individually or collectively, to project decisive force into regions of conflict beyond the continent was negligible. Europeans could provide peacekeeping forces in the Balkans – indeed, they could and eventually did provide the vast bulk of those forces in Bosnia and Kosovo. But they lacked the wherewithal to introduce and sustain a fighting force in potentially hostile territory, even in Europe. Under the best of circumstances, the European role was limited to filling out peacekeeping forces after the United States had, largely on its own, carried out the decisive phases of a military mission and stabilized the situation. As some Europeans put it, the real division of labor consisted of the United States "making the dinner" and the Europeans "doing the dishes."

This inadequacy should have come as no surprise, since these were the limitations that had forced Europe to retract its global influence in the first place. Those Americans and Europeans who proposed that Europe expand its strategic role beyond the continent set an unreasonable goal. During the Cold War, Europe's strategic role had been to defend itself. It was unrealistic to expect a return to international great-power status, unless European peoples were willing to shift significant resources from social programs to military programs.

Clearly they were not. Not only were Europeans unwilling to pay to project force beyond Europe. After the Cold War, they would not pay for sufficient force to conduct even minor military actions on the continent without American help. Nor did it seem to matter whether European publics were being asked to spend money to strengthen NATO or an independent European foreign and defense policy. Their answer was the same. Rather than viewing the collapse of the Soviet Union as an opportunity to flex global muscles, Europeans took it as an opportunity to cash in on a sizable peace dividend. Average European defense budgets gradually fell below 2 percent of GDP. Despite talk of establishing Europe as a global superpower, therefore, European military capabilities steadily fell behind those of the United States throughout the 1990s.

The end of the Cold War had a very different effect on the other side of the Atlantic. For although Americans looked for a peace dividend, too, and defense budgets declined or remained flat during most of the 1990s, defense spending still remained above 3 percent of GDP. Fast on the heels of the Soviet empire's demise came Iraq's invasion of Kuwait and the largest American military action in a quarter-century. Thereafter American administrations cut the Cold War force, but not as dramatically as might have been expected. By historical standards, America's military power and particularly its ability to project that power to all corners of the globe remained unprecedented.

Meanwhile, the very fact of the Soviet empire's collapse vastly increased America's strength relative to the rest of the world. The sizable American military arsenal, once barely sufficient to balance Soviet power, was now deployed in a world without a single formidable adversary. This "unipolar moment" had an entirely natural and predictable consequence: it made the United States more willing to use force abroad. With the check of Soviet power removed, the United States was free to intervene practically wherever and whenever it chose – a fact reflected in the proliferation of overseas military interventions that began during the first Bush administration with the invasion of Panama in 1989, the Persian Gulf War in 1991, and the humanitarian intervention in Somalia in 1992, continuing during the Clinton years with interventions in Haiti, Bosnia, and Kosovo. While American politicians talked of pulling back from the world, the reality was an America intervening abroad more frequently than it had throughout most of the Cold War. Thanks to new technologies, the United States was also freer to use force around the world in more limited ways through air and missile strikes, which it did with increasing frequency.

How could this growing transatlantic power gap fail to create a difference in strategic perceptions? Even during the Cold War, American military predominance and Europe's relative weakness had produced important and sometimes serious disagreements. Gaullism, Ostpolitik, and the various movements for European independence and unity were manifestations not only of a European desire for honor and freedom of action. They also reflected a European conviction that America's approach to the Cold War was too confrontational, too militaristic, and too dangerous. Europeans believed they knew better how to deal with the Soviets: through engagement and seduction, through commercial and political ties, through patience and forbearance. It was a legitimate view, shared by many Americans. But it also reflected Europe's weakness relative to the United States, the fewer military options at Europe's disposal, and its greater vulnerability to a powerful Soviet Union. It may have reflected, too, Europe's memory of continental war. Americans, when they were not themselves engaged in the subtleties of détente, viewed the European approach as a form of appeasement, a return to the fearful mentality of the 1930s. But appeasement is never a dirty word to those whose genuine weakness offers few appealing alternatives. For them, it is a policy of sophistication.

The end of the Cold War, by widening the power gap, exacerbated the disagreements. Although transatlantic tensions are now widely assumed to have begun with the inauguration of George W. Bush in January 2001, they were already evident during the Clinton administration and may even be traced back to the administration of George H. W. Bush. By 1992, mutual recriminations were rife over Bosnia, where the United States refused to act and Europe could not act. It was during the Clinton years that Europeans began complaining about being lectured by the "hectoring hegemon." This was also the period in which Védrine coined the term *hyperpuissance* to describe an American behemoth too worryingly powerful to be designated merely a superpower. (Perhaps he was responding to then-Secretary of State Madeleine Albright's insistence that the United States was the world's "indispensable nation.") It was also during the 1990s that the transatlantic disagreement over American plans for missile defense emerged and many Europeans began grumbling about the American propensity to choose force and punishment over diplomacy and persuasion.

The Clinton administration, meanwhile, though relatively timid and restrained itself, grew angry and impatient with European timidity, especially the unwillingness to confront Saddam Hussein. The split in the alliance over Iraq didn't begin with the 2000 election but in 1997, when the Clinton administration tried to increase the pressure on Baghdad and found itself at odds with France and (to a lesser extent) Great Britain in the United Nations Security Council. Even the war in Kosovo was marked by nervousness among some allies – especially Italy, Greece, and Germany – that the United States was too uncompromisingly militaristic in its approach. And while Europeans and Americans ultimately stood together in the confrontation with Belgrade, the Kosovo war produced in Europe less satisfaction at the successful prosecution of the war than unease at America's apparent

omnipotence. That apprehension would only increase in the wake
of American military action after September 11, 2001.

The Psychology of Power and Weakness

Today's transatlantic problem, in short, is not a George Bush
problem. It is a power problem. American military strength has
produced a propensity to use that strength. Europe's military
weakness has produced a perfectly understandable aversion to the
exercise of military power. Indeed, it has produced a powerful
European interest in inhabiting a world where strength doesn't
matter, where international law and international institutions predominate, where unilateral action by powerful nations is forbid-
den, where all nations regardless of their strength have equal rights
and are equally protected by commonly agreed-upon international
rules of behavior. Europeans have a deep interest in devaluing and
eventually eradicating the brutal laws of an anarchic, Hobbesian
world where power is the ultimate determinant of national security and success.

This is no reproach. It is what weaker powers have wanted from
time immemorial. It was what Americans wanted in the eighteenth and early nineteenth centuries, when the brutality of a
European system of power politics run by the global giants of
France, Britain, and Russia left Americans constantly vulnerable to
imperial thrashing. It was what the other small powers of Europe
wanted in those years, too, only to be sneered at by Bourbon kings
and other powerful monarchs, who spoke instead of *raison d'état*.
The great proponent of international law on the high seas in the
eighteenth century was the United States; the great opponent was
Britain's navy, the "Mistress of the Seas." In an anarchic world,
small powers always fear they will be victims. Great powers, on
the other hand, often fear rules that may constrain them more
than they fear the anarchy in which their power brings security
and prosperity.

This natural and historic disagreement between the stronger
and the weaker manifests itself in today's transatlantic dispute
over the question of unilateralism. Europeans generally believe

their objection to American unilateralism is proof of their greater commitment to certain ideals concerning world order. They are less willing to acknowledge that their hostility to unilateralism is also self-interested. Europeans fear American unilateralism. They fear it perpetuates a Hobbesian world in which they may become increasingly vulnerable. The United States may be a relatively benign hegemon, but insofar as its actions delay the arrival of a world order more conducive to the safety of weaker powers, it is objectively dangerous.

This is one reason why in recent years a principal objective of European foreign policy has become, as one European observer puts it, the "multilateralising" of the United States.[4] It is not that Europeans are teaming up against the American hegemon, as Huntington and many realist theorists would have it, by creating a countervailing power. After all, Europeans are not increasing their power. Their tactics, like their goal, are the tactics of the weak. They hope to constrain American power without wielding power themselves. In what may be the ultimate feat of subtlety and indirection, they want to control the behemoth by appealing to its conscience.

It is a sound strategy, as far as it goes. The United States *is* a behemoth with a conscience. It is not Louis XIV's France or George III's England. Americans do not argue, even to themselves, that their actions may be justified by *raison d'état*. Americans have never accepted the principles of Europe's old order, never embraced the Machiavellian perspective. The United States is a liberal, progressive society through and through, and to the extent that Americans believe in power, they believe it must be a means of advancing the principles of a liberal civilization and a liberal world order. Americans even share Europe's aspirations for a more orderly world system based not on power but on rules – after all, they were striving for such a world when Europeans were still extolling the laws of *Machtpolitik*.

But while these common ideals and aspirations shape foreign policies on both sides of the Atlantic, they cannot completely negate the very different perspectives from which Europeans and Americans view the world and the role of power in international affairs. Europeans oppose unilateralism in part because they have no capacity for unilateralism. Polls consistently show that Americans support multilateral action in principle – they even support acting under the rubric of the United Nations – but the fact remains that the United States can act unilaterally, and has done so many times with reasonable success. For Europeans, the appeal to multilateralism and international law has a real practical payoff and little cost. For Americans, who stand to lose at least some freedom of action, support for universal rules of behavior really is a matter of idealism.

Even when Americans and Europeans can agree on the kind of world order they would strive to build, however, they increasingly disagree about what constitutes a threat to that international endeavor. Indeed, Europeans and Americans differ most these days in their evaluation of what constitutes a tolerable versus an intolerable threat. This, too, is consistent with the disparity of power.

Europeans often argue that Americans have an unreasonable demand for "perfect" security, the product of living for centuries shielded behind two oceans.[5] Europeans claim they know what it is like to live with danger, to exist side by side with evil, since they've done it for centuries. Hence their greater tolerance for such threats as may be posed by Saddam Hussein's Iraq or the ayatollahs' Iran. Americans, they claim, make far too much of the dangers these regimes pose.

Even before September 11, this argument rang a bit hollow. The United States in its formative decades lived in a state of substantial insecurity, surrounded by hostile European empires, at constant risk of being torn apart by centrifugal forces that were encouraged by threats from without: national insecurity formed the core of Washington's Farewell Address. As for the Europeans' supposed tolerance for insecurity and evil, it can be overstated. For the better part of three centuries, European Catholics and Protestants more often preferred to kill than to tolerate each other; nor have the past two centuries shown all that much mutual tolerance between Frenchmen and Germans.

Some Europeans argue that precisely because Europe has suffered so much, it has a higher tolerance for suffering than America and therefore a higher tolerance for threats. More likely the opposite is true. The memory of their horrendous suffering in World

War I made the British and French publics more fearful of Nazi Germany, not more tolerant, and this attitude contributed significantly to the appeasement of the 1930s.

A better explanation of Europe's greater tolerance for threats is, once again, Europe's relative weakness. Tolerance is also very much a realistic response in that Europe, precisely because it is weak, actually faces fewer threats than the far more powerful United States.

The psychology of weakness is easy enough to understand. A man armed only with a knife may decide that a bear prowling the forest is a tolerable danger, inasmuch as the alternative – hunting the bear armed only with a knife – is actually riskier than lying low and hoping the bear never attacks. The same man armed with a rifle, however, will likely make a different calculation of what constitutes a tolerable risk. Why should he risk being mauled to death if he doesn't need to?

This perfectly normal human psychology is helping to drive a wedge between the United States and Europe today. Europeans have concluded, reasonably enough, that the threat posed by Saddam Hussein is more tolerable for them than the risk of removing him. But Americans, being stronger, have reasonably enough developed a lower threshold of tolerance for Saddam and his weapons of mass destruction, especially after September 11. Europeans like to say that Americans are obsessed with fixing problems, but it is generally true that those with a greater capacity to fix problems are more likely to try to fix them than those who have no such capability. Americans can imagine successfully invading Iraq and toppling Saddam, and therefore more than 70 percent of Americans apparently favor such action. Europeans, not surprisingly, find the prospect both unimaginable and frightening.

The incapacity to respond to threats leads not only to tolerance but sometimes to denial. It's normal to try to put out of one's mind that which one can do nothing about. According to one student of European opinion, even the very focus on "threats" differentiates American policymakers from their European counterparts. Americans, writes Steven Everts, talk about foreign "threats" such as "the proliferation of weapons of mass destruction, terrorism, and 'rogue states.'" But Europeans look at "challenges," such as "ethnic conflict, migration, organized crime, poverty and environmental degradation." As Everts notes, however, the key difference is less a matter of culture and philosophy than of capability. Europeans "are most worried about issues . . . that have a greater chance of being solved by political engagement and huge sums of money." In other words, Europeans focus on issues – "challenges" – where European strengths come into play but not on those "threats" where European weakness makes solutions elusive. If Europe's strategic culture today places less value on power and military strength and more value on such soft-power tools as economics and trade, isn't it partly because Europe is militarily weak and economically strong? Americans are quicker to acknowledge the existence of threats, even to perceive them where others may not see any, because they can conceive of doing something to meet those threats.

The differing threat perceptions in the United States and Europe are not just matters of psychology, however. They are also grounded in a practical reality that is another product of the disparity of power. For Iraq and other "rogue" states objectively do *not* pose the same level of threat to Europeans as they do to the United States. There is, first of all, the American security guarantee that Europeans enjoy and have enjoyed for six decades, ever since the United States took upon itself the burden of maintaining order in far-flung regions of the world – from the Korean Peninsula to the Persian Gulf – from which European power had largely withdrawn. Europeans generally believe, whether or not they admit it to themselves, that were Iraq ever to emerge as a real and present danger, as opposed to merely a potential danger, then the United States would do something about it – as it did in 1991. If during the Cold War, Europe by necessity made a major contribution to its own defense, today Europeans enjoy an unparalleled measure of "free security" because most of the likely threats are in regions outside Europe, where only the United States can project effective force. In a very practical sense – that is, when it comes to actual strategic planning – neither Iraq nor Iran nor North Korea nor any other "rogue" state in the world is primarily a European problem. Nor, certainly, is China. Both Europeans and Americans agree that these are primarily American problems.

This is why Saddam Hussein is not as great a threat to Europe as he is to the United States. He would be a greater threat to the United States even were the Americans and Europeans in complete agreement on Iraq policy, because it is the logical consequence of the transatlantic disparity of power. The task of containing Saddam Hussein belongs primarily to the United States, not to Europe, and everyone agrees on this[6] – including Saddam, which is why he considers the United States, not Europe, his principal adversary. In the Persian Gulf, in the Middle East, and in most other regions of the world (including Europe), the United States plays the role of ultimate enforcer. "You are so powerful," Europeans often say to Americans. "So why do you feel so threatened?" But it is precisely America's great power that makes it the primary target, and often the only target. Europeans are understandably content that it should remain so.

Americans are "cowboys," Europeans love to say. And there is truth in this. The United States does act as an international sheriff, self-appointed perhaps but widely welcomed nevertheless, trying to enforce some peace and justice in what Americans see as a lawless world where outlaws need to be deterred or destroyed, and often through the muzzle of a gun. Europe, by this Old West analogy, is more like a saloonkeeper. Outlaws shoot sheriffs, not saloonkeepers. In fact, from the saloonkeeper's point of view, the sheriff trying to impose order by force can sometimes be more threatening than the outlaws who, at least for the time being, may just want a drink.

When Europeans took to the streets by the millions after September 11, most Americans believed it was out of a sense of shared danger and common interest: the Europeans knew they could be next. But Europeans by and large did not feel that way and still don't. Europeans do not really believe they are next. They may be secondary targets – because they are allied with the US – but they are not the primary target, because they no longer play the imperial role in the Middle East that might have engendered the same antagonism against them as is aimed at the United States. When Europeans wept and waved American flags after September 11, it was out of genuine human sympathy, sorrow, and affection for Americans. For better or for worse, European displays of solidarity were a product more of fellow-feeling than self-interest.

The Origins of Modern European Foreign Policy

Important as the power gap may be in shaping the respective strategic cultures of the United States and Europe, it is only one part of the story. Europe in the past half-century has developed a genuinely different perspective on the role of power in international relations, a perspective that springs directly from its unique historical experience since the end of World War II. It is a perspective that Americans do not share and cannot share, inasmuch as the formative historical experiences on their side of the Atlantic have not been the same.

Consider again the qualities that make up the European strategic culture: the emphasis on negotiation, diplomacy, and commercial ties, on international law over the use of force, on seduction over coercion, on multilateralism over unilateralism. It is true that these are not traditionally European approaches to international relations when viewed from a long historical perspective. But they are a product of more recent European history. The modern European strategic culture represents a conscious rejection of the European past, a rejection of the evils of European *Machtpolitik*. It is a reflection of Europeans' ardent and understandable desire never to return to that past.

Who knows better than Europeans the dangers that arise from unbridled power politics, from an excessive reliance on military force, from policies produced by national egoism and ambition, even from balance of power and *raison d'état*? As German Foreign Minister Joschka Fischer put it in a speech outlining his vision of the European future at Humboldt University in Berlin (May 12, 2000), "The core of the concept of Europe after 1945 was and still is a rejection of the European balance-of-power principle and the hegemonic ambitions of individual states that had emerged following the Peace of Westphalia in 1648." The European Union is itself the product of an awful century of European warfare.

Of course, it was the "hegemonic ambitions" of one nation in particular that European integration was meant to contain. And it is the integration and taming of Germany that is the great accomplishment of Europe – viewed historically, perhaps the greatest feat of international politics ever achieved. Some Europeans recall, as Fischer does, the central role played by the United States in solving the "German problem." Fewer like to recall that the military destruction of Nazi Germany was the prerequisite for the European peace that followed. Most Europeans believe that it was the transformation of European politics, the deliberate abandonment and rejection of centuries of *Machtpolitik*, that in the end made possible the "new order." The Europeans, who invented power politics, turned themselves into born-again idealists by an act of will, leaving behind them what Fischer called "the old system of balance with its continued national orientation, constraints of coalition, traditional interest-led politics and the permanent danger of nationalist ideologies and confrontations."

Fischer stands near one end of the spectrum of European idealism. But this is not really a right–left issue in Europe. Fischer's principal contention – that Europe has moved beyond the old system of power politics and discovered a new system for preserving peace in international relations – is widely shared across Europe. As senior British diplomat Robert Cooper recently wrote in the *Observer* (April 7, 2002), Europe today lives in a "postmodern system" that does not rest on a balance of power but on "the rejection of force" and on "self-enforced rules of behavior." In the "postmodern world," writes Cooper, "*raison d'état* and the amorality of Machiavelli's theories of statecraft . . . have been replaced by a moral consciousness" in international affairs.

American realists might scoff at this idealism. George F. Kennan assumed only his naive fellow Americans succumbed to such "Wilsonian" legalistic and moralistic fancies, not those war-tested, historically minded European Machiavels. But, really, why shouldn't Europeans be idealistic about international affairs, at least as they are conducted in Europe's "postmodern system"? Within the confines of Europe, the age-old laws of international relations have been repealed. Europeans have stepped out of the Hobbesian world of anarchy into the Kantian world of perpetual

peace. European life during the more than five decades since the
end of World War II has been shaped not by the brutal laws of
power politics but by the unfolding of a geopolitical fantasy, a
miracle of world-historical importance: the German lion has lain
down with the French lamb. The conflict that ravaged Europe ever
since the violent birth of Germany in the nineteenth century has
been put to rest.

The means by which this miracle has been achieved have
understandably acquired something of a sacred mystique for
Europeans, especially since the end of the Cold War. Diplomacy,
negotiations, patience, the forging of economic ties, political
engagement, the use of inducements rather than sanctions, the
taking of small steps and tempering ambitions for success – these
were the tools of Franco-German rapprochement and hence the
tools that made European integration possible. Integration was not
to be based on military deterrence or the balance of power. Quite
the contrary. The miracle came from the rejection of military
power and of its utility as an instrument of international affairs –
at least within the confines of Europe. During the Cold War, few
Europeans doubted the need for military power to deter the
Soviet Union. But within Europe the rules were different.

Collective security was provided from without, meanwhile,
by the *deus ex machina* of the United States operating through
the military structures of NATO. Within this wall of security,
Europeans pursued their new order, freed from the brutal laws
and even the mentality of power politics. This evolution from the
old to the new began in Europe during the Cold War. But the end
of the Cold War, by removing even the external danger of the
Soviet Union, allowed Europe's new order, and its new idealism,
to blossom fully. Freed from the requirements of any military
deterrence, internal or external, Europeans became still more confident that their way of settling international problems now had
universal application.

"The genius of the founding fathers," European Commission
President Romano Prodi commented in a speech at the Institut
d'Études Politiques in Paris (May 29, 2001), "lay in translating
extremely high political ambitions . . . into a series of more specific, almost technical decisions. This indirect approach made

further action possible. Rapprochement took place gradually. From confrontation we moved to willingness to cooperate in the economic sphere and then on to integration." This is what many Europeans believe they have to offer the world: not power, but the transcendence of power. The "essence" of the European Union, writes Everts, is "all about subjecting inter-state relations to the rule of law," and Europe's experience of successful multilateral governance has in turn produced an ambition to convert the world. Europe "has a role to play in world 'governance,'" says Prodi, a role based on replicating the European experience on a global scale. In Europe "the rule of law has replaced the crude interplay of power . . . power politics have lost their influence." And by "making a success of integration we are demonstrating to the world that it is possible to create a method for peace."

No doubt there are Britons, Germans, French, and others who would frown on such exuberant idealism. But many Europeans, including many in positions of power, routinely apply Europe's experience to the rest of the world. For is not the general European critique of the American approach to "rogue" regimes based on this special European insight? Iraq, Iran, North Korea, Libya – these states may be dangerous and unpleasant, even evil. But might not an "indirect approach" work again, as it did in Europe? Might it not be possible once more to move from confrontation to rapprochement, beginning with cooperation in the economic sphere and then moving on to peaceful integration? Could not the formula that worked in Europe work again with Iran or even Iraq? A great many Europeans insist that it can.

The transmission of the European miracle to the rest of the world has become Europe's new *mission civilisatrice*. Just as Americans have always believed that they had discovered the secret to human happiness and wished to export it to the rest of the world, so the Europeans have a new mission born of their own discovery of perpetual peace.

Thus we arrive at what may be the most important reason for the divergence in views between Europe and the United States. America's power, and its willingness to exercise that power – unilaterally if necessary – represents a threat to Europe's new sense of mission. Perhaps the greatest threat. American policymakers find it hard to believe, but leading officials and politicians in Europe worry more about how the United States might handle or mishandle the problem of Iraq – by undertaking unilateral and extralegal military action – than they worry about Iraq itself and Saddam Hussein's weapons of mass destruction. And while it is true that they fear such action might destabilize the Middle East and lead to unnecessary loss of life, there is a deeper concern.[7] Such American action represents an assault on the essence of "postmodern" Europe. It is an assault on Europe's new ideals, a denial of their universal validity, much as the monarchies of eighteenth- and nineteenth-century Europe were an assault on American republican ideals. Americans ought to be the first to understand that a threat to one's beliefs can be as frightening as a threat to one's physical security.

As Americans have for two centuries, Europeans speak with great confidence of the superiority of their global understanding, the wisdom they have to offer other nations about conflict resolution, and their way of addressing international problems. But just as in the first decade of the American republic, there is a hint of insecurity in the European claim to "success," an evident need to have their success affirmed and their views accepted by other nations, particularly by the mighty United States. After all, to deny the validity of the new European idealism is to raise profound doubts about the viability of the European project. If international problems cannot, in fact, be settled the European way, wouldn't that suggest that Europe itself may eventually fall short of a solution, with all the horrors this implies?

And, of course, it is precisely this fear that still hangs over Europeans, even as Europe moves forward. Europeans, and particularly the French and Germans, are not entirely sure that the problem once known as the "German problem" really has been solved. As their various and often very different proposals for the future constitution of Europe suggest, the French are still not confident they can trust the Germans, and the Germans are still not sure they can trust themselves. This fear can at times hinder progress toward deeper integration, but it also propels the European project forward despite innumerable obstacles. The European project must succeed, for how else to overcome what Fischer, in his

Humboldt University speech, called "the risks and temptations objectively inherent in Germany's dimensions and central situation"? Those historic German "temptations" play at the back of many a European mind. And every time Europe contemplates the use of military force, or is forced to do so by the United States, there is no avoiding at least momentary consideration of what effect such a military action might have on the "German question."

Perhaps it is not just coincidence that the amazing progress toward European integration in recent years has been accompanied not by the emergence of a European superpower but, on the contrary, by a diminishing of European military capabilities relative to the United States. Turning Europe into a global superpower capable of balancing the power of the United States may have been one of the original selling points of the European Union – an independent European foreign and defense policy was supposed to be one of the most important byproducts of European integration. But, in truth, the ambition for European "power" is something of an anachronism. It is an atavistic impulse, inconsistent with the ideals of postmodern Europe, whose very existence depends on the rejection of power politics. Whatever its architects may have intended, European integration has proved to be the enemy of European military power and, indeed, of an important European global role.

This phenomenon has manifested itself not only in flat or declining European defense budgets, but in other ways, too, even in the realm of "soft" power. European leaders talk of Europe's essential role in the world. Prodi yearns "to make our voice heard, to make our actions count." And it is true that Europeans spend a great deal of money on foreign aid – more per capita, they like to point out, than does the United States. Europeans engage in overseas military missions, so long as the missions are mostly limited to peacekeeping. But while the EU periodically dips its fingers into troubled international waters in the Middle East or the Korean Peninsula, the truth is that EU foreign policy is probably the most anemic of all the products of European integration. As Charles Grant, a sympathetic observer of the EU, recently noted, few European leaders "are giving it much time or energy."[8]

EU foreign policy initiatives tend to be short-lived and are rarely backed by sustained agreement on the part of the various European powers. That is one reason they are so easily rebuffed, as was the case in late March when Israeli Prime Minister Ariel Sharon blocked EU foreign policy chief Javier Solana from meeting with Yasser Arafat (only to turn around the next day and allow a much lower-ranking American negotiator to meet with the Palestinian leader).

It is obvious, moreover, that issues outside of Europe don't attract nearly as much interest among Europeans as purely European issues do. This has surprised and frustrated Americans on all sides of the political and strategic debate: recall the profound disappointment of American liberals when Europeans failed to mount an effective protest against Bush's withdrawal from the ABM [antiballistic missile] treaty. But given the enormous and difficult agenda of integration, this European tendency to look inward is understandable. EU enlargement, the revision of the common economic and agricultural policies, the question of national sovereignty versus supranational governance, the so-called democracy deficit, the jostling of the large European powers, the dissatisfaction of the smaller powers, the establishment of a new European constitution – all of these present serious and unavoidable challenges. The difficulties of moving forward might seem insuperable were it not for the progress the project of European integration has already demonstrated.

American policies that are unwelcome on substance – on a missile defense system and the ABM treaty, belligerence toward Iraq, support for Israel – are all the more unwelcome because for Europe, they are a distraction. Europeans often point to American insularity and parochialism. But Europeans themselves have turned intensely introspective. As Dominique Moïsi noted in the *Financial Times* (March 11, 2002), the recent French presidential campaign saw "no reference . . . to the events of September 11 and their far-reaching consequences." No one asked, "What should be the role of France and Europe in the new configuration of forces created after September 11? How should France reappraise its military budget and doctrine to take account of the need to maintain some kind of parity between Europe and the United States, or at least between France and the UK?" The Middle East conflict became an issue in the campaign because of France's large Arab and Muslim population, as the high vote for [Jean-Marie] Le Pen demonstrated. But Le Pen is not a foreign policy hawk. And as Moisi noted, "for most French voters in 2002, security has little to do with abstract and distant geopolitics. Rather, it is a question of which politician can best protect them from the crime and violence plaguing the streets and suburbs of their cities."

Can Europe change course and assume a larger role on the world stage? There has been no shortage of European leaders urging it to do so. Nor is the weakness of EU foreign policy today necessarily proof that it must be weak tomorrow, given the EU's record of overcoming weaknesses in other areas. And yet the political will to demand more power for Europe appears to be lacking, and for the very good reason that Europe does not see a mission for itself that requires power. Its mission is to oppose power. It is revealing that the argument most often advanced by Europeans for augmenting their military strength these days is not that it will allow Europe to expand its strategic purview. It is merely to rein in and "multilateralize" the United States. "America," writes the pro-American British scholar Timothy Garton Ash in the *New York Times* (April 9, 2002), "has too much power for anyone's good, including its own." Therefore Europe must amass power, but for no other reason than to save the world and the United States from the dangers inherent in the present lopsided situation.

Whether that particular mission is a worthy one or not, it seems unlikely to rouse European passions. Even Védrine has stopped talking about counterbalancing the United States. Now he shrugs and declares there "is no reason for the Europeans to match a country that can fight four wars at once." It was one thing for Europe in the 1990s to increase its collective expenditures on defense from $150 billion per year to $180 billion when the United States was spending $280 billion per year. But now the United States is heading toward spending as much as $500 billion per year, and Europe has not the slightest intention of keeping up. European analysts lament the continent's "strategic irrelevance." NATO Secretary General George Robertson has taken to calling

Europe a "military pygmy" in an effort to shame Europeans into spending more and doing so more wisely. But who honestly believes Europeans will fundamentally change their way of doing business? They have many reasons not to.

The US Response

In thinking about the divergence of their own views and Europeans', Americans must not lose sight of the main point: the new Europe is indeed a blessed miracle and a reason for enormous celebration – on both sides of the Atlantic. For Europeans, it is the realization of a long and improbable dream: a continent free from nationalist strife and blood feuds, from military competition and arms races. War between the major European powers is almost unimaginable. After centuries of misery, not only for Europeans but also for those pulled into their conflicts – as Americans were twice in the past century – the new Europe really has emerged as a paradise. It is something to be cherished and guarded, not least by Americans, who have shed blood on Europe's soil and would shed more should the new Europe ever fail.

Nor should we forget that the Europe of today is very much the product of American foreign policy stretching back over six decades. European integration was an American project, too, after World War II. And so, recall, was European weakness. When the Cold War dawned, Americans such as Dean Acheson hoped to create in Europe a powerful partner against the Soviet Union. But that was not the only American vision of Europe underlying US policies during the twentieth century. Predating it was Franklin Delano Roosevelt's vision of a Europe that had been rendered, in effect, strategically irrelevant. As the historian John Lamberton Harper has put it, he wanted "to bring about a radical reduction in the weight of Europe" and thereby make possible "the retirement of Europe from world politics."[9]

Americans who came of age during the Cold War have always thought of Europe almost exclusively in Achesonian terms – as the essential bulwark of freedom in the struggle against Soviet tyranny. But Americans of Roosevelt's era had a different view. In the late 1930s the common conviction of Americans was that "the European system was basically rotten, that war was endemic on that continent, and the Europeans had only themselves to blame for their plight."[10] By the early 1940s Europe appeared to be nothing more than the overheated incubator of world wars that cost America dearly. During World War II Americans like Roosevelt, looking backward rather than forward, believed no greater service could be performed than to take Europe out of the global strategic picture once and for all. "After Germany is disarmed," FDR pointedly asked, "what is the reason for France having a big military establishment?" Charles de Gaulle found such questions "disquieting for Europe and for France." Even though the United States pursued Acheson's vision during the Cold War, there was always a part of American policy that reflected Roosevelt's vision, too. Eisenhower undermining Britain and France at Suez was only the most blatant of many American efforts to cut Europe down to size and reduce its already weakened global influence.

But the more important American contribution to Europe's current world-apart status stemmed not from anti-European but from pro-European impulses. It was a commitment to Europe, not hostility to Europe, that led the United States in the immediate postwar years to keep troops on the continent and to create NATO. The presence of American forces as a security guarantee in Europe was, as it was intended to be, the critical ingredient to begin the process of European integration.

Europe's evolution to its present state occurred under the mantle of the US security guarantee and could not have occurred without it. Not only did the United States for almost half a century supply a shield against such external threats as the Soviet Union and such internal threats as may have been posed by ethnic conflict in places like the Balkans. More important, the United States was the key to the solution of the German problem and perhaps still is. Germany's Fischer, in the Humboldt University speech, noted two "historic decisions" that made the new Europe possible: "the USA's decision to stay in Europe" and "France's and Germany's commitment to the principle of integration, beginning with economic links." But of course the latter could never have

occurred without the former. France's willingness to risk the reintegration of Germany into Europe – and France was, to say the
least, highly dubious – depended on the promise of continued
American involvement in Europe as a guarantee against any resurgence of German militarism. Nor were postwar Germans unaware
that their own future in Europe depended on the calming presence of the American military.

The United States, in short, solved the Kantian paradox for the
Europeans. Kant had argued that the only solution to the immoral
horrors of the Hobbesian world was the creation of a world government. But he also feared that the "state of universal peace"
made possible by world government would be an even greater
threat to human freedom than the Hobbesian international order,
inasmuch as such a government, with its monopoly of power,
would become "the most horrible despotism."[11] How nations
could achieve perpetual peace without destroying human
freedom was a problem Kant could not solve. But for Europe the
problem was solved by the United States. By providing security
from outside, the United States has rendered it unnecessary for
Europe's supranational government to provide it. Europeans did
not need power to achieve peace and they do not need power to
preserve it.

The current situation abounds in ironies. Europe's rejection of
power politics, its devaluing of military force as a tool of international relations, have depended on the presence of American
military forces on European soil. Europe's new Kantian order
could flourish only under the umbrella of American power exercised according to the rules of the old Hobbesian order. American
power made it possible for Europeans to believe that power was
no longer important. And now, in the final irony, the fact that
United States military power has solved the European problem,
especially the "German problem," allows Europeans today to
believe that American military power, and the "strategic culture"
that has created and sustained it, are outmoded and dangerous.

Most Europeans do not see the great paradox: that their passage
into post-history has depended on the United States not making
the same passage. Because Europe has neither the will nor the
ability to guard its own paradise and keep it from being overrun,

spiritually as well as physically, by a world that has yet to accept the rule of "moral consciousness," it has become dependent on America's willingness to use its military might to deter or defeat those around the world who still believe in power politics.

Some Europeans do understand the conundrum. Some Britons, not surprisingly, understand it best. Thus Robert Cooper writes of the need to address the hard truth that although "within the post-modern world [i.e., the Europe of today], there are no security threats in the traditional sense," nevertheless, throughout the rest of the world – what Cooper calls the "modern and pre-modern zones" – threats abound. If the postmodern world does not protect itself, it can be destroyed. But how does Europe protect itself without discarding the very ideals and principles that undergird its pacific system?

"The challenge to the postmodern world," Cooper argues, "is to get used to the idea of double standards." Among themselves, Europeans may "operate on the basis of laws and open coopera-tive security." But when dealing with the world outside Europe, "we need to revert to the rougher methods of an earlier era – force, preemptive attack, deception, whatever is necessary." This is Cooper's principle for safeguarding society: "Among ourselves, we keep the law but when we are operating in the jungle, we must also use the laws of the jungle."

Cooper's argument is directed at Europe, and it is appropriately coupled with a call for Europeans to cease neglecting their defenses, "both physical and psychological." But what Cooper really describes is not Europe's future but America's present. For it is the United States that has had the difficult task of navigating between these two worlds, trying to abide by, defend, and further the laws of advanced civilized society while simultaneously employing military force against those who refuse to abide by those rules. The United States is already operating according to Cooper's double standard, and for the very reasons he suggests. American leaders, too, believe that global security and a liberal order – as well as Europe's "postmodern" paradise – cannot long survive unless the United States does use its power in the dan-gerous, Hobbesian world that still flourishes outside Europe.

What this means is that although the United States has played the critical role in bringing Europe into this Kantian paradise, and still plays a key role in making that paradise possible, it cannot enter this paradise itself. It mans the walls but cannot walk through the gate. The United States, with all its vast power, remains stuck in history, left to deal with the Saddams and the ayatollahs, the Kim Jong Ils and the Jiang Zemins, leaving the happy benefits to others.

An Acceptable Division?

Is this situation tolerable for the United States? In many ways, it is. Contrary to what many believe, the United States can shoulder the burden of maintaining global security without much help from Europe. The United States spends a little over 3 percent of its GDP on defense today. Were Americans to increase that to 4 percent – meaning a defense budget in excess of $500 billion per year – it would still represent a smaller percentage of national wealth than Americans spent on defense throughout most of the past half-century. Even Paul Kennedy, who invented the term "imperial overstretch" in the late 1980s (when the United States was spending around 7 percent of its GDP on defense), believes the United States can sustain its current military spending levels and its current global dominance far into the future. Can the United States handle the rest of the world without much help from Europe? The answer is that it already does. The United States has maintained strategic stability in Asia with no help from Europe. In the Gulf War, European help was token; so it has been more recently in Afghanistan, where Europeans are once again "doing the dishes"; and so it would be in an invasion of Iraq to unseat Saddam. Europe has had little to offer the United States in strategic military terms since the end of the Cold War – except, of course, that most valuable of strategic assets, a Europe at peace.

The United States can manage, therefore, at least in material terms. Nor can one argue that the American people are unwilling to shoulder this global burden, since they have done so for a decade already. After September 11, they seem willing to continue doing so for a long time to come. Americans apparently feel no resentment at not being able to enter a "postmodern" utopia. There is no evidence most Americans desire to. Partly because they are so powerful, they take pride in their nation's military power and their nation's special role in the world.

Americans have no experience that would lead them to embrace fully the ideals and principles that now animate Europe. Indeed, Americans derive their understanding of the world from a very different set of experiences. In the first half of the twentieth century, Americans had a flirtation with a certain kind of internationalist idealism. Wilson's "war to end all wars" was followed a decade later by an American secretary of state putting his signature to a treaty outlawing war. FDR in the 1930s put his faith in non-aggression pacts and asked merely that Hitler promise not to attack a list of countries Roosevelt presented to him. But then came Munich and Pearl Harbor, and then, after a fleeting moment of renewed idealism, the plunge into the Cold War. The "lesson of Munich" came to dominate American strategic thought, and although it was supplanted for a time by the "lesson of Vietnam," today it remains the dominant paradigm. While a small segment of the American elite still yearns for "global governance" and eschews military force, Americans from Madeleine Albright to Donald Rumsfeld, from Brent Scowcroft to Anthony Lake, still remember Munich, figuratively if not literally. And for younger generations of Americans who do not remember Munich or Pearl Harbor, there is now September 11. After September 11, even many American globalizers demand blood.

Americans are idealists, but they have no experience of promoting ideals successfully without power. Certainly, they have no experience of successful supranational governance; little to make them place their faith in international law and international institutions, much as they might wish to; and even less to let them travel, with the Europeans, beyond power. Americans, as good children of the Enlightenment, still believe in the perfectibility of man, and they retain hope for the perfectibility of the world. But they remain realists in the limited sense that they still believe in the necessity of power in a world that remains far from perfection. Such law as there may be to regulate international behavior, they believe, exists because a power like the United States defends it by force of arms. In other words, just as Europeans claim, Americans can still sometimes see themselves in heroic terms – as Gary Cooper at high noon. They will defend the townspeople, whether the townspeople want them to or not.

The problem lies neither in American will or capability, then, but precisely in the inherent moral tension of the current international situation. As is so often the case in human affairs, the real question is one of intangibles – of fears, passions, and beliefs. The problem is that the United States must sometimes play by the rules of a Hobbesian world, even though in doing so it violates European norms. It must refuse to abide by certain international conventions that may constrain its ability to fight effectively in Robert Cooper's jungle. It must support arms control, but not always for itself. It must live by a double standard. And it must sometimes act unilaterally, not out of a passion for unilateralism but, given a weak Europe that has moved beyond power, because the United States has no choice *but* to act unilaterally.

Few Europeans admit, as Cooper does implicitly, that such American behavior may redound to the greater benefit of the civilized world, that American power, even employed under a double standard, may be the best means of advancing human progress – and perhaps the only means. Instead, many Europeans today have come to consider the United States itself to be the outlaw, a rogue colossus. Europeans have complained about President Bush's "unilateralism," but they are coming to the deeper realization that the problem is not Bush or any American president. It is systemic. And it is incurable.

Given that the United States is unlikely to reduce its power and that Europe is unlikely to increase more than marginally its own power or the will to use what power it has, the future seems certain to be one of increased transatlantic tension. The danger – if it is a danger – is that the United States and Europe will become positively estranged. Europeans will become more shrill in their attacks on the United States. The United States will become less inclined to listen, or perhaps even to care. The day could come, if

it has not already, when Americans will no more heed the pronouncements of the EU than they do the pronouncements of
ASEAN or the Andean Pact.

To those of us who came of age in the Cold War, the strategic
decoupling of Europe and the United States seems frightening. De
Gaulle, when confronted by FDR's vision of a world where
Europe was irrelevant, recoiled and suggested that this vision
"risked endangering the Western world." If Western Europe was
to be considered a "secondary matter" by the United States, would
not FDR only "weaken the very cause he meant to serve – that of
civilization?" Western Europe, de Gaulle insisted, was "essential to
the West. Nothing can replace the value, the power, the shining
example of the ancient peoples." Typically, de Gaulle insisted this
was "true of France above all." But leaving aside French *amour
propre*, did not de Gaulle have a point? If Americans were to
decide that Europe was no more than an irritating irrelevancy,
would American society gradually become unmoored from what
we now call the West? It is not a risk to be taken lightly, on either
side of the Atlantic.

So what is to be done? The obvious answer is that Europe
should follow the course that Cooper, Ash, Robertson, and others
recommend and build up its military capabilities, even if only marginally. There is not much ground for hope that this will happen.
But, then, who knows? Maybe concern about America's over-
weening power really will create some energy in Europe. Perhaps
the atavistic impulses that still swirl in the hearts of Germans,
Britons, and Frenchmen – the memory of power, international
influence, and national ambition – can still be played upon. Some
Britons still remember empire; some Frenchmen still yearn for *la
gloire*; some Germans still want their place in the sun. These urges
are now mostly channeled into the grand European project, but
they could find more traditional expression. Whether this is to be
hoped for or feared is another question. It would be better still if
Europeans could move beyond fear and anger at the rogue colossus and remember, again, the vital necessity of having a strong
America – for the world and especially for Europe.

Americans can help. It is true that the Bush administration
came into office with a chip on its shoulder. It was hostile to the
new Europe – as to a lesser extent was the Clinton administration

– seeing it not so much as an ally but as an albatross. Even after September 11, when the Europeans offered their very limited military capabilities in the fight in Afghanistan, the United States resisted, fearing that European cooperation was a ruse to tie America down. The Bush administration viewed NATO's historic decision to aid the United States under Article V less as a boon than as a booby trap. An opportunity to draw Europe into common battle out in the Hobbesian world, even in a minor role, was thereby unnecessarily lost.

Americans are powerful enough that they need not fear Europeans, even when bearing gifts. Rather than viewing the United States as a Gulliver tied down by Lilliputian threads, American leaders should realize that they are hardly constrained at all, that Europe is not really capable of constraining the United States. If the United States could move past the anxiety engendered by this inaccurate sense of constraint, it could begin to show more understanding for the sensibilities of others, a little generosity of spirit. It could pay its respects to multilateralism and the rule of law and try to build some international political capital for those moments when multilateralism is impossible and unilateral action unavoidable. It could, in short, take more care to show what the founders called a "decent respect for the opinion of mankind."

These are small steps, and they will not address the deep problems that beset the transatlantic relationship today. But, after all, it is more than a cliché that the United States and Europe share a set of common Western beliefs. Their aspirations for humanity are much the same, even if their vast disparity of power has now put them in very different places. Perhaps it is not too naively optimistic to believe that a little common understanding could still go a long way.

Notes

*This chapter was previously published in *Policy Review*, 113 (June–July 2002) and in Robert Kagan, *Of Paradise and Power* (New York: Knopf; London: Atlantic), © 2003 by Robert Kagan, used by permission of Alfred A. Knopf, a division of Random House, Inc.

1   One representative French observer describes "a U.S. mindset" that "tends to emphasize military, technical and unilateral solutions to

international problems, possibly at the expense of co-operative and political ones." See Gilles Andreani, "The Disarray of U.S. Non-Proliferation Policy," *Survival* (Winter 1999–2000).

2   The case of Bosnia in the early 1990s stands out as an instance where some Europeans, chiefly British Prime Minister Tony Blair, were at times more forceful in advocating military action than first the Bush and then the Clinton administration. (Blair was also an early advocate of using air power and even ground troops in the Kosovo crisis.) And Europeans had forces on the ground in Bosnia when the United States did not, although in a UN peacekeeping role that proved ineffective when challenged.

3   Samuel P. Huntington, "The Lonely Superpower," *Foreign Affairs* (March–April 1999).

4   Steven Everts, "Unilateral America, Lightweight Europe?: Managing Divergence in Transatlantic Foreign Policy," Centre for European Reform working paper (February 2001).

5   For that matter, this is also the view commonly found in American textbooks.

6   Notwithstanding the British contribution of patrols of the "no-fly zone."

7   The common American argument that European policy toward Iraq and Iran is dictated by financial considerations is only partly right. Are Europeans greedier than Americans? Do American corporations not influence American policy in Asia and Latin America, as well as in the Middle East? The difference is that American strategic judgments sometimes conflict with and override financial interests. For the reasons suggested in this essay, that conflict is much less common for Europeans.

8   Charles Grant, "A European View of ESDP," Centre for European Policy Studies working paper (April 2001).

9   John Lamberton Harper, *American Visions of Europe: Franklin D. Roosevelt, George F. Kennan, and Dean G. Acheson* (Cambridge University Press, 1996), 3. The following discussion of the differing American perspectives on Europe owes much to Harper's fine book.

10 William L. Langer and S. Everett Gleason, *The Challenge to Isolation, 1937–1940* (Harper Bros, 1952), 14.

11 See Thomas L. Pangle and Peter J. Ahrensdorf, *Justice Among Nations: On the Moral Basis of Power and Peace* (University Press of Kansas, 1999), 200–1.

6

The Goals of Diplomacy, Hard Power, and Soft Power*

Robert Cooper

America seems to be hard power incarnate and Europe the embodiment of soft power. America has military capabilities second to none. It is not just that the US defense budget is equal to the sum of the defense budgets of the next 20 countries – or more since it grows all the time; nor that its supplementary estimates often turn out to be greater than the total defense expenditure of some of its more capable partners. The sum of defense expenditure is always greater than its parts: economies of scale and the ability to focus resources mean that the United States possesses military assets that others cannot dream of. The military world divides neatly into two classes: the USA and everyone else. And the gap between the two is growing.

The US has long had a superior defense capability: since 9/11 it has acquired the will to use it. The approach of the administration is set out clearly in its National Security Strategy: alliances are important but the central objective is the maintenance of US military superiority. For the moment this does not seem a difficult task. The US is far ahead of all its allies and even further ahead of any possible enemy. During the Afghan campaign of 2001 it was turning assistance from allies away. In the run up to the invasion of Iraq the US Defense Secretary made clear that the US could, if necessary, manage quite well without its most capable ally, the UK.

The influence of the military also seems greater in the US than in many European countries. The formidable power of the five US commanders in chief is one aspect: they have budgets and authority that far exceeds those of any ambassador. The fact that generals can make political careers in the USA is another. Even in the State Department, US officials think far more in military terms than their European counterparts do. The attitude of US policymakers is always "can do"; and often it is the military who do the doing. Moreover the United States' most important relationships are expressed primarily in military terms: NATO for Europe and the Security Treaty for Japan.

By contrast Europe has been seen as a civilian power. The European Union has no army although this is one of the areas where unity would bring obvious increase in efficiency and influence. It relies on law, on negotiation, on multilateral organization. Its relationships are often in the form of "contractual agreements," itself a revealing phrase. It seems a model of soft power, as America is of hard power. These concepts however require a closer look: neither hard power nor soft power is so straightforward as it seems at first glance.

Hard power is coercive force. Soft power (it seems) can be just about anything else. We all know what hard power looks like. We see pictures of it every day in the newspapers and on the television. We read about it in our history books and the government spends its defense budget on hard power. Most of us have not encountered it directly. The experience is probably frightening and unpleasant.

Realists have a preference for hard power. Bismarck is famous for the remark that "This policy cannot succeed through speeches . . . and songs; it can be carried out only through blood and iron." Mao Zedong took the view that power grew out of the barrel of a gun. Lyndon B. Johnson thought that "when you've got them by the balls the hearts and minds will follow." Machiavelli says it is better to be feared than loved – to compel, that is, rather than to attract: "men love at their own pleasure and fear at the pleasure of the Prince."

And yet each of these examples contains some irony. Bismarck's "blood and iron" was not the solution to the German question. By 1945 Germany had had enough of both: they had undermined Bismarck's achievement of unification and had led to the ruin of Germany. President Johnson was, to put it simply, wrong. The hearts and minds manifestly did not follow in Vietnam. Indeed the war came to an end not just because of the stubborn military resistance by the North Vietnamese/Vietcong but also because of their superior ability to win hearts and minds in Vietnam, and because of the US government's inability to do the same in its own home territory. Whereas Johnson seems genuinely to have believed in the efficacy of hard power (perhaps his lack of military experience accounts for his trusting the military more than Kennedy did), the quotation from Mao is something of an aberration. The man who wrote of the guerrilla swimming among the peasants like a fish in the sea had a keen understanding that power did not just grow out the rifle's mouth. Besides he may have noticed that it was little red books and not guns that his supporters in the Cultural Revolution waved.

A society based solely on hard power never existed: if it did it would not deserve the name of society. It would in the most literal sense amount to Hobbes's war of all against all. If every relationship depends on coercion or the threat of coercion even alliances would be impossible (not to mention families, religions, corporations, or crime syndicates). Taken to its extreme, hard power equals anarchy at the level of the individual. This is why, in Hobbes's state of nature, life is solitary as well as nasty, brutish, and short. Some collapsing states in Africa have come near to this; but even among the lawless bands there is some order; this rests upon a soft power in which ethnicity, magic, and money may all play a part.

Hard power may not be as powerful as it might seem at first sight but we do at least know what it is. Soft power is a more elusive idea. Joe Nye – perhaps the best-known authority on the subject – defines power as the ability to obtain the outcomes one wants, and soft power as the ability to do that by attraction and persuasion rather than by coercion.[1] In the terms of Hollywood this sounds like Marilyn Monroe rather than Arnold

Schwarzenegger. But is attraction the same thing as power? There are many aspects of the USA that are extremely attractive. Sometimes Hollywood itself is held up as an important source of soft power. But both Saddam Hussein and Kim Jong-il are said to have a passion for Hollywood movies without this having done much for American ability to obtain the outcomes it seeks in Iraq or North Korea. If Hollywood put out US propaganda it might do more for American influence; but then if it put out propaganda it would be less popular. Nor can it even be said that in some more subtle way American films and music spread American values. *Jaws, Psycho, Some Like it Hot, Animal House II*, and *The Godfather* are all deeply American but all present different views of the world and the viewer is free to make his choice. Where people adopt the values of a particular slice of American output – the rather admirable values preached by *Star Trek*, for example, had a following in East Germany – they choose the film because of the values not the other way round. As it happens *The Godfather* is said to be a particular favorite of both Saddam Hussein and Kim Jong-il. Perhaps that is because it is about power.

The fact that the USA makes good films is probably good for its image generally just as Germany's reputation for making good cars makes people think well of Germany. Coca Cola and McDonalds also stand for America – at least they are targets for anti-American demonstrators – but here too the connection with American influence is not obvious. (Saddam Hussein used to be the licensee for Pepsi Cola.) So while the USA can feel good about its widespread cultural impact and American companies almost certainly profit from it, it is not clear that it amounts to power. The other effect of course that America's attractiveness has is that it brings in lots of immigrants. These may be a source of wealth one day – and ability to compete for workers with key skills may be increasingly important – but this too is not power in the normal sense. Both opinion polls and anecdotes suggest that many people like American values, American society, even American people; but this does not mean they like American policy.

Another approach to soft power would be to say that it consists in getting people to do what you want by getting them to want what you want.[2] In this interpretation success itself represents a form of soft power since it encourages imitation. A striking example is the impact that Japan had on East and Southeast Asia. Some time in the 1960s people noticed that Japan was more of a success story than China and tried to imitate it. In fact they had quite a lot of success and some version of the Japanese model can be seen in a range of countries from South Korea through China, Malaysia, and many others in Southeast Asia. This has created a more comfortable environment for Japan than if all its neighbors had taken up Maoist ideas. Japan may not have been powerful in a conventional sense but it has had a powerful influence on its neighbors in a way that has produced desirable outcomes for Japan itself.

The difficulty with describing this as power is that while the influence is undoubted (if unintentional), the desirability of the outcome depends on the particular circumstances. For example, if we had been facing acute raw material shortages it might be against Japan's interests to have other countries imitate its high growth economic policies. Would that mean its soft power had suddenly gone (though its influence remained unchanged)? Or, to take a genuine historical case should we consider that the European and American Empires of the early twentieth century were examples of soft power because their success caused Japan to imitate them in seeking an empire aggressively in its region, or that this was a failure of soft power because this outcome was the opposite of what they wanted?

Sometimes those who write about soft power tell you that it is to do with setting the agenda, establishing norms and values, creating rules that suit you. This comes closer to the idea of power. But not in every case. For example, in Belgium (where I happen to live at the moment) the rules are set by Roman law overlaid by the Napoleonic code. It is good to know that the soft power of the Roman Empire and of the rather briefer Napoleonic Empire has lasted so well but it hasn't done much for its creators.

Perhaps the best way to clarify the idea of soft power may be to look at a couple of historical examples.

The greatest historical example of soft power must be the Catholic Church. Indeed the distinction between spiritual and temporal power may be more or less the same as that between soft and hard power. Stalin (who was something of an enthusiast for hard power) was right that the Pope did not have very many divisions – though there were times when, apart from owning vast areas of land, the Church could always enlist one or other of the lords temporal to fight for it. What the Pope did have was perhaps the greatest organization the world has ever known. And he had potentially at least the obedience of a large part of the population. Above all he was the source of legitimacy at a time when legitimacy came from above rather than below. In fact the Pope was the source of legitimacy in its most literal sense through his power to pronounce marriages legal or illegal – and so their off-spring legitimate or illegitimate. This was a critical capability in a world linked by a network of obligations based on kinship. He was in some sense the source of all soft power in the feudal world. Kings went to him to have their cause pronounced just or their marriage invalid. (On the importance of kinship see the way in which Shakespeare's Henry V seeks to legitimate his claim to the French throne – act 1, scene 2, lines 33 onwards.)

Eventually this formidable mass of soft power was pushed into the background not so much by the accumulating hard power of the European nation-states as by the weakening of its own monopoly on legitimacy through the split in Christendom. Then came an alternative source of legitimacy offered by the state first through its capacity to protect and organize people and later through its ability to represent them.

A second example, less impressive and more short-lived, but closer to our experience is the British Empire. The tiny quantities of military force used to control the lives of millions of imperial subjects are in retrospect astonishing. It is true that a certain amount of hard power was also available to sustain the Empire when needed; but in every case when the Empire had to be defended with hard power it was the beginning of the end. The survival of the Empire depended first and last on prestige: the prestige of technology and organization, perhaps even of a certain kind of justice, but also the prestige supplied by myths of racial superiority. When these were punctured by people who did not believe in white superiority such as the Japanese and Mahatma Gandhi there was nothing for the British to do but to get out.

These two examples concern soft power in its hardest form: when it represents real power, even power over life and death rather than a general good feeling about a country or organization. Strikingly they are both examples of semi-domestic situations. At the core of soft power is legitimacy. Armies obey civilian governments, junior gangsters obey their bosses, and children obey parents because they accept some rules or some authority. The most developed version of soft power is the legal and constitutional order by which most states are governed. It is true that behind this power remains the possibility of using force but for the most part obedience is obtained without this being mentioned or even thought of. People obey the state because that is what you do with a legitimately constituted state. Most power in a domestic context is soft power: authority without force. And if soft power sometimes seems to be a complicated, many-sided, and elusive concept, that may be because legitimacy, which lies at its heart, is also a complex and elusive concept.

The arguments about soft and hard power have however generally been applied in the international sphere where, it is normally held, might – hard power, that is – is right. It is therefore worth considering an example further removed from the internal ordering of a state than those already cited of the Church or an empire.

The Warsaw Pact was a good example of hard power at work. Its continued existence depended on coercion from the Soviet Union; this was demonstrated successively in East Germany, Hungary, Czechoslovakia, and Poland. The attempt to legitimize this in the Brezhnev Doctrine may have been a symptom of the declining conviction with which these interventions were carried out. NATO on the other hand was a kinder, gentler organization, one which conducted its business through consensus, footnotes, and astonishingly boring debates – in other words, soft power. Does the fact that NATO is still there and the Warsaw Pact has gone mean that soft power beats hard power?

It is interesting to consider how the Warsaw Pact failed. It was not through want of hard power. The Soviet Union could undoubtedly have suppressed Solidarity and the Polish Round Table and could have closed the Hungarian border. But it didn't

want to. It was not a failure of hard power but a failure of will
and confidence. Probably this should be considered as an element
of soft power. The Soviet system ultimately lost legitimacy even
in the eyes of the people that owned it. That is because, in a way,
they were rather decent people. "Evil empire" was definitely the
wrong phrase. Gorbachev wanted to do the right thing by the
Russian people and was honest enough to see the lack of success
of the Soviet system. If he had been in the game purely for power
or for profit, then he might still be there today. But the Soviet
system lost legitimacy because of its lack of success in economic
terms and lack of an external threat that might have legitimized
the use of hard power. In terms of threat reduction the European
Union may also have played a part. NATO certainly did too. What
mattered above all was that Germany was not perceived as threatening. But the real drama was on the Soviet side where there was
a radical failure of legitimacy – a failure, that is, of soft power.

In comparison to the Warsaw Pact, NATO looks like a soft organization; but in practice there was quite a lot of hard power
involved too. It was after all a military organization that, right up
to the end, was seen as a threat, at least by the Soviet military.
There must be a good chance that, without the threat of force
that NATO, or perhaps the USA, represented, the Soviet Union
would at some time have taken the opportunity to deal with the
Berlin problem. If that had succeeded, or if there had been no
security guarantees at all, it might have developed larger ambitions. So NATO's hard power was important too. But the real
battles of the Cold War were intra-alliance battles, the attempt to
find compromises between different sets of interests and different
points of views. Keeping the Alliance together was what mattered,
through the long debates on the Harmel report, on the two-track
decision, and many others. These you could say were the devices
by which NATO's soft power (its legitimacy) was maintained.
On the other side the use of Soviet hard power undermined the
Warsaw Pact's legitimacy almost from the beginning.

It is worth noting in passing that it was important that success
was defined in terms of prosperity. This was not an achievement
for the soft power of the capitalist system; economic success was
also the promise of the Soviet system. That, in a way, was one of

the things that helped make the Cold War winnable: both sides were playing on the same field. The difficulty in dealing with countries such as North Korea may be precisely that Kim Jong-il and Western governments have quite different notions of what constitutes success.

NATO was a success for soft power. It was cheaper for the USA to secure cooperation from West European allies by being friendly and giving them some say in the system than it would have been if it had tried to operate like the Soviet Union.[3] It is also questionable whether the American people would have permitted that. The USA may not have chosen soft power consciously nor did the USSR choose hard power consciously: that is just the way that they were. Within the Soviet Union, Stalin's terror came close to achieving the ultimate horror of a pure hard power system – where people were disoriented and even normal social life ceased to function. Earlier, however, it had seemed that the Soviet Union had quite a lot of soft power at its disposal. For a period it seemed to represent some attractive ideals, to be a force for modernization ("I have seen the future and it works" – a sentence that has outlived the memory of its author Lincoln Steffens), and in the 1930s communists seemed to be the only people who were resisting Hitler. But in fact it didn't work and just as tanks can break down and airplanes can crash if the hardware fails, so states can break down if the software is badly designed. What looked attractive turned out to be a failure.

When you have succeeded with hard power the normal thing to do is to try and turn it to soft power. Endless coercion provokes resistance and is too costly. All conquerors try to set up a new order, following Rousseau's advice: "The strongest is never strong enough always to be master unless he transforms strength into right and obedience into duty" – hard power into soft power he might have said today (with rather less force). The Soviet Union made a mess of the transformation. Hitler's New Order was so unattractive that it could not function without coercion. The order that America promoted after the war including both NATO and the European Union, the OECD, the WTO, and much else was simply a more competent job. Perhaps the most competent job anyone has ever done. But this New Order was still based on hard power. The

Marshall Plan was important but the American security guarantees were the critical factor. They were vital not just in persuading European countries to take the American side against the Soviet Union but also in enabling them to organize their own relations with each other better. Without American guarantees there would have been a large German army to deal with the Soviet threat and a large French army to deal with the German threat. So the soft power of the European Union is a remarkable success; but ultimately this order was based on hard power.[4]

This case – and there are many others – demonstrates that soft power can play a crucial role in international relations as well as in a domestic order. In both cases it is about establishing legitimacy. Whereas in domestic situations our ideas of legitimacy are well explored and, in the West at least, well established, in the international sphere the position is less clear. There are many sources of legitimacy and so also of soft power.

There is, first and foremost, a legitimacy that comes from sustaining the international order. If the USA is seen by others as the guarantor of the international system or the ultimate guarantor of security, and if its actions are seen as contributing to sustaining order, they will be accepted as legitimate. (Views on this may of course differ, as the Iraq War has made clear.) The provision of public goods such as security, or the function of lender of last resort, confers a degree of legitimacy internationally just as it does domestically.

It is a mistake, however, to think that soft power is a natural strength of Europe although the EU seems in some respects the apotheosis of soft power. Internally it operates by law; externally it uses force largely in peacekeeping mode. But soft power goes with hard power internationally as it does domestically. A country may be respected and trusted, as for example Norway is; this will bring it influence but not, when the chips are down, power. American supremacy in hard power on the other hand gives it equally enormous potential for soft power. If you want to exercise soft power you must have something to offer – a recipe for success, resources to help others get there, and probably armed force to protect them on the way. Hard power begets soft power.

Success is also a great legitimizer. At the end of the Cold War the US had enormous prestige. It was seen as owning the secret of the good life that everyone wanted and that communism had promised but failed to deliver. All across Central and Eastern Europe people listened to American economists, Baptists, constitutional experts, and other gurus. This was the great moment of soft power. There were European voices also but these are always less confident and less clear than those from the United States. Europe is a continent of skepticism, lacking the conviction of the USA. Besides there are always any number of European alternatives while there is one single model of American success. What gives a country influence however is not so much its own achievement, though this will excite admiration, as the conviction that this can be turned into success for someone else. Each wants their own success on their own terms, achieved by their own decisions and not handed to them by someone else (not that this is possible). But if another country is felt to have the recipe and to be willing to share it, that gives them, potentially, a good deal of soft power.

It is in this area that the softer forms of soft power can make a difference. If, through the media, people have the impression that the USA is an ideal society and a disinterested provider of peace and freedom they may respond to its appeals, be willing to provide intelligence about its enemies, and even welcome its armies. If its good intentions are undermined by hostile broadcasting they may not. A good public image can be a support for legitimacy.

The third and most important source of legitimacy internationally is participation. The United Nations remains the most important source of legitimacy because of the (sometimes contradictory) aspirations and norms it represents, because of its established place in the international legal framework, but above all because it is a forum in which everyone has a voice. The world cannot be governed by the same kind of representative democracy that has become the norm domestically (though it is still not fully observed in most countries). But the more those affected are seen to be involved in the decision-making process the more the decisions taken are likely to be considered legitimate.

Thus the magnitude of America's soft power on the European continent after World War II came not just from the protection it has offered and its role in managing the Western/world order but above all from its willingness to listen to the views of its allies and to involve them in decision making.[5] Legitimizing great power rule makes it all the more powerful. It adds soft power to hard. For the US it was worth the sacrifice of speed and decisiveness inherent in the switch to collective decision-making if the result was to obtain long-term sustainability. Rousseau would have admired the strategy. If NATO should come to be seen either as subservient to the USA or as not really involved in the important decisions its legitimacy will decline – and with it an important instrument of American power.

The European Union's soft power derives from the same range of factors. It offers less in the way of protection than NATO but this dimension is not completely absent. In multinational negotiations, where an increasing number of important decisions are made, EU members are able to defend their interests and to protect themselves better against other big players such as the US than if they operated on their own. And even without the formal setting of a multilateral negotiation EU membership provides some soft protection. Russia is likely to think more carefully about bullying one of the Baltic states when they are members of the EU than if they were on their own. The European Union also appears as a recipe for success in overcoming the historical problems of peace among the nation-states in Europe, and its aspirations – peace, prosperity, unity, while preserving diversity – are likely to be acceptable to most countries. But above all its soft power derives from its readiness to offer others a seat at the decision-making table.

A striking illustration is the case of Turkey, where the EU's influence in the core areas of Turkish sovereignty has been far greater than that of the USA in spite of the latter's long-standing military and political links. The massive changes taking place in Turkey, which is undergoing the most dramatic constitutional revision since its foundation (including for example the abolition of the death penalty and language rights for minority populations, notably the Kurds), are based on the expectation that, in return, it will secure a place in the European Union. This is regime change without violence, and it is all the more effective for being executed through soft rather than hard power. If Turkey's hopes in this should be disappointed it will be a blow to the EU's credibility from which it will take a long time to recover.

Hard power and soft power are two sides of the same coin. Legitimacy has many sources but the first requirement of legitimate government is that the citizens are protected. That is why revolutions almost always follow lost wars. Behind every law there stands a policeman, willing in the end to use force. And behind every constitution there stands an army willing to defend the state against outside interference or against attempts to overthrow it. The great battles of history – between Catholics and Protestants, monarchists and republicans, liberals and fascists or communists – were battles between rival legitimacies. They were fought with hard power to establish what sort of soft power system would govern men's lives. Soft power is the velvet glove, but behind it there is always the iron fist.

On the other hand the policeman does not arrest and the army does not fight or defend the state because someone coerces them. Ultimately they do these things because they accept authority. As Hume points out even Caesar has to command the loyalty of the Praetorian Guard. If that loyalty is to survive and flourish it needs to be based on some generally accepted legitimacy. Weber's definition of the state rightly includes both force and legitimacy. There is no soft power without hard power. But there is also no hard power without soft power. And in the international arena too, even with its supposed anarchy and power politics, lasting change requires legitimacy – soft power that is, as well as hard power.

It is no surprise that those of us who live in developed countries rarely encounter hard power. One of the objectives of civilization is precisely to transform hard power into soft power: anarchy into order, force into law, power into legitimate authority. These are the goals for which domestic political orders are established. They are also the goals of diplomacy.

Notes

*This chapter is written in a personal and not an official capacity.

1   Joseph Nye, *The Paradox of American Power* (New York: Oxford University Press, 2002), and his chapter in this volume.

2 Nye, *Paradox*, p. 9.
3 See for instance Thomas Risse-Kappen, *Cooperation among Demo-cracies: The European Influence on U.S. Foreign Policy* (Princeton, NJ: Princeton University Press 1995).
4 See Robert Kagan's chapter in this volume.
5 See Risse-Kappen, *Cooperation among Democracies*.

7

American Power: From "Compellance" to Cosmopolitanism?*

Mary Kaldor

"American democracy requires the repression of democracy in the rest of the world." So spoke an Asian human rights activist in a democracy seminar in Cracow. I pondered this sentence when I read it in an op-ed article last summer.[1] On the face of it, it seemed so paradoxical. After all, America is the "Crusader State"; a state based on an idea rather than a national identity, and that idea is democracy. Moreover, it is a state committed not only to preserving the idea within America but extending it to the rest of the world.[2] And yet, when I thought about it, the sentence did express what appears to the rest of the world to be the introverted nature of current American foreign policy. Seen from the outside, the war on terrorism seems to be less about defeating terrorism than a performance staged to meet the requirements of American democracy. What matters is the appearance, the spectacle, not what happens on the ground except insofar as what happens on the ground seeps through into the performance.

In all the discussions, especially in Europe, about the new American Empire, this aspect seems to be missing – the difference between appearance and reality, the mimetic character of American foreign policy. When Robert Kagan talks about American power and European weakness or when the former

French foreign minister Hubert Védrine refers to *hyperpuissance*, they assume that billions of dollars spent on defense, or that numbers of weapons or men under arms, can be translated into power.[3] Power means the ability to influence others, to control events elsewhere, to impose our will on others, what Thomas Schelling called "compellance."[4] But, in practice, American power is much less effective than is generally assumed, at least on its own. If America were truly an empire, surely it would be able to extend democracy to other regions, to impose its system on the rest of the world? The United States has the capability to be immensely destructive but much less the capability to do "compellance." From the point of view of American policymakers, however, this may not matter. The policy they pursue may be rational in terms of American domestic concerns, in attempting to dominate the American political landscape, in winning or nearly winning elections.

In this article, I argue that there is a mismatch between American domestic concerns, how the world is perceived inside America, and the reality in the rest of the world. Or to put it another way, American political culture and institutions were shaped by the experiences of World War II and the Cold War. The ideology of that period continues to exert a powerful influence on American perceptions and American foreign policy and yet it is badly suited to the changed world that we inhabit. The American foreign-policymakers continue to stage a drama drawn from the past, even though the enemies and the technologies have changed. And they will continue to do so, as long as this performance satisfies the American public, whatever the consequences for the rest of the world – unless reality begins to hit home, as it did briefly (and intensely) on September 11, 2001.

In developing the argument, I will start by describing what has changed, why traditional approaches no longer work; in particular I will emphasize the changed meaning of sovereignty in the context of globalization and the changed functions of military force primarily as a consequence of increased destructiveness. I will then set out four different policy approaches to the current conjecture based on different assumptions about the meaning of sovereignty and the nature of military power, and I will argue that

America's ability to do "compellance" can only be restored within a multilateral framework, underpinned by humanitarian norms. In the final section, I will speculate on the ways in which reality might impinge on American policymakers; in particular, the ways in which the need, at the least, to contain terrorism might propel a changed agenda.

The Changing Global Context

A decade ago, a number of scholars were predicting American decline. The United States, as the world hegemon, was becoming overstretched in the same way that earlier empires had declined under the burden of military power. Just as Britain was overtaken by the United States in the mid-twentieth century, so, it was predicted, Japan and Western Europe would lead in the next phase of capitalism.[5] Yet, today no one talks about the decline of America. Rather, the predominant debate both in scholarly and political circles concerns unipolarity and whether this is conducive to stability or whether it is dangerous. So what happened in between? Was it just the collapse of the Soviet Empire, the only challenger to the United States? Or is there some deeper explanation?

It is worth revisiting the arguments of those who predicted America's decline because of their arguments about the relationship between phases of capitalism and security frameworks.[6] They argued that different phases of capitalist growth were ushered in by war, which determined the shape of the regulatory framework. Thus the Napoleonic wars led to the first phase of industrialization, underpinned by the Concert of Europe and later the interimperial order, together with Britain's financial hegemony. Then came two world wars and a new phase of industrialization, characterized by mass production and mass consumption and known as Fordism. Global economic growth based on the Fordist model was underpinned by the Cold War order and the hegemonic role of the United States in the noncommunist world.

What was happening in the 1970s and 1980s was the decline of Fordism; the saturation of the markets for cars; the rising oil price; the boredom of workers with the routines of mass production. Declining international competitiveness and the growing cost of overseas defense and foreign economic and military assistance led many people to conclude that the American era was coming to an end. Japan and Western Europe, it was argued, less burdened by military spending and other overseas commitments, would take the lead in the new phase of capitalist technology, based on information technology.

In fact, the favorable environment generated in the 1990s in the United States as a consequence of deregulation and the investment boom has given America the leading edge in the so-called new economy. But it would be wrong to conclude that this explains the new role of the United States. I believe that we are still in a transition phase and that the outcome of the "war on terror" will determine the future regulatory framework of the new economy. The situation at the beginning of the twenty-first century can be compared with the early 1930s. In Kindleberger's classic book on the Depression, he argued that the huge productivity increases resulting from the introduction of mass production were not matched by changes in the structure of demand, and he explained this mismatch in terms of the continued dominance of Britain and the pound sterling.[7] It was not until after World War II that a global institutional framework was established for the "golden age" of Fordist economic growth. (It was not necessarily the best institutional framework but it worked.) Today, as in the 1920s, dramatic increases in productivity brought about by computers and by new communication technologies have not been matched by corresponding shifts in the pattern of global demand. Like that of the 1920s, the boom of the 1990s, it can be argued, was a false boom brought about by overexpectation, by excitement about the promise of the new technology.[8]

The problem today is how to construct the institutional framework that can guarantee the spread of the new economy, and that can lead to a new golden age. Unlike in the 1930s, this is not about whether hegemony passes from the United States to another state or groups of states; rather it is about the character of the new institutional framework. As long as American foreign-policymaking remains embedded in the Cold War framework, it can be argued, this will provide a constraint on future economic development and the decline thesis could still turn out to be true. In other words, the old Cold War model of hegemony is declining and, at this moment, we face a choice about the appropriate model for the future. America will continue to be dominant in any future model because of its size and wealth but differently from in the past. In particular, this new phase of capitalist development has certain important differences in comparison with Fordism and any new institutional framework would have to take these differences into account.

The changed meaning of sovereignty

The first difference has to do with the changed meaning of sovereignty. Fordism was associated with big government, with high levels of welfare and military spending, and with the growth of the public sector. The Cold War framework allowed for the liberalization of international trade and capital and for a great extension of state intervention at home. The new economy is associated with globalization, by which I mean the increasing interconnectedness of economies, polities, and societies, and with the withdrawal of the state from a range of activities as a consequence of liberalization and privatization. Interconnectedness, as those who write about globalization point out, is an uneven process involving homogeneity and diversity, integration and fragmentation, as well as decentralization and individuation.[9]

I agree with those who argue that globalization does not mean the demise of the state but rather its transformation. However, the direction of transformation is as yet unclear. The factors that shape that transformation include:

- The difficulty of sustaining closed societies or spheres of influence. In a sense the 1989 revolutions can be explained in these terms. The Soviet Union could not maintain control over Central Europe in the face of the growing interpenetration of societies as a consequence of increases in travel and communication. Both liberalization of trade and the increasingly transnational character of civil society make it difficult for traditional authoritarian leaders to insulate their societies from the rest of the world. This is why there are only a handful of apparently stable authoritarian regimes in the world today.

- The growing importance of new layers of political institutions – global, regional, and local. The growing interconnectedness of political institutions – the growth of treaties and international agreements – and the growing complexity of decision-making in the new economy have greatly increased the number of political decision points. These new institutions are in the process of generating new overlapping and sometimes contradictory loyalties – multiple "communities of fate," as David Held puts it.[10]
- Growing awareness of and growing resistance to the influence of events that take place far away. With the advent of the so-called new media, new imagined communities are displacing traditional patriotism. On the one hand, an emerging human consciousness has provided a basis for the new human rights regime and the popular reactions to massive human rights violations or to genocide. On the other hand, the construction of transnational networks has stimulated new or revived ethnic and religious identities that cross boundaries.

Essentially, these factors imply a move away from absolute control of territory and from geopolitics, that is to say, the control of foreign territory in the national interest. Sovereignty is increasingly conditional – dependent both on domestic consent and international respect. In traditional authoritarian states, the impact of globalization may result in state "failure" or "weakness." In other states, it may mean greater insertion within a multilateral framework of global governance. Both the notion of humanitarian intervention, the idea that humanitarian concerns override the norm of nonintervention that gained ground during the 1990s, and "new wars" based on identity politics, which aim to establish new absolutist exclusive statelets, can be viewed as differing responses to the current global conjuncture.

The changed functions of military forces

The second difference has to do with the decline of military power; that is to say the declining ability of states to use military force for "compellance." The growing destructiveness of all weapons means that superior military technology rarely confers a decisive advantage in conflicts between armed opponents. Moreover, it is not just weapons of mass destruction that can inflict mass destruction; the attacks of September 11 were equivalent to a small nuclear weapon. Nowadays, it is extremely difficult to control territory militarily and to win an outright military victory.

This proposition, I believe, was already becoming true at the end of World War II. Schelling's argument about "compellance" derived from the discovery of nuclear weapons; the question he asked was whether military force loses its utility in a world of mutual vulnerability, where nuclear weapons can inflict mass destruction. Nuclear weapons, it can be argued, became emblematic of the destructive nature of war. The allies did win a decisive victory in World War II, but only after 50 million people had died. The success of deterrence in the postwar period, it can be argued, was less due to nuclear weapons per se than to the unthinkability of another war on the scale of World War II. Indeed, the Soviet Union did not have a separate concept for deterrence; rather their concepts of *ustrashenie* (intimidation) or *sderzhivanie* (restraining or holding back) referred to the possibility of war in general.[11] It can be argued that these concepts, both deterrence and the Soviet equivalents, were ways of keeping alive the memory of what happened in World War II.

In World War II, platforms (particularly tanks and aircraft, but also submarines), using internal combustion engines and fueled by oil, broke through the stalemate of World War I where the use of artillery and machine guns on both sides had prevented any territorial advances. In contrast to World War I, World War II was a war of offense and of maneuver. With developments in information technology and, indeed, improvements in the destructiveness and accuracy of all types of weapons, including small arms, artillery, and missiles, however, the platforms that were typical of the Fordist era have become increasingly vulnerable as well. The Iran-Iraq War of the 1980s was much more like World War I than World War II.

It is argued that the one area where superior military technology conveys an advantage is in the air. The Americans do have the capacity to destroy or evade all known air defenses. Through the use of precision-guided munitions (PGMs) and unmanned aerial vehicles (UAVs), they can destroy targets from long distance with a high degree of accuracy, as we have seen in all recent wars fought by the United States. But this is not the same as controlling territory or achieving outright military victory. In the Gulf War, the United States and its allies did succeed in liberating Kuwait with a massive deployment of force; if undertaken today, it would occupy some 80 percent of American military manpower.[12] In Yugoslavia, the air attacks could not prevent the acceleration of ethnic cleansing in Kosovo; as Wesley Clark, then SACEUR (Supreme Allied Command Europe), put it at the time, "you cannot stop para-military murder from the air."[13] One of the problems was that it was very difficult to lure Serb forces into the open where they could be attacked from the air, as was done in the Gulf War. In the end, Milosevic capitulated, Kosovo was liberated, and the refugees returned home, but the experience left a legacy of hatred within Kosovo and undoubtedly contributed to the persistence of embittered anti-Western nationalism in Serbia today.[14] In the case of Afghanistan, the American effort succeeded in toppling the Taliban, with the help of the Northern Alliance and, at a crucial moment, some of the Pashtun warlords. In the critical battle for Mazar-i-Sharif, Taliban forces were stranded in the open and, altogether in the course of the war, thousands of Taliban troops were killed from the air. But the war effort did not succeed in capturing Osama bin Laden and many Al-Qaeda leaders, and it has not succeeded in stabilizing Afghanistan.

Military commentators suggest that reluctance to use troops on the ground is a consequence of the risk averseness of American leaders. In the case of Afghanistan, in particular, it is argued that had more American troops been committed to the battle for Tora Bora (December 2001) or later to Operation Anaconda (an operation in March 2002 in the Shah-e-Kot valley where Al-Qaeda operatives were hiding), Osama bin Laden would not have got away, even though many more Americans might have died.[15] But it is not at all clear whether ground forces could be any more effective. Ground superiority is much harder to achieve than air superiority. Would the Americans have been more efficient than the Afghan fighters in Tora Bora? The Russians and the Israelis, for example, are not casualty averse. The Russians are losing two to three Russian soldiers a day in Chechnya but they are still not able to defeat the rebels. They have been immensely destructive; Grozny is reduced to rubble; there has been massive population displacement, but they have not brought stability to the region. Unlike the Russians, the Israelis are better trained, equipped, and paid and claim to be operating within the laws of war and trying to avoid civilian casualties. Yet they cannot defeat the intifada and stabilize Palestine.

The 2003 war in Iraq validates these points. With the help of accurately targeted air power, the Coalition forces were able to topple the Iraqi regime at a speed unprecedented in history. The United States had a huge information advantage; it was able to process information received both from satellite pictures and from reports from the ground so that at any one moment, the wireless Internet system could show the deployment of troops with enemy forces in red and friendly forces in blue. Known as Force XXI Battle Command, Brigade and Below, it was installed on nearly every vehicle. This allowed red forces to be directly destroyed from the air; no one knows the extent of the military casualties, those that were not killed took off their uniforms and ran away. But toppling the regime is not the same as occupying the country, as has become painfully apparent. To some extent, the problem can be attributed to inadequate troop levels and unwillingness to risk casualties.[16] But as in Chechnya and Palestine, the spread of weapons has allowed for much more effective unconventional warfare and has resulted in daily attacks against American forces, Iraqis who collaborate with the American forces, and also foreign diplomats. It has also greatly complicated reconstruction efforts, undermining the promise of oil revenues, and greatly increasing the cost of occupation – both financially and in terms of casualties. At the time of writing, American soldiers killed since the war was proclaimed over have exceeded the number killed during the war.

To argue that military compellance is very difficult nowadays against an armed opponent is not to say that military forces have no rational functions. Rather, the classic function of capturing territory militarily reached its end point in the Fordist era. First of all, military forces can be used against civilian populations. This is the typical strategy of what I call "new wars," where a combination of state and non-state actors try to gain political control over territory by killing or expelling dissenters or those of a different religion or ethnicity. In general, these are wars fought in the name of exclusive identities – religion or ethnicity. The goal is to sow "fear and hatred" so that the local population supports the project of an exclusive ethnic or religious state. Battles between armed opponents are very rare; almost all violence is inflicted on civilians. Terrorist attacks on symbolic targets like the center of global capitalism (the World Trade Center towers) or a place of secular entertainment (the Sari nightclub in Bali) have similar goals – they spread fear and insecurity, they polarize society, they convey a dramatic message about modernity.

Secondly, military forces still represent a symbol of the nation, especially among current and former superpowers like the United States, Russia, or Britain. Modern state building was so bound up with war and the development of modern military forces that our idea of stateness is inextricably linked to military rituals, uniforms, and even war. Hence the deployment of military forces serves important domestic political functions, helping to instill a sense of pride and loyalty, underscoring domestic cohesion. It is commonplace nowadays to argue that some military adventures, for example current Russian threats against Georgia, are best explained in terms of forthcoming elections. Just as Bush has widespread support for the war on terror, so Putin used the second Chechen war to gain power, and, so it can be argued, the current Middle East conflict helps sustain Sharon's political support.

Thirdly, there is a role for military forces in containment, especially in new wars. It may not be possible to win outright victory, but the implication of equal destructiveness is that the advantage passes to the defender. Thus it is possible to envisage defensive non-escalatory military operations designed to defend civilians where the new warriors threaten them. These operations cannot win or even stop wars but they can reduce fear and insecurity and create a breathing space where political solutions can be discussed. Essentially, this was, for all its flaws and mistakes, the British strategy in Northern Ireland and also, more recently, in Sierra Leone. Techniques like safe havens, humanitarian corridors, pioneered in Bosnia but not effectively carried out, could be conceived as part of a strategy of containment. To be effective, such a strategy does require risking casualties and this is one reason why the strategy failed in Bosnia, and indeed in Somalia. But it does not require the same level of risk as for example in the case of offensive war. At present, such risks are borne by human rights activists and journalists but rarely soldiers. Thus, in Afghanistan, more foreign journalists were killed than Americans in combat (although more Americans were killed if you include those killed by friendly fire).

Alternative Visions of American Power

Assumptions about sovereignty and about military power are the axes that define different visions of America's role in the world. The distinction between idealists and realists can be explained in terms of conceptions of sovereignty. The realists hold to a traditional conception of sovereignty. For them, international relations consist of sovereign units each pursuing their individual self-interest; what happens inside these sovereign units is irrelevant. The job of the state is to protect the state from external enemies; tyrants only matter if they are also potential aggressors. The idealists, on the other hand, hold that sovereignty is conditional and that there are values and norms, for example human rights, which override the claims to sovereignty.

The distinction I make between unilateralists and multilateralists applies primarily to the use of military forces. Unilateralists share a belief in the efficacy of military power. By and large, those that favor multilateral approaches start from the assumption that relations among states can no longer be settled by military force.

Table 7.1 Different visions of America's role in the world

	Idealist	Realist
Unilateralist	Spectacle war	Neorealists and anti-imperialists
Multilateralist	Cosmopolitans	Cooperative security

Although multilateralists might consider it necessary to exercise power within the framework of rules, the basic point is that they believe in a rule-based system not a might-based system. A parallel can be drawn with the evolution of peaceful societies within nation-states. Governments reserve the right to exercise legitimate force even though they are governing a system in which it is illegitimate to settle domestic conflicts by force.

It is possible to be unilateralist in the military field and multilateralist as regards the economy. Unilateralists tend to favor a liberal world economy, especially free trade and capital movements, but they reserve the right to behave unilaterally sometimes, as for example in the case of steel tariffs.

In what follows, I describe four different visions of America's role in the world based on different assumptions about sovereignty and military power, as shown in table 7.1.

Spectacle war

The first vision is that of the Bush administration, which I call "spectacle war."[17] By "spectacle war" I mean the kind of long-distance, high-technology air war described in the previous section. I call this type of war a "spectacle" to emphasize its imaginary nature from the point of view of Americans. These wars do not risk American casualties and, indeed, do not even require additional taxes; American citizens merely have to watch the war on television and applaud. James Der Derian uses the term "virtuous war" in order to combine both the virtual character of the war and the notion of virtue, the idea that the war is being fought in a noble cause.[18] "Virtuous war relies on virtual simulation, media manipulation, global surveillance and networked warfare to deter and if need be to destroy potential enemies. It draws on just war doctrine (when possible) and holy war doctrine (when necessary)."[19]

The origins of "spectacle war" can be traced back to the Cold War framework. During the Cold War, deterrence had a similar imaginary form.[20] Throughout the period of the Cold War, both sides behaved as though they were at war, with military buildups, technological competition, espionage and counterespionage, war games and exercises. This activity was an important way to remind people of World War II and, on the American side, to sustain a belief in the American mission to defend the world against evil through the use of superior technology. Technological developments responded to what planners imagined the Soviet Union might acquire – the so-called worst case scenario. This introverted planning, as I have argued elsewhere, meant that American and Soviet technological change was better explained as though they were both arming against a phantom German military machine that continued to evolve in the planners' imaginations, rather than against each other.[21] For example, air power was always central to the American conception of deterrence and this derived from the wartime experience of strategic bombing. Intercontinental missiles developed in the 1950s and 1960s were envisaged as an extension of strategic air power. The Russians never had a separate air arm and did not engage in strategic bombing in World War II; instead, they regarded missiles as an extension of artillery.

The advent of information technologies generated a debate about the future direction of military strategy in the 1970s and 1980s. The so-called military reform school argued that the platforms of the Fordist era were now as vulnerable as people were in World War I because of the use of Precision Guided Munitions (PGMs), and that the advantage had shifted to the defense. High attrition rates in the Vietnam and Middle East wars as a result of the use of handheld missiles seemed to confirm that argument. The advocates of traditional American strategy argued that the offensive maneuvers of World War II were even more important since the use of area destruction munitions could swamp defensive forces and missiles, and unmanned aerial vehicles (now known as UAVs) could replace vulnerable manned aircraft. The consequence was the AirLand Battle strategy of the 1980s, with its centerpiece, "deep strike," to be carried out by the then new Tomahawk cruise missiles, at that time armed with nuclear warheads.

During the 1990s, this thinking was taken a stage further with the Revolution in Military Affairs (RMA). For RMA enthusiasts, the advent of information technology was as important in revolutionizing warfare as was the discovery of the stirrup or the internal combustion engine. RMA is spectacle war; it is war carried out at long distance using computers and new communications technologies. The cruise missile, in particular, is the "paradigmatic" weapon of the RMA.[22] After the end of the Cold War, US military spending declined by one-third but this mainly affected personnel. Military Research and Development (R&D) declined by much less than military spending as a whole and this allowed for the development both of follow-ons to traditional Cold War platforms and the new technologies associated with the RMA. An important aspect of the new technologies is the improvement in virtual war gaming, which further underscores the imaginary nature of spectacle war. Increasingly, the Defense Department has recruited Hollywood producers to help invent future worst-case scenarios, giving rise to what James Der Derian describes as MIME-NET, the military-industrial-entertainment network.[23] One of the most quoted remarks of the Iraq War was that of General William Wallace, commander of the army's V Corps, in charge of all US Army units in Iraq, that "the enemy we're fighting is a bit different from the one we war-gamed against."[24]

For the Bush administration, the term "defense transformation" has come to supplant RMA as the new jargon. As one enthusiast for defense transformation has put it:

> However jerky the transmission belt, the qualities of the modern American economy – its adventurousness, spontaneity and willingness to share information – eventually reach the American military. Just as the teenager who grew up tinkering with automobile engines helped to make the motorised armies of WWII work, so

do the sergeants accustomed to playing video games, surfing web pages, and creating spread sheets make the information-age military of to-day effective.[25]

Donald Rumsfeld claims that defense transformation "is about more than building new high-tech weapons – although that is certainly part of it. It is also about new ways of thinking and new ways of fighting."[26]

Yet it is hard to escape the conclusion that information technology is being grafted onto traditional assumptions about the ways in which military forces should be used and to traditional institutional defense structures. The methods have not changed much since World War II.[27] They involve a combination of aerial bombardment at long distance, and rapid offensive maneuvers, despite the changed names every decade – AirLand Battle, Revolution in Military Affairs, and now Defense Transformation. The very use of video gaming feeds in the assumptions of the gamers who have been schooled in the Cold War framework. September 11 allowed President Bush to ask for a big increase in defense spending. Defense spending had already begun to increase again in 1998 as the new expensive systems developed during the 1990s came to fruition. During his election campaign, Bush had suggested that it might be possible to skip a generation of weapons systems to save money and focus on the cutting-edge technologies like PGMs and UAVs (both of which were in short supply in Afghanistan). In fact the 2003 budget is sufficient to accommodate everything – the F22 fighter, for example, which replaces the F15, which already enjoys air superiority over any known enemy.[28] The expensive program for National Missile Defense will also go ahead. It is unlikely to work but the point is rather to underscore the vision of American defense; to provide the appearance of defense against incoming missiles and, therefore, a psychological insurance for unilateral military action.

"Spectacle war" is also linked to a powerful moral crusade. There was always an idealist strain in American Cold War thinking. Bush's "axis of evil" echoes Ronald Reagan's "evil empire." The Bushites believe or appear to believe that America is a cause not a nation, with a mission to convert the rest of the world to the

American dream and to rid the world of terrorists and tyrants. For them, sovereignty is conditional for other states, but unconditional for the United States because the United States represents "good." Hence the United States can act unilaterally; it can reject treaties like the Climate Change Protocol, the Land Mines Convention, the Biological Weapons Convention, and, above all, the International Criminal Court because America is right; but others do not have the same option. This view was expressed by Assistant Secretary of State, Richard Haas:

> What you are seeing in this administration is the emergence of a new principle or body of ideas . . . about what you might call the limits of sovereignty. Sovereignty entails obligations. One is not to massacre your own people. Another is not to support terrorism in any way. If a government fails to meet these obligations, then it forfeits some of the advantages of sovereignty, including the right to be left alone inside your own territory. Other governments, including the United States, gain the right to intervene. In the case of terrorism, this can even lead to a right of preventive . . . self-defense. You essentially can act in anticipation, if you have grounds to think it's a question of when, and not if, you're going to be attacked.[29]

This dual approach to sovereignty is well expressed in Bush's new security strategy, which argues that it is America's duty to protect freedom "across the globe." "Some worry" says Bush "that it is somehow undiplomatic or impolite to speak the language of right and wrong. I disagree. Different circumstances require different methods, but not different moralities."[30] What is alarming about the new security strategy is that through the use of new concepts, the administration has claimed an extraordinarily wide mandate for military action. First of all, the enemy is no longer defined. The enemy is anyone who might be a terrorist and who might acquire weapons of mass destruction (WMD). During the 1990s, great efforts were expended in "imagining" new "worst-case scenarios" and new post-Soviet threats. With the collapse of the Soviet military-industrial complex, US strategists came up with all sorts of inventive new ways in which America might be attacked, through spreading viruses, poisoning water systems, causing the collapse of the banking system, disrupting air traffic control or power transmission. Of particular importance was the idea of state-sponsored terrorism and the notion of "rogue states" that sponsor terrorism and acquire long-range missiles as well as weapons of mass destruction. These new threats emanating from a collapsing Russia or from Islamic fundamentalism were known as "asymmetric" threats, as weaker states or groups develop weapons of mass destruction or other horrific techniques to attack US vulnerabilities to compensate for conventional inferiority. Since September 11, these ideas appear to have been substantiated and the notion of the "enemy" extended even further to those we don't necessarily know; hence the shift from a "threat-based approach" to a "capabilities-based" approach. According to Rumsfeld:

> There are things we know that we know. There are known unknowns. That is to say, there are things we know that we don't know. But there are also unknown unknowns. There are things we don't know we don't know . . . each year, we discover a few more of these unknown unknowns.[31]

Secondly, against these new unknown enemies, the US has developed new doctrines of "preemption" in place of deterrence and "proactive counterproliferation" instead of nonproliferation. According to Bush, deterrence no longer works; that was the lesson of September 11: "Traditional concepts of deterrence will not work against a terrorist enemy whose avowed tactics are wanton destruction and the targeting of innocents; whose so-called soldiers seek martyrdom in death and whose most potent protection is statelessness."[32] Hence, the United States reserves the right to act preemptively, using the tools of "spectacle war" against those states who are believed to harbor terrorists or possess weapons of mass destruction. Interestingly, the rhetoric seems to switch between states that pose a threat to their own people (tyrants) and those that pose a threat to the United States (through the possession of WMD or through sponsoring terrorists).

This expanded mandate for military action amounts to an agenda for a permanent war much like the Cold War, in which periodic victories sustain public support and the rightness of the cause stifles dissent. If it is the case that military compellance is much more difficult than the Bushites claim, then "spectacle war" cannot be expected to defeat terrorism. On the contrary, it may stimulate the spread of terrorism because the strategy itself discredits the claim to political legitimacy. This is for three reasons. First, the crusade, the "war on terrorism", raises the profile of the terrorists and dignifies them as enemies rather than criminals. The moment that Bush chose to describe what happened on September 11 as an attack on the United States rather than a "crime against humanity," he firmly placed the event in a traditional war paradigm. By using the term "war," Bush constructed a language of polarization, accentuated by his famous sentence "You are either with us or against us."[33] Moreover, the language of "war on terrorism" has spread throughout the world, legitimizing a range of local "wars on terrorism" (Chechnya, Palestine, Kashmir, Karabakh, to name but a few).

Secondly, the US administration has put together a global coalition to fight terrorism but it is an alliance on the Cold War model where the criterion for membership is support for the United States not adherence to international principles, as would be the case for a truly multilateral arrangement. The inclusion of undemocratic states like Saudi Arabia, Pakistan, or Uzbekistan and states responsible for massive human rights violations like Israel or Russia undermines the claim to be pursuing a just cause. Moreover, this is compounded by the use of the "war on terrorism" to justify increased surveillance and curtailment of rights.[34] Pressure on states to agree to exemptions for the United States in relation to the International Criminal Court, as in the case of the so-called "new Europeans," actually undermines multilateral arrangements.

Thirdly, because "spectacle war" does not risk casualties, it undermines any claims for legitimacy in the struggle to defeat terrorism. US attacks are accurate but nevertheless they cannot avoid "collateral damage" or "mistakes" nor can they prevent humanitarian catastrophes as a result of war. In the war in Afghanistan, there were around 1,000–3,000 civilian casualties from "collateral

damage" but thousands more died as a consequence of the worsening humanitarian crisis and some 500,000 people fled from
their homes; in addition some thousands of Taliban and Al-Qaeda
troops were killed.[35] In the case of the Iraq War, civilian casualty
figures are still not available. Estimates suggest that around 8,000
people were killed.[36] Again, this is low by the standards of war
but very high by human rights standards – the same number were,
for example, killed in the massacre at Srebrenica. These experiences demonstrate that American lives are privileged over other
lives, thus belying Bush's globalist claims.

In the combination of violence and morality, there is a parallel
with Al-Qaeda and other religious fundamentalists. I do not want
to suggest symmetry. But nevertheless, the parallel is significant
because it allows for a process of mutual reinforcement. Religion
provides a justification for violence that excludes compromise and
that overrides rules and procedures. The spectacular nature of
attacks like those of September 11 or in Bali are not intended to
defeat an enemy, or to be victorious. Rather, they are proof of a
struggle between good and evil, ways of mobilizing supporters. It
is the struggle itself that matters, the sense of participating in a
sacred battle, not victory or defeat. Mark Juergensmeyer writes:

> What the perpetrators of such acts of terror expect – and indeed
> welcome – is a response as vicious as the acts themselves. By
> goading secular authorities into responding to terror with terror,
> they hope to accomplish two things. First, they want tangible evi-
> dence for their claim that the secular enemy is a monster. Second,
> they hope to bring to the surface the great war – a war that they
> have told their potential supporters was hidden, but real.[37]

For Donald Rumsfeld and George W. Bush, the war against the
"unknowables" has something of the same character. "Spectacle
war" seems to confirm the conceptions of cosmic war promoted
by Al-Qaeda and others and to justify further acts of terrorism.
By the same token, their response sustains a permanent crusading
war mentality in the United States, drawn from the experience of
the Cold War, which in turn underpins the position of the Republican right and justifies further increases in the defense budget.

Neorealists and anti-imperialists

There has always been a tension in American foreign-policy making between idealists and realists, between those who believe in the American mission to spread the American Way, and those who argue that America is a Great Power like any other and must pursue a strategy of survival. For the former, the Cold War was a struggle between good and evil, between democracy and totalitarianism; for the latter the Cold War was the inevitable consequence of bipolarity – a strategic order that some described as the "long peace."[38]

I have used the term "neorealist" to describe that strand of opinion that favors the hardheaded pursuit of national interest, in which humanitarian concerns are largely irrelevant. They are uni-lateralist because they believe in the use of force by the United States, whether or not it is sanctioned by international rules, and, like the Bushites, they act on the assumption that compellance is still possible. The neorealists became prominent in the 1970s and 1980s when they argued that the relationship between the United States and the Soviet Union could be better managed. Famously, when Nixon and Kissinger went to Moscow in 1972 to negotiate the first SALT (Strategic Arms Limitation Talks) Treaty, they ignored the Jewish refuseniks demonstrating at the Kremlin gates.

The neorealists are critical of the Bush strategy because they do not think it is in the US national interest. Many of them opposed the Iraq War because, although Saddam Hussein was a tyrant, he did not at that time pose a direct threat to the United States. Moreover, a war in Iraq might have diverted resources from the main threat from Al-Qaeda. Thirty-four international scholars, including such luminaries as Kenneth Walz, often considered the father of neorealism, Thomas Schelling, the inventor of "com-pellance," and John Mearsheimer of the "Long Peace," placed an advertisement in the *New York Times* opposing the war in Iraq.[39]

Of course, there is a range of views among the neorealists. Some, like Henry Kissinger, favored war with Iraq on geopolitical grounds. Others, while reserving the right to use military power unilaterally, consider that military power is less important nowadays. Joseph Nye, a former assistant secretary of defense, draws a threefold classification of power – military, economic, and what he calls "soft" power. Nowadays, power resources have shifted away from military power towards economic and "soft" power. Whereas military power is unipolar, dominated by the United States, economic power is multipolar, and "soft" power is "the realm of transnational relations that cross borders outside of government control. . . . [Soft] power is widely dispersed and it makes no sense to speak of unipolarity, multipolarity or hegemony."[40] For Nye, values are part of the national interest. Nevertheless, he considers that what he calls C list priorities – wars in places like Bosnia and Rwanda which do not threaten US interests – are less important than A or B list priorities, direct threats to the US from a "peer competitor" or threats to strategic US interests in places like the Persian Gulf or the Korean peninsula. For this reason the US has to be able to act unilaterally and cannot accept constraints like the International Criminal Court, which might lead to "unjustified charges of war crimes" by US troops.[41]

The anti-imperialist leftists are the inverse of the neorealists. Whereas the realists believe that the United States should act in the national interest and some criticize the current administration for not doing so, the anti-imperialists believe that the United States does act in the national self-interest and criticize the United States because of the impact on the rest of the world, as well as poor Americans. It might seem paradoxical to call the anti-imperialists "realists" since presumably they favor world revolutions and have an idealistic vision of a system in which there are no Great Powers. My point is rather that their analysis is realist. By accepting the thesis that America pursues its hardheaded national interest, they actually help to legitimate American power since many Americans believe that it is a good thing to pursue the national interest; Bush Senior always defended the first Gulf War in terms of the threat to American oil supplies.

The anti-imperialists see the United States as a Great Power, an Empire, pursuing geopolitical interests like oil, and they consider that the idealism of the Bush administration (and indeed of earlier administrations) is merely a cover or legitimation for more hardheaded self-interest. Thus Chomsky talks about the new "military humanism."[42] They assume that military compellance still works. Hence they view with great suspicion, in Peter Gowan's words,

> Washington's central strategic initiative of the past decade – not the winding down of Nato after the end of the Cold War . . . but its first deployment in action in the Balkans, and then expansion full-steam ahead to the frontiers of Russia itself. Since September 11, of course, the "revolution in military affairs" has carried the American war machine still further, into hitherto unimagined terrain, with bases in five or six Central Asian states, and forward posts in the Caucasus, to add to the eighty countries in Eurasia, Africa and Oceania already in its keep. The staggering scale of this armed girdling of the planet tells its own story.[43]

The positions of the neorealists and the anti-imperialists are well illustrated by the new interest in resource wars (primarily oil). Both the neorealists and anti-imperialists often argue that underlying the "war on terrorism" is a strategic interest in controlling the sources of oil and oil transportation routes. In support of this argument, the Cheney report on energy is often cited. The report advocates seeking new sources of oil apart from the Persian Gulf (Alaska or the Caspian Sea) to ensure cheap oil supplies to the United States for the foreseeable future.[44]

It was always the case that, in the wars of the twentieth century, control over oil supplies was a central part of strategy. Oil was the key factor of production and of warfare in the Fordist era, and, in a global conflict, the various sides sought ways to cut their enemies off from the supply of this vital commodity. World War II, in particular, depended on the mass mobilization of tanks, aircraft, and ships fueled by oil. Both Germany and Japan were obsessed by the need to seek autonomous sources of oil. Nowadays, however, the world has changed. The market for oil is much more globalized and war is much more localized. There are threats to oil supplies but they derive much more from instability and conflict, "new wars," than from the risk of hostile control of oil. Indeed, it can be argued, especially, for example, in the Southern Caucasus, that geopolitical interests actually stimulate local conflicts and make oil supplies less, not more, secure. There may, of course, be a private greed element, in that the oil companies have a powerful influence on the Bush administration and they see the acquisition of bases as a way of exerting influence to win contracts. But that is not the same as a national or geopolitical interest. Some argue that oil was the main reason for going to war with Iraq. But if this was the case, were there not easier ways, short of war, to secure the oil?

Indeed, it can be argued that, by stressing the importance of oil, the anti-imperialists endorse the realist justification for unilateral action. In the 1991 Gulf War, George Bush Senior was able to make much of the possibility that Saddam Hussein could strangle Western oil supplies.

Like the Bushites, the neorealists and the anti-imperialists have an old-fashioned view of military power, drawn from earlier wars. They are perhaps more prudent than the Bushites. Unlike the Bushites, they also have an old-fashioned view of sovereignty. For the anti-imperialists, this tends to mean that they do not take human rights violations or terrorist attacks sufficiently seriously – regarding these concerns merely as justifications for imperialism. For the neorealists, terrorist threats to the United States are important but not human rights violations or terrorist threats in other countries.

One difference between the neorealists and the anti-imperialists is in the economic field. Neorealists tend to support a liberal world economy. Anti-imperialists are often protectionist, believing that sovereignty is the best way to defend against imperialist exploitation.

Cooperative security

European leaders often deplore the unilateralism of the United States. One strand of European multilateralism continues to be realist. That is to say, the European realists have a vision of the world composed of sovereign states, but based on a set of rules and norms. Underpinning this vision is the philosophy of the so-called English School – people like Hedley Bull or Martin Wight, who trace their thinking to early international legalists like

Grotius. According to the English School, there is no single world power but there is, nevertheless, world society, because even in an anarchical context states operate according to certain principles – the most important of which is nonintervention. Hedley Bull, for example, was opposed to humanitarian intervention because it challenged this principle: "The growing moral conviction that human rights should have a place in relations among states has been deeply corrosive of the rule of non-intervention, which once drew strength from the general acceptance that states alone have rights in international law."[45] It was assumptions of this kind that underpinned the détente policies during the 1970s and 1980s pioneered by European social democrats, who were deeply distrustful of American idealism. They strongly favored disarmament and arms control as well as openings to the East but opposed the muscular language of human rights. I remember Dennis Healey, former Labour foreign secretary, saying in the early 1980s when the Polish Solidarity movement was at its height: "I prefer stability to solidarity."

International lawyers in the United States also made this argument in opposition to the war in Iraq and to the Bush administration's doctrine of preemption. Douglass Cassel of North Western University argued that a "preemptive strike in these circumstances would rupture the framework of international law built since World War II and provide a precedent for future aggression by powerful states whose agendas might be quite different from the United States."[46] Possible examples are a Chinese attack on Taiwan, India or Pakistan attacking each other, or Russia invading Georgia.

Robert Kagan has criticized the multilateralist view on the grounds that it reflects Europe's weakness. He argues that the multilateralist view is only possible because Europeans can rely on American military force.[47] Of course, Kagan assumes that compellance works and that American military force does preserve stability. But he has a point about Europe's weakness. Can nonintervention nowadays be sustained in the face of crimes against humanity, genocide, or massive violations of human rights? Do not Nye's C list threats impinge on the rest of the world? "New wars" do, after all, create the black holes that generate criminals, refugees, and terrorists. Spectacle war is not the answer. But are there alternative means?

Cosmopolitanism

At the heart of the cosmopolitan position is the notion that a new form of political legitimacy needs to be constructed, which offers an alternative to various forms of fundamentalism and exclusivism. The cosmopolitan position is idealist and multilateralist. It draws its inspiration from Immanuel Kant's "Perpetual Peace" project published in 1795. Kant argued that perpetual peace could be achieved in a world of states, based on republican (democratic) constitutions, where these states sign a permanent peace treaty with each other (the principle of nonintervention) but where cosmopolitan right (human rights) overrides sovereignty. He argued that cosmopolitan right need only be confined to the right of hospitality – that strangers should be tolerated and respected. It was Kant who pointed out that the global community had shrunk to the point where "a right violated anywhere could be felt everywhere."[48]

Thus the cosmopolitan ideal combines a commitment to humanist principles and norms, an assumption of human equality, with a recognition of difference, and indeed a celebration of diversity.[49] To be idealist does not mean to be unrealistic. In a world where compellance no longer works, the only alternative is containment. And this has to be done through political and legal means. Politically, the cosmopolitan ideal has to offer an alternative that can undercut support for extremists. Religious fundamentalism and ultranationalism are rarely popular; their support depends on the weakness of alternatives. These exclusive ideologies are bred primarily but not only in "weak" or "failing" states, out of the despair of the excluded. In legal terms, the cosmopolitan ideal has to be situated within a multilateralist set of rules and procedures that apply equally to all individuals and can be seen to be fair.

There is a role for military means in this vision but as containment not spectacle war. A cosmopolitan global community cannot stand aside when genocide is committed, as in Rwanda, for example. But military tasks should be confined to the protection of civilians and the arrest of war criminals and should be authorized through the appropriate multilateral procedures. Normally, this means UN Security Council authorization but there could be a set of principles in exceptional cases; if such principles were violated, then there would have to be procedures for appeal. The task of military containment may well include air power but it would have to be viewed as tactical power in support of protection forces. Hence there is an argument for defense transformation to develop military forces that are neither trained for spectacle war nor for classic peacekeeping, but it is a transformation of roles and tactics rather than technology. Military containment needs to be conceived as international law enforcement not as war fighting.

The cosmopolitans thus share the Bushite assumption that sovereignty is conditional. But conditionality applies to all states and, moreover, the conditions cannot be determined unilaterally but only through a set of multilaterally agreed procedures. The cosmopolitans are, for example, deeply critical of the current American attempts to undermine the International Criminal Court by reaching bilateral agreements, which would exempt Americans from criminal charges. The United States cannot be exempted from the ICC because this would imply that Americans are exceptionally privileged – a position which directly challenges the fundamental assumption of human equality.

Cosmopolitanism has to be able to offer an alternative reality. Paradoxically, it is the current American administration and its enemies who get away with an unreal vision of the world. War, for them, is a form of escapism, which diverts attention from everyday life. Especially for the religious fundamentalists and ultranationalists, war is a way of reminding people of a purer less difficult past, a form of nostalgia, where spiritual values are more important than the material present. They are often master manipulators of the new media, using television, videocassettes, and radio to convey their message.

This is another reason why cosmopolitans also need to have an economic program, a multilateralist commitment not just to a liberal world economy but also to global social justice. The commitment to an international rule of law and to global security, based on cosmopolitan principles, is the precondition for improving everyday life. But human rights do also include economic and social rights.

Many European social democrats stress this aspect of multilateralism, as do some parts of the anti-imperialist camp. This argument acquired increased momentum in the aftermath of September 11. Tony Blair, for example, made a strong appeal for a new global justice agenda. "One illusion has been shattered on 11 September," he said on a trip to the United States, "that we can have the good life of the West irrespective of the state of the rest of the world . . . the dragon's teeth are planted in the fertile soil of wrongs unrighted, of disputes left to fester for years, of failed states, of poverty and deprivation."[50] Or as George Soros put it in his latest book: "The terrorist attacks on September 11 have brought home to us in a tragic fashion how interdependent the world has become and how important it is for our internal security what internal conditions prevail in other countries."[51] The French government proposed a Tobin tax and the British and Scandinavian governments have been pushing for a big increase and untying of development aid. The New Partnership for Africa's Development (NEPAD) is also part of the concern for global justice. Nevertheless these efforts are so far modest and, despite some nods in this direction, have drawn little serious response from the Bush administration. Moreover, especially in the European case, the commitment to a liberal world economy still does not extend to the free movement of people.

Conclusion

The war on terrorism is not working. At the time of writing, Iraq seems to be becoming a safe haven for all kinds of Islamic jihadis who have made common cause with the remnants of the Iraqi regime, turning Bush's assertions about the links between Saddam Hussein and Al-Qaeda into a self-fulfilling prophecy.[52] Two and a half years after the collapse of the World Trade Center, an Al-Qaeda cell exploded several bombs on four trains in Madrid, killing some 200 people. In May 2003, bombings in Casablanca and Riyadh led to over 70 deaths. There have also been "raids" in Pakistan, Yemen, and Kenya, not to mention the bombing of the Sari nightclub in Bali or the Chechens holding hostage a theater in Moscow. Since 2001, the FBI has frozen some $125 million in assets; some 2,700 known or suspected operatives have been arrested, and perhaps a third of the leadership has been killed.[53] This may have prevented attacks in the United States and Europe. Nevertheless, by all accounts the network known as Al-Qaeda continues to grow. What is important is the ability to recruit young men to the cause; that is what makes possible the multiplication of cells. As Jason Burke has put it: "Al Qaeda can only be understood as an ideology, an agenda, a way of seeing the world that is shared by an increasing number of young predominantly male Muslims."[54] I have argued that only a cosmopolitan vision can, at least, contain the new sources of violence. We live in a world where privileging groups of people is counterproductive because it is no longer possible to insulate territory. We also live in a world where the utility of military force is much more limited than formerly. A political, legal, and social approach is much more important as a way of dealing with terrorism. American power, despite its wealth and huge military forces, can only be effective within a cosmopolitan framework. This is why we need Americans to be what Richard Falk calls "cosmopolitan patriots."[55]

It is sometimes argued that the war on terrorism will be good for the global economy and help to prevent a recession in the United States. Expenditure on the war has permitted deficit financing, and overspending may help to stimulate global growth. Unlike at the beginning of the Cold War, however, the United States no longer enjoys an external surplus. At that time, the world was desperate for dollars, and overseas military spending helped to stimulate both domestic growth in other countries and increases in US exports. Today the US has a substantial current account deficit and is heavily indebted. Some argue that this does not matter because foreign investors are attracted by high American productivity growth. But increased overseas spending, especially going to states with weak rule of law and inadequate governance, could merely end up increasing the deficit. For a new "golden age," the US needs global growth stimulated through a multilateral program of assistance that offers the possibility of reconstructing legitimate authority.

Are there any prospects for reorienting American power, for dismantling the straitjacket of the Cold War heritage, and harnessing American power to a set of cosmopolitan goals? In the immediate aftermath of September 11, when even *Le Monde* proclaimed that we are all Americans, many people hoped that such a reorientation might happen because the threat was real. Wars often bring about dramatic restructuring although not immediately. If terrorism continues to spread, if the economy fails to pick up, and if, above all, American democracy still has some life in it, then change is possible. On the one hand, wars of the new type tend to be polarizing, entrenching extremists on all sides; this is the experience of the Balkans or the Middle East. On the other hand, the global protests against the war in Iraq were unprecedented. Some 15 million people demonstrated worldwide, including in the United States.[56] American war weariness is growing and new connections are being made among generals, who understand the limitations of war, global companies, whose profits depend on global stability, and immigrant groups, especially the Muslim community.

I conclude, therefore, that the Asian human rights activist I quoted at the beginning is wrong. If the American political system continues to be distorted by the manipulation of public opinion through spectacle war, then it no longer represents the ideal of democratic deliberation propounded by the Founding Fathers, which has been such an inspiration to the rest of the world. The current strategy of "spectacle war" may have the effect of repressing democracy. But if America is to remain a truly open reasoning society, then it needs democracy in the rest of the world. There is no such thing as democracy in one country any longer.

Notes

*An earlier version of this chapter appeared in *International Affairs*, 79, 1 (2003).

1 Jeffrey C. Goldfarb, "America Versus Democracy? Losing Young Allies in the War Against Terror," *International Herald Tribune* (August 21, 2002).

2 See Walter A. McDougall, *Promised Land, Crusader State: The American Encounter with the World since 1776* (Boston, MA: Houghton Mifflin, 1997).

3 Robert Kagan, "The Power Divide" *Prospect* (August 2002); Hubert Védrine, with Dominique Moisi, *France in the Age of Globalization* (Washington, DC: Brookings Institution, 2001).

4 Thomas C. Schelling, *Arms and Influence* (New Haven, CT: Yale University Press, 1966).

5 See, for example, Paul Kennedy, *The Rise and Fall of the Great Powers: Economic Change and Military Conflict from 1500–2000* (New York: Random House, 1987); Robert Gilpin, *War and Change in World Politics* (Cambridge: Cambridge University Press, 1981).

6 See, for example, Joshua Goldstein, *Long Cycles: Prosperity and War in the Modern Age* (London and New Haven, CT: Yale University Press, 1988).

7 Charles P. Kindleberger, *The World in Depression, 1929–1939* (London: Penguin, 1987).

8 For a brilliant exposition of this argument, see Carlota Perez, *Technological Revolutions and Financial Capital: The Dynamics of Bubbles and Golden Ages* (Cheltenham: Edward Elgar, 2002).

9 David Held, Anthony McGrew, David Goldblatt, and Jonathan Perraton, *Global Transformations* (Cambridge: Polity, 1999); Anthony Giddens, *Runaway World: How Globalisation is Reshaping Our Lives* (London: Profile Books, 1999).

10 Held et al., *Global Transformations*.

11 See David Holloway, *The Soviet Union and the Arms Race* (New Haven, CT: Yale University Press, 1983).

12 For this argument, see James Fallows, "The Fifty-First State?" *Atlantic Monthly* (November 2002).

13 General Wesley Clark, press conference, April 1, 1999.

14 In the autumn 2002 elections, the radical nationalist Seselj, who had advocated expelling all Kosovars from Kosovo, and even at one point, infecting them with the AIDS/HIV virus, obtained 23 percent of the vote.

15 See Michael O'Hanlon, "A Flawed Masterpiece," *Foreign Affairs* (May–June 2002).

16 The Germans blitzkrieg against France, Netherlands, and Belgium cost them 27,000 casualties.

17   The term was first used by Michael Mann in "The Roots and Contradictions of Modern Militarism," in his *States, War and Capitalism* (Oxford: Blackwell, 1988), pp. 166–87. Colin McInnes uses the term "spectator-sport" warfare.

18   See James Der Derian, *Virtuous War: Mapping the Military-Industrial-Media-Entertainment Network* (Boulder, CO: Westview Press, 2001).

19   James Der Derian, "9/11: Before, After and Between," in Craig Calhoun, Paul Price, and Ashley Timmer, eds, *Understanding September 11* (New York: New Press, 2002), p. 180.

20   See Mary Kaldor, *Imaginary War: Understanding the East–West Conflict* (Oxford: Basil Blackwell, 1990).

21   Ibid., chapters 11 and 12.

22   See Lawrence Freedman, "The Revolution in Strategic Affairs," *Adelphi Paper 318* (London: International Institute of Strategic Affairs, 1998).

23   In the aftermath of September 11, the military have recruited the University of Southern California's Institute of Creative Technology to involve Hollywood in imagining terrorist worstcase scenarios. See James Der Derian, "9/11: Before, After and Between."

24   According to Max Boot, the *New York Times* report left out the phrase "a bit," thereby exaggerating American difficulties. See Max Boot, "The New American Way of War," *Foreign Affairs* (July–August 2003).

25   Elliott A. Cohen, "A Tale of Two Secretaries," *Foreign Affairs* (May–June 2002), p. 39.

26   Donald H. Rumsfeld, "Transforming the Military," *Foreign Affairs* (May–June 2002), p. 21.

27   Kersti Hakansson has demonstrated this point in a comparison of tactics in Vietnam and Afghanistan. See "New Wars, Old Warfare? Comparing US Tactics in Afghanistan and Vietnam," in Jan Angstrom and Isabelle Duyvesteyn, eds, *The Nature of Modern War: Clausewitz and his Critics Revisited* (Stockholm: Swedish National Defense College, Department of War Studies, 2003).

28   See David Gold, "US Military Expenditure and the 2001 Quadrennial Defense Review," Appendix 6E, *SIPRI Yearbook 2002: Armaments, Disarmament and International Security* (Oxford: Oxford University Press, 2002).

29   Quoted in G. John Ikenberry, "America's Imperial Ambition," *Foreign Affairs* (September/October 2002), p. 52.

30 *The National Security Strategy of the United States*, at www.nytimes.com/2002/09/20/politics/20STEXT_FULL.html.
31 Quoted in G. John Ikenberry, "America's Imperial Ambition," p. 50.
32 *National Security Strategy of the United States.*
33 See Michael Howard, "What's in a Name?" *Foreign Affairs* (January–February 2002).
34 For a partial list of these types of actions, see Box 1.3 in Marlies Glasius and Mary Kaldor, "The State of Global Civil Society Before and After September 11," in Marlies Glasius, Mary Kaldor, and Helmut Anheier, eds, *Global Civil Society 2002* (Oxford: Oxford University Press, 2002).
35 See Carl Connetta, "Strange Victory: A Critical Appraisal of Operation Enduring Freedom and the Afghanistan War," *Project on Defense Alternatives, Research Monograph No. 6* (30 January 2002). Estimates of Taliban and Al-Qaeda troops killed vary from 4,000 to 10,000.
36 The independent website iraqbodycount.net reports that as at the end of September 2003, a minimum of 7,377 and a maximum of 9,180 civilians had been killed since the beginning of the war.
37 Mark Juergensmeyer, "Religious Terror and Global War," in Calhoun, et al., *Understanding September 11*, p. 40.
38 John Lewis Gaddis, *The Long Peace: Inquiries into the History of the Cold War* (Oxford: Oxford University Press, 1987).
39 "War with Iraq is not in America's National Interest," advertisement, *New York Times* (September 26, 2002).
40 Joseph S. Nye, Jr, *The Paradox of American Power* (Oxford: Oxford University Press, 2002, p. 39).
41 Ibid., p. 160.
42 Noam Chomsky, *The New Military Humanism: Lessons from Kosovo* (London: Pluto Press, 1999).
43 Peter Gowan, "The Calculus of Power," *New Left Review* (July–August 2002), p. 63.
44 Michael Klare "Global Petro-Politics: The Foreign Policy Implications of the Bush Administration's Energy Plan," *Current History* (March 2002).
45 Hedley Bull, ed., *Intervention in World Politics* (Oxford: Clarendon Press, 1984), p. 183.
46 Quoted in Adele Simmons, "Iraq: Who's Leading the Protest," *Chicago Sun-Times* (October 13, 2002).
47 Kagan, "The Power Divide."

48   Immanuel Kant, "Perpetual Peace" (1795), in Hans Reiss, ed., *Kant's Political Writings* (Cambridge: Cambridge University Press, 1992).

49   Anthony Appiah, "Cosmopolitan Patriots," in Joshua Cohen, ed., *For Love of Country – Debating the Limits of Patriotism: Martha C. Nussbaum and Respondents* (Cambridge, MA: Beacon Press, 1996).

50   Tony Blair, quoted in *Human Development Report 2002: Deepening Democracy in a Fragmented World* (New York: Oxford University Press, 2002), p. 101.

51   George Soros, *George Soros on Globalization* (London: Perseus Books, 2002), p. 17.

52   Interestingly something similar seems to have happened after the 1998 air strikes on Afghanistan in response to the bombings of American embassies in Kenya and Tanzania. Jason Burke shows how the Taliban were initially deeply suspicious of Al-Qaeda on doctrinal as well as political grounds despite Osama bin Laden's offers of financial support. But they were thrown together after the air strikes. See Jason Burke, *Al Qaeda: Casting a Shadow of Terror* (London: I. B. Taurus & Co., 2003).

53   International Institute for Strategic Studies, *Strategic Survey 2003* (London, 2003).

54   Ibid.

55   Richard Falk, "Testing Patriotism and Citizenship in the Global Terror War," in Ken Booth and Tim Dunne, eds, *Worlds in Collision: Terror and the Future of World Order* (London: Palgrave, 2002).

56   See Mary Kaldor, Helmut Anheier, and Marlies Glasius, eds, *Global Civil Society 2003* (Oxford: Oxford University Press, 2003).

8

Beyond Iraq: The Crisis of the Transatlantic Security Community*

Thomas Risse

Introduction

There is little doubt that the transatlantic relationship is in a deep crisis despite the patching-up work being done on either side of the Atlantic after the Iraq War. Therefore, it is time to re-evaluate US–European relations and to take stock of its current evolution. Such an effort has to take into account, however, that the history of the transatlantic relationship is a history of crises. Compare the crowds marching against George W. Bush, his rhetoric of an "axis of evil," and the Iraq War with the demonstrations against Ronald Reagan, his talk of an "evil empire," and the euro-missiles!

If the current conflicts are supposed to be different from the past, we need convincing analytical arguments pointing to structural changes in world politics rather than editorial adhocery. Three such changes come to mind: the end of the Cold War; unprecedented American preponderance; and September 11, 2001, and the rise of transnational terrorism.

In what follows I will argue that none of these changes (alone or in combination) offers sufficient evidence to conclude that structural changes in the international system are about to spell the end of the transatlantic community as we have known it over the past fifty years. The transatlantic security community rests on (a) collective identity based on common values; (b) (economic) interdependence grounded in common material interests; and (c) common institutions based on norms regulating the relationship. The current conflicts stem from domestic developments on both sides of the Atlantic leading to different perceptions of contemporary security threats and, more importantly, different prescriptions on how to handle them. Such differences have existed before and they have been dealt with through the institutions of the transatlantic community including European use of domestic access opportunities into the US political system. There is little to suggest that these transatlantic channels of mutual influence do not work any longer. This is the good news.

The bad news is that unilateral and even imperial tendencies in contemporary US foreign policy and particularly its official discourse violate constitutive norms on which the transatlantic security community has been built over the years, namely multilateralism and close consultation with the allies. Building "coalitions of the willing" to deal with world problems rather than using enduring alliances has become the official talk in Washington. The more US foreign policy in general acts unilaterally and the more it renounces international agreements and institutions which the US itself has helped to build, the more it touches upon fundamental principles of world order and the rule of (international) law in dealing with international conflicts. The "National Security Strategy" of the US is indeed partly at odds with some principles of world order which have been part of the Western consensus in the post–World War II era.[1] In this sense, the current disagreements between Europe and the US go beyond ordinary policy conflicts and touch issues of common values.

In short, the transatlantic community faces a deep crisis. It is no longer possible to paper over the differences in joint communiqués and nice photo opportunities. Rather, we need a new transatlantic bargain.[2] As a result, a European response to the challenges of the Bush administration should be articulated. A European countervision is already expressed through practice – from European efforts in conflict prevention and peacekeeping to

European support for the International Criminal Court and multilateral efforts at dealing with global environmental challenges. But the neoconservative discourse emanating from Washington requires a European response in terms of an alternative vision of world order based on the rule of law and liberal principles.

Yet, a European (counter-)vision of world order is not meant to wreck the transatlantic security community. In fact, the rhetoric of building a counterweight to American hyperpower emanating from politicians and intellectuals mostly in "old Europe" is bound to fail, since it will split Europe further apart in foreign policy. It will lead to further "letters of the eight." Rather, efforts at a common European foreign policy and a European "grand strategy" should revive a serious transatlantic dialogue and (re-)create the transnational alliances across the Atlantic among like-minded groups that seem to have been silenced after 9/11.

I proceed in three steps. First, I take stock of and discuss the fundamentals of the transatlantic security community including some alternative accounts. Second, I analyze domestic developments in the US and Europe in order to account partially for the current crisis. I conclude with some suggestions for the necessary transatlantic dialogue concerning world order questions.

The Crisis of the Transatlantic Security Community

Crisis, what crisis?

It is wrong to argue that policy disagreements between Europeans and North Americans dominate the transatlantic agenda. There is still quite some variation across policy areas concerning the extent to which the US and European governments disagree among each other. In transatlantic economic affairs, for example, things are fundamentally intact. The two main powers in the world economy – the US and the European Union – still cooperate in managing international economic relations through multilateral institutions, particularly the World Trade Organization. Even in security issues, it would be hard to argue that disagreements prevail. As to the top priority on the current international security agenda – the fight against transnational terrorism – both sides have established a rather smooth cooperative relationship concerning transnational law enforcement and intelligence sharing. Military and political security cooperation on the Balkans, in Afghanistan, and elsewhere has not been affected by the crisis in the transatlantic relationship. And as long as the Bush administration continues to actively pursue the "road map," Europeans and Americans are in agreement as to how to deal with the Israeli–Palestinian conflict. Thus, not all is bad in the transatlantic relationship.

Yet, policy disagreements between the US and Europe do extend over a wide range of issues these days. During the Cold War, such conflicts were rather normal, but they were mostly confined to specific questions. Today, things seem to be different. "Regime change" by force, "preventive war," and other policies of the Bush administration are not considered legitimate means of international politics in Europe. And this includes even the United Kingdom and those European countries who have been part of the "coalition of the willing" in the Iraq War. Moreover, European and US foreign policies are at odds with each other on almost all issues of global governance (except for international economic affairs). This relates to, among others, nuclear and conventional arms control, international human rights (the fight over the International Criminal Court only constitutes the tip of the iceberg here), and the international environment.[3] The underlying problematic of these policy disagreements concerns rather fundamental world order questions, such as the role of multilateral institutions including the United Nations in global governance, understandings of international law, and the like. It has to be noted here that many of these policy conflicts predate both September 11, 2001, and the Bush administration. The International Criminal Court and the European–American rift on the climate change regime have been with us already during the Clinton administration.

So, how can we explain the increasing policy disagreements between the US and Europe? Is something wrong with the fundamentals of the relationship?

Three Claims on the Contemporary Crisis in US–European Relations

The end of the Cold War

John J. Mearsheimer and Kenneth N. Waltz have already argued more than ten years ago that the end of the Cold War and the resulting end of the bipolar international system would lead to a decline of the Western alliance.[4] The argument was straightforward and came out of the structural realist theory of international relations: alliances are partnerships of convenience and joint interest to balance the power of an adversary. Once the power of the adversary has collapsed, the forces that bind an alliance together decrease. NATO and the transatlantic relationship are no exceptions. More than ten years after the end of the Cold War, it is still unclear whether the argument is right or wrong. Worse, the neo-realist claim is too indeterminate to tell us precisely what would count as evidence confirming or falsifying it. In 1990, for example, Mearsheimer predicted not only the collapse of NATO, but also of the EU, and he expected Germany to go nuclear. Even if one concedes that NATO is in a deep crisis, the EU is certainly not in decline and Germany still has no intention to acquire nuclear weapons.

US power (and European weakness)

A second argument holds that the end of the Cold War has led to an unprecedented supremacy of US power in the international system.[5] The US does no longer require allies to pursue its goals and can go it alone. At the same time, Europe is militarily weak and its military expenditures have declined sharply after the end of the Cold War. Robert Kagan argued in this context that the US lives in a Hobbesian "dog-eat-dog" world and sees itself as the world's policeman, while Europeans have made themselves comfortable in a Kantian world of peace and multilateralism.[6]

There are various problems and inherent contradictions with these claims. First, it is certainly true that we live in a unipolar world when it comes to military power. Concerning economic power, though, the argument only holds true if the European Union is treated as 25 single states rather than an economic power with a single market and a single currency (and shortly a constitution). Concerning various categories of "soft power" (knowledge, ideas, etc.),[7] it is rather unclear whether the US is in a league of its own, since "soft power" seems to be rather diffuse and more widely spread in the contemporary world system.

Second, as to superpower behavior in a unipolar world, we need to distinguish clearly between (benign) hegemony and imperialism. *Hegemonic* power rests on the willingness of the superpower to sustain an international order, on its preparedness to commit itself to the rules of that order, and on the smaller states' acceptance of this order as legitimate. The latter is a function of the former as a result of which small states gain "voice opportunities" to influence the hegemon's behavior, as G. John Ikenberry has convincingly argued.[8] *Imperial* power also rests on the willingness of the superpower to sustain world order, but the main difference to hegemony is that the superpower only plays by the rules when it suits its interests. In other words, imperial power is above the rules of the order.[9]

Yet, unipolarity as a structural condition of the international system does not tell us whether we live in a hegemonic or an imperial order. The behavioral consequences of a unipolar world for US foreign policy are unclear. Yet, for allies and for the sustainability of the transatlantic alliance it makes all the difference in the world whether they are faced with a hegemon or an imperial power. US hegemony and leadership has been readily accepted by the European allies throughout the post–World War II period. US imperialism, however, would indeed lead to the end of the transatlantic partnership and would have to be maintained by the use of US power against its allies in the long run. The crucial point is that we need to look inside the US itself in order to explain whether it behaves like a benign hegemon or like a malign imperialist. In other words, domestic politics and domestic structures become central to accounting for US foreign policy, even if we accept realist assumptions about the (unipolar) structure of the international system.

September 11, 2001, and the rise of transnational terrorism

There is a final claim that 9/11 and the reactions to it constitute a watershed in the transatlantic relationship. If this means that differences in domestic responses to transnational terrorist threats result in transatlantic conflicts over the means to handle the threat, there is some truth to it.[10] If it means that the transatlantic community as such is endangered because of 9/11, the argument makes no sense. On the contrary, the transatlantic alliance faces a new threat which endangers the survival of highly industrialized democracies precisely because transnational terrorist networks exploit the vulnerabilities of open and liberal societies.[11] As a result, increased transatlantic cooperation in intelligence and law enforcement is necessary, which should strengthen alliance cohesion rather than weaken it.

In sum, neither the end of the Cold War nor US unipolarity nor the new threats of terrorist networks constitute changes in world politics that spell the end of the transatlantic community as such. These processes have in common that they are indeterminate with regard to their consequences for the US–European relationship. Let us now have a closer look at the fundamentals of this relationship to determine whether they are still intact.

The Transatlantic Alliance: A Liberal Security Community

Debates about US foreign policy, unipolarity, and the transatlantic relationship mostly overlook the obvious fact that the Western world consists of liberal and capitalist democracies tied together through strong economic relations and common institutions. Joint democracy, economic interdependence, and highly institutionalized international relations – these are indicators for what Karl W. Deutsch already in 1957 called a "pluralistic security community," defined as "a group of people which has become 'integrated.' By integration we mean the attainment, within a territory, of a 'sense of community' and of institutions and practices strong enough and widespread enough to assure, for a 'long' time, dependable expectations of 'peaceful change' among its population."[12] A security community constitutes a particular social structure of international relations which then generates peaceful relations among the members.[13]

But what explains the expectations of peaceful change among members of a security community? Three factors – "three Is" – mutually reinforce each other and serve to account for the democratic peace in the contemporary security community of major powers:[14]

1 collective *identity*;
2 stable and interdependent *interactions* across societies creating strong social interests in each other's well-being; and
3 strong *institutionalization* of relationships creating social order and enduring norms among the members of the community.

Collective identity

Among the three factors, collective identity is probably the most difficult to measure. Yet, there are sufficient examples to sustain the argument that the often proclaimed "value community" of the Western alliance does not simply represent sheer rhetoric.[15] After the end of the Cold War, the Western security community did fight for its principles several times, from the second Gulf War to the war in Kosovo.

But is anti-Americanism on the rise in Europe, while there is growing anti-Europeanism in the US? We need to distinguish mass public and elite opinion here. Concerning the former, the main measurement problem is not to confuse support for each other's foreign policies with collective identification. All public opinion polls agree that many Europeans – including British, Italian, Spanish, and Central Eastern European citizens – disagree sharply with the Bush administration's foreign policy.[16] How rejection of particular US foreign policies translates into "anti-Americanism," however, is hard to tell. The Iraq crisis and war has led to some decline in mutual sympathy for each other.[17] Interestingly enough, the image of the US in Europe leading up to the war was more negative than the postwar image. In summer 2002, 75% of the

British, 61% of the Germans, and 63% of the French held favorable views of the US. These numbers declined to 48% (British), 25% (German), and 31% (French) in March 2003. In June 2003, once again 70% of the British, 45% of the Germans, and 43% of the French have favorable views of the US. In contrast, American citizens seem to sharply distinguish between those who were with the US and those who were opposed to the Iraq War. While US citizens still hold the British in very high esteem (82%), the previously positive image of the French and the Germans has declined sharply (French: 29%, down from 79% in February 2002; Germans: 44%, down from 83% in early 2002). It is too early to tell whether this negative image of US citizens toward the French and the Germans is going to last.

As to European views of the US, however, it is abundantly clear that negative feelings toward America stem from the Bush administration's policies rather than from some underlying resentments of the US in general. Take the data in table 8.1 for the "old Europeans" Germany and France. It is very hard to discern from these data that anti-Americanism should be on the rise in Germany and France.

On the contrary, opinion poll data still confirm a remarkable degree of transatlantic consensus with regard to mutual sympathy for each other, threat perceptions, and support for a multilateral world order. While Europeans regard the US less favorably in 2002

Table 8.1   Views of Americans in Germany and France (June 2003)

	Favorable views of Americans	What's the problem with the US?	
		Mostly Bush	America in general
Germany	67% (70% in 2002)	74%	21%
France	58% (71% in 2002)	74%	22%

Source: The Pew Global Attitudes Project, *Views of a Changing World* (Washington, DC: The Pew Research Center for the People and the Press, June 2003), pp. 21–2.

than in 1999–2000, more than two-thirds still hold a positive image of America. The same holds true for American feelings toward major European allies.[18] Threat perceptions in Europe and the US are still remarkably similar, even though support for the "U.S. led war on terrorism" declined in France and Germany.[19] Europeans and Americans also agree that religious and ethnic hatred constitutes one of the greatest dangers in the world, while US citizens seem to be somewhat more concerned about the spread of nuclear weapons than their European counterparts. Finally and perhaps most significantly in the light of the current transatlantic disputes, it is significant to note that support for multilateral institutions remains equally high in Western Europe and in the United States. These data have remained stable for a long period of time.[20] It is true, though, that support for the UN suffered quite a bit after the Iraq War, but on either side of the Atlantic (US: 43%, down from 72% in 2002; Great Britain: 41%, down from 78%; France: 47%, down from 75%; Germany: 46%, down from 79%).[21] Yet, international organizations in general are still held in very high esteem on either side of the Atlantic.[22]

In sum, it is hard to construct a widening gap in the overall worldviews, general foreign policy outlook, and a strong decline in mutual sympathy and we-feeling between Americans and Europeans, even though the latter's views have been affected negatively by the Iraq War. It is in the evaluation of the Bush administration's foreign policy that US and European public opinions differ sharply. Yet, while we do not see widening cleavages in mass public opinion on either side of the Atlantic, elite opinion appears to be a different matter, particularly regarding the foreign policy elites now in charge in Washington. I will comment on this aspect later in this article.

Transnational interdependence

Concerning the second factor contributing to a security community, transnational (economic) interdependence, I can be brief. Here, the transatlantic community is alive and kicking. Combined indicators for trade, foreign investment, and capital flows show that the transatlantic region is highly integrated economically and is only surpassed by the EU's single market itself. In 1999, 45.2 percent of all US foreign investment went to Europe, while 60.5 percent of all European foreign investment went to the United States. European investments in Texas alone are higher than all Japanese investments in the US combined. Moreover, intra-firm trade constitutes a large portion of transatlantic trade. EU subsidiaries of US companies import more than one-third of all US exports to the EU, while US subsidiaries of EU companies import more than two-fifths of all EU exports to the United States. Six million jobs on each side of the Atlantic depend on transatlantic economic relations.[23]

In sum, the transatlantic market is highly integrated and remains so despite the ups and downs in the political relationship. The US and the EU not only constitute each other's most important economic partners, but are also the two leading world economic powers. As a result, the current international economic order is largely guaranteed and stabilized by the transatlantic economic relationship. What is less clear, though, is the degree to which high economic interdependence serves to smooth increasing political conflicts. The spill-over effects from one area to the other are not clear, in either direction.

Multilateral institutions

This leads to the third factor constituting a security community, multilateral institution-building. Again and in parallel to the density of transnational interdependence, Europe and the transatlantic region constitute the most tightly coupled institutionalized settings within the larger security community. This region of the world also hosts the two strongest political, economic, and security institutions in terms of robustness of norms, rules, and decision-making procedures, the EU and NATO. The multilateral institutions of the transatlantic community serve to manage the inevitable conflicts inside a security community.[24] Strong procedural norms of mutual consultation and policy coordination secure that the members of the community have regular input and influence on each other's policymaking processes. These procedural norms and regulations are among the major tools mitigating power asymmetries among community members.

Of course, these "voice opportunities"[25] suffer the more US foreign policy pursues a unilateralist course or falls victim to "imperial ambitions."[26] US unilateralism violates fundamental norms of multilateralism that are constitutive for the transatlantic community. If unilateral tendencies – which have always been a temptation in American foreign policy – become the prevailing practice, the transatlantic security community's constitutive norms are endangered. The dominant discourse emanating from Washington concerning "coalitions of the willing," which is now enshrined in the foreign policy doctrine of the United States,[27] stands in sharp contrast to the idea of multilateralism on which the transatlantic alliance has been based over the past 50 years. NATO was so successful in the past as an instrument of alliance management precisely because it served as a clearinghouse for potential policy disputes *before* firm decisions were taken on either side of the Atlantic. The more consultations in the alliance framework are reduced to merely inform each other about decisions already taken, the more NATO becomes irrelevant for the future of the transatlantic relationship. This is why the North Atlantic alliance has taken such a toll in the past years, even before 9/11 and certainly before the Iraq crisis. In sum, if we are in a fundamental crisis of the transatlantic relationship, it primarily concerns the norms governing this relationship which have been enshrined in its institutions. If the US continues to build its foreign policy on "coalitions of the willing," this constitutes unilateralism in disguise and is fundamentally at odds with the norms of the transatlantic security community.

In sum, if we use the "three Is" – identity, interdependence, institutions – as indicators for the state of the transatlantic security community, we get a rather precise picture of its current situation. While the collective identification with each other seems to have declined slightly in 2002 and 2003, the basis of common values and shared principles is still intact. In the wider world community, European and North American societies still have more in common than any other societies in the world. The transatlantic

economic interdependence remains equally strong. Current challenges to the community mostly concern its institutions and the
constitutive norms on which they are based. Growing US unilateralism and imperial ambitions violate fundamental community
norms and, thus, give rise to increased transatlantic conflicts. To
understand the sources of these conflicts, however, we need to
open up the black boxes of the states on both sides of the Atlantic
and look at domestic politics.

Domestic Sources of the Transatlantic Disputes

If we want to understand the current transatlantic troubles, we
need to look at domestic politics on either side of the Atlantic. To
some extent, one is reminded of the transatlantic tensions during
the times of the first Reagan administration in the early 1980s.[28]
While George W. Bush is widely perceived as a unilateralist president in Europe, Ronald Reagan was seen as abandoning nuclear
arms control in a similar fashion. These similarities run deeper
than perceptions in public opinion.

The domestic side of US foreign policy

Most importantly, US foreign policy is currently controlled by a
domestic coalition whose worldviews differ substantially from
dominant European foreign policy coalitions. Three competing
groups are dominating the Bush administration's foreign policy
and they hold strikingly similar worldviews to the prevailing and
equally competing domestic coalitions during Reagan's first
term.[29]

During the early 1980s, a neoconservative group hating détente
and arms control as well as despising the "wimpish" European
allies were largely in control of the Pentagon. Some members of
this group, such as Richard Perle, are still around in the Bush
administration. Now and then, this group consists of devoted
militant internationalists preferring American unilateralism over
entangling alliances. During the early 1980s, neoconservatives

were convinced that arms control had to be abandoned in favor of an arms race in order to ruin the Soviet economy and, thus, to win the Cold War. Twenty years later, this group believes in the "unipolar moment" as a unique opportunity for the US to (re-)create an international order following an American design. Their "imperial ambition"[30] is prepared to accept temporary alliances, but their fundamental beliefs reject stable partnerships such as the transatlantic community as too entangling to suit US interests. In other words, this group of neoconservatives rejects the principles upon which the security community between the US and Europe has been built. It is anti-European to the degree that it considers the transatlantic alliance as largely superfluous and a constraint on US foreign policy.

However, we need to distinguish between two versions of neo-conservative thinking in foreign policy.[31] They are both unilateral and aggressive internationalists and prepared to use American power offensively when they see US interests at stake. But they differ in how they view the world and which values they want to promote. One group – among them Vice President Dick Cheney and Secretary of Defense Donald Rumsfeld – see the world in Hobbesian terms as a "dog-eat-dog" world. They are aggressive realists who believe in the US role as world policeman to keep order in an anarchic international system.[32] But there is also another group of neoconservative hawks who are prepared to use American power to promote liberal values and to construct a world order based on liberal democracies, universal human rights, and American-style capitalism. Undersecretary of Defense Paul Wolfowitz is among the most prominent representatives of this group which Pierre Hassner has aptly called "Wilsonians in boots," analogous to Napoleon's "revolution in boots."[33] In their view, the purpose of American power in the world is to promote democracy and capitalism. US power is to be used to aggressively push a liberal world order. This is why they supported regime change in Iraq. The two groups of unilateralist neoconservatives constitute what can be called the "Pentagon party" in the current US administration.

Yet, the neoconservatives of the early Reagan as well as the current Bush administration have been balanced domestically and

bureaucratically by a more moderate and traditional conservative group. Officials such as Richard Burt, Paul Nitze, and George
Shultz in the early 1980s, Bush senior's foreign policy team of the
late 1980s, as well as Colin Powell in the current Bush administration see the world in more moderate realist terms. While they
certainly share liberal values, they are not Wilsonians in the sense
of supporting a multilateral liberal world order. But they resent
the "imperial ambition" of the unilateralists and are convinced that
the US cannot go it alone – even in a unipolar system. At the same
time, this group is rather skeptical of the nation-building implications which the neoconservatives' liberal visions imply. Today as
well as 20 years ago, this group has remained committed to the
transatlantic security community. With a little help from their
European friends, the traditional conservatives succeeded in gradually moving Ronald Reagan toward the resumption of nuclear
arms control – and in having George W. Bush go to the United
Nations to seek support for his Iraq policy. As to the Bush administration, Powell's fellow conservatives at the State Department
are supported by the disgruntled US military,[34] on the one hand,
and – not to be overlooked – by the foreign policy establishment
in the US Senate, for instance Senators Richard Lugar and Joe
Biden, the current and the former chairman of the Senate Foreign
Relations Committee.

From the beginning of the Bush administration, a tug-of-war
between the neoconservatives and the traditional conservatives –
between the "Pentagon party" and the "State Department party"
– characterized the foreign policy decision-making process in
Washington. The President himself was not known initially for
favoring the liberal vision of the neoconservatives, even though
US foreign policy had already become more unilateralist than
during the Clinton administration. In particular, the Bush administration abandoned most efforts at seeking multilateral solutions
for the world's most urgent problems. Then came September 11,
2001, and the attack against the US homeland by transnational
terrorists. 9/11 and the understandable shock and sense of vulnerability it generated among Americans had profound consequences for the domestic balance of power in US foreign policy.
It created a policy window of opportunity for neoconservative

policy entrepreneurs such as Wolfowitz. As a result, the domestic balance of power in the US changed in favor of the neoconservative group whose liberal vision including "Wilsonianism in boots" was increasingly shared by the President.[35]

The presidential "National Security Strategy" of September 2002 as well as the focus on Iraq constituted expressions of this new domestic balance of power in Washington. Nevertheless, both examples also show that neoconservative unilateralists of the offensive realist and the liberal variety both had to make concessions to the traditional conservatives and their allies in Congress and in Europe. As to the "National Security Strategy" document, for example, it does express a liberal vision of world politics: "Finally, the United States will use this moment of opportunity to extend the benefits of freedom across the globe. We will actively work to bring the hope of democracy, development, free markets, and free trade to every corner of the world."[36] Incorporating the foreign policy views of the neoconservatives, the document commits the US to:

- preemptive, if not preventive, warfare against terrorism and "rogue states" with weapons of mass destruction;
- unilateralism "when our interests and unique responsibilities require";[37] and
- military superiority "to dissuade potential adversaries from pursuing a military buildup in hopes of surpassing, or equaling, the power of the United States."[38]

None of these statements as such is new. However, it is the combination of a liberal vision with unilateral action "if necessary" (but who decides?) that represents quite a shift from previous foreign policy strategies of the United States. Yet, the document also contains quite a few paragraphs expressing the standard repertoire of the traditional conservatives, such as the commitment to NATO, the EU, and other allies. It also commits the US to active engagement in regional crises and to a substantial increase in foreign aid. Finally and significantly, the US remains committed to a multilateral and liberal international economic order. This latter point is often overlooked in Europe, but it is of utmost importance for the future world order. In sum, the much criticized "National Security Strategy" document actually represents a policy compromise between neoconservative unilateralists and traditional conservatives in the Bush administration.

The domestic side of European foreign policy

While the dominant coalition in charge of US foreign policy is composed of neoconservatives (realist as well as liberal unilateralists) and traditional conservatives (realists with a preference for traditional alliances), the dominant coalitions running the EU's foreign policy as well as the foreign policies of the most important member states look rather different (see figure 8.1). The figure depicts the dominant coalitions on both sides of the Atlantic in a two-dimensional space. A third dimension which is often used to describe foreign policy attitudes – isolationism versus internationalism – is omitted here, since the dominant foreign policy elites in the US and in Europe share a commitment to internationalism. Rather, the various groups differ from each other with regard to:

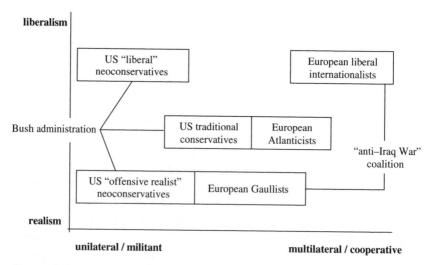

Figure 8.1 Dominant foreign policy coalitions in the US and Europe

1 a "*realist–liberal*" continuum (y-axis) which depicts whether people view the world in realist terms and, thus, security interests dominate their vision of foreign policy, or whether they are primarily committed to the promotion of a liberal vision (i.e. the spread of human rights, democracy, and market economy); and

2 a "*unilateral/militant–multilateral / cooperative*" continuum (x-axis) delineating whether foreign policymakers favor unilateralism and the use of force to promote foreign policy goals or whether they support a cooperative foreign policy working with and through multilateral institutions.

The three factions dominating the Bush administration's foreign policy are situated on the left-hand side of the figure.[39] The figure also depicts three European foreign policy groups according to their views.

The first group in the upper right corner of the figure could be called "liberal internationalists." It is often overlooked that the European center-left shares with American "liberal" neoconservatives a commitment to the promotion of democracy and human rights as their foreign policy priorities. In sharp contrast to the US right, however, this group is equally firmly committed to a cooperative foreign policy and to work with and through multilateral institutions. This group, which is currently in charge of, for example, German foreign policy, pursues the foreign policy of a "civilian power,"[40] and, thus, shares a Kantian vision of world order in the true sense of the "perpetual peace" – that is, building a pacific federation of democratic states and strengthening the rule of law in international affairs.[41] European Kantians are not pacifists; they do support the use of military force if necessary (cf. Chancellor Schröder's stance on Kosovo and Afghanistan). Yet, military power has to be embedded in political and diplomatic efforts. Unilateralism is anathema for the European center-left (see also the new EU foreign policy document).

Then there is a second group among the European foreign policy elites which holds a more realist view of the world than either the American neoconservatives or the European center-left. Since this group thinks primarily in realist "balance of power" terms, it is very much concerned about the growth of US power and promotes a European foreign policy of balancing and building a counterweight to US primacy. One could call this group the "European Gaullists." Their mantra is to build a multipolar world in contrast to a unipolar one dominated by US hyperpower. Interestingly and strangely enough, the Franco-German anti–Iraq War coalition brought together the European center-left and the European "Gaullists," who joined forces for different reasons. Both were concerned about American unilateralism. But the center-left was primarily opposed to using force for liberal purposes ("regime change"), while the "Gaullists" opposed the war because of concern over US "hyperpower."

The third group among European foreign policy elites can be located in a similar position to the American traditional conservatives. This group holds rather moderate worldviews on either the "liberal-realist" axis or the "militant-cooperative" axis. Above all, however, this group is strongly committed to preserving the transatlantic partnership almost no matter what. This group of "European Atlanticists," which formed the core of the European "coalition of the willing" during the Iraq War, is strongly motivated to avoid policy disagreements with Washington that could weaken the transatlantic community.

Two main conclusions follow from this attempt at locating the various foreign policy groupings on either side of the Atlantic in a two-dimensional political space:

1 The core of the transatlantic disagreements does not concern value commitments such as the goals of promoting democracy or human rights. When it comes to the question whether foreign policy should primarily promote liberal values rather than serving strategic or economic interests (the realist view), Europeans are as much divided among themselves as Americans. Despite the different positions on the Iraq War, however, Europeans are overwhelmingly in favor of multilateralism and cooperative foreign policies, while the two groups of neoconservatives in Washington are unilateralists. Thus, the main dividing line between the US and Europe concerns the

commitment to multilateral norms which have been constitutive of the transatlantic security community.

2　It is also obvious that the two opposing camps in Europe that emerged during the Iraq crisis ("new" versus "old" Europe) constitute anything but stable foreign policy coalitions. To put it more bluntly: neither European Gaullism nor European Atlanticism of the old kind can form the basis of a common European foreign policy consensus. I will come back to that point in the conclusions.

To sum up this point: the current crisis in the transatlantic relationship has to be explained on the basis of the differing worldviews of dominant foreign policy coalitions on either side of the Atlantic. It is domestic politics, stupid!, rather than structural changes in the international system that has made the Atlantic a wider ocean. This is not to imply that the crisis is less serious. In fact, one of the dominant groups currently running US foreign policy does not believe in the values and norms of the security community anymore. Whether this group will be strengthened or weakened in the future is impossible to predict.

Conclusions: European Responses to American Unilateralism

The argument of this article can be summarized as follows. As to the fundamentals of the transatlantic security community, a mixed picture emerges. Two of the "three Is" – interdependence and identity as a commitment to collective value – appear to be still intact. Yet its institutional basis as well as the norms governing the security community appear to be eroding. These conflicts stem from domestic developments on both sides of the Atlantic leading to different perceptions of contemporary security threats and, more importantly, different prescriptions on how to handle them. Unilateral and even imperial tendencies in contemporary US foreign policy violate constitutive norms on which the transatlantic community has been based for more than 50 years. They also touch upon fundamentals concerning the future world order and the rule of (international) law in dealing with international conflicts. American neoconservatives are as committed as the European center-left to the global promotion of human rights and democracy, but they are also convinced that the unprecedented American power position in the world requires unilateral action to promote these goals including the unilateral use of (preventive) force. In contrast, a strong European consensus favors a cooperative foreign policy geared to strengthening international institutions and the rule of international law.

What policy consequences follow from this assessment, particularly for European responses to America's "imperial ambitions"? I see three major implications. First, neither balancing nor bandwagoning can be a valid basis for a European response to American imperial ambitions. Building Europe as a "counterweight" to US power is not feasible in practical terms, nor can a European consensus be built around it which would have to include the United Kingdom as well as the new EU member states in Central Eastern Europe. Nor is bandwagoning an option, since it would betray core principles of European foreign policy when dealing with US unilateralist tendencies. Thus, there is a European paradox: On the one hand, Europe and the EU need to speak out with one voice in order to be listened to in Washington. On the other hand, a European common foreign policy will fail immediately and split Europe further apart if it is constructed as a counter-hegemonic project.

Second, however, there is a way out. I would argue against Charles Kupchan that the social structure of the transatlantic relationship and its institutional basis in particular can be repaired.[42] Moreover, the traditional European reaction to US unilateralist impulses remains valid. In the past, Europeans have usually responded to transatlantic conflicts by increased binding through strengthening the transatlantic institutional ties rather than counterbalancing. They have used the open US domestic system for their purposes by successfully forming transnational and transgovernmental coalitions across the Atlantic in order to increase their leverage on American foreign policy.[43] There is no compelling reason why this strategy, which worked well during the first Reagan administration with a similar domestic configuration of forces, cannot be successfully employed today. Now and then, the natural allies of Europeans inside the administration and in Congress are the moderate conservatives who care about the transatlantic community. Moreover, European foreign policy can exploit the fact that American public opinion continues to hold views much closer to European outlooks than to those of the neoconservatives inside and outside the administration.

Third, it is important that European voices are being heard loud and clear in Washington. While European governments should pick carefully their conflicts with the US administration and cannot fight simultaneously on all fronts, the "National Security Strategy" document deserves a common European response. Of course, one can argue that this response already exists in practice given the emerging European foreign policy focusing on human rights, democracy, and multilateralism. Yet, European practice has to be complemented by a European foreign policy discourse. The goal is not to weaken the institutional ties in the transatlantic community, but to strengthen similar voices inside the US domestic system. Such a European foreign policy strategy needs to tackle the world order conflicts that constitute the root causes of the transatlantic policy disagreements:

1   A clear expression of a *liberal vision of world order* based on the rule of law, democracy, human rights, and market economy: it would be disastrous to leave liberal visions to American neoconservatives and not to recognize that Western foreign policy is first and foremost about promoting liberal values. This entails in particular the necessity of a European response to the neoconservatives' political agenda of promoting democracy in the world's crisis regions, particularly in the Middle East.[44] A proactive European foreign policy is needed in this regard.

2   An equally unambiguous commitment to *multilateralism and the rule of international law*: this is the characteristic feature and trademark of contemporary European foreign policy that distinguishes a European foreign policy strategy from some of the ideas articulated in the recent US "National Security Strategy." The point is that a liberal vision of world order

cannot be promoted unilaterally without being inherently contradictory. If it is constitutive for domestic liberal orders that nobody – not even the most powerful – is above the law, this is also true for a world order based on democratic principles. A liberal world order requires recognition of the rule of law as a constitutive feature – together with democracy and human rights. This is also the ultimate reason why European foreign policy must not give in to US pressures concerning the International Criminal Court. However, one has to recognize that contemporary international law is in serious need of reform. This concerns first and foremost norms of national sovereignty, which are increasingly at odds with commitments to international human rights.

3 Europe also has to articulate a clear *strategy on how to deal with the new security threats*, such as weapons of mass destruction in the hands of dictators and the dangers emanating from transnational terrorism. Transnational terrorist networks and weapons of mass destruction are real threats to liberal societies that require not just political, but also military answers. The current transatlantic division of labor – the US as the military fighting force and the world's policeman, Europe as the main provider of political nation-building and cleaning-up afterwards – is not sustainable. Once again, it would be disastrous to let the use of military force be dictated by American unilateralists. This is particularly true if one rejects the idea of preventive war in the absence of a clear and present danger. We need a serious transatlantic debate, not on preventive war, but on preventive action to stem the double dangers of weapons of mass destruction and of transnational terrorism. The emerging EU foreign policy strategy constitutes a step in the right direction.

In short, a new "transatlantic bargain" is required if the US–European alliance is to survive the coming challenges. Whether this can be done by reforming NATO or by building new US–EU security institutions remains to be seen. But current and future world order problems require a strong transatlantic relationship to meet these challenges jointly.

Notes

*This is an updated and abbreviated version of a paper first presented at the American Institute for Contemporary German Studies, Washington, DC, January 24, 2003, published as AICGS Seminar Papers. The present version was first published in *Die Friedens-Warte*, 78, 2–3 (2003). I owe a lot to discussions in my research seminar at the Free University. I thank the students as well as Tanja Börzel for their critical comments.

1 President of the United States, *The National Security Strategy of the United States of America* (Washington, DC, September 2002).
2 Andrew Moravcsik, "Striking a New Transatlantic Bargain," *Foreign Affairs*, 4 (2003), pp. 74–89.
3 For details see Gert Krell, *Arroganz der Macht, Arroganz der Ohnmacht: Der Irak, die Weltordnungspolitik der USA und die transatlantischen Beziehungen*, HSFK-Report 1/2003 (Frankfurt/ Main: Hessische Stiftung Friedens- und Konfliktforschung, 2003), pp. 22–5; and Peter Mayer, Volker Rittberger, and Fariborz Zelli, "Risse im Westen? Betrachtungen zum transatlantischen Verhältnis heute," *Leviathan*, 31, 1 (2003), pp. 32–52.
4 John J. Mearsheimer, "Back to the Future: Instability in Europe after the Cold War," *International Security*, 15, 1 (1990), pp. 5–56; Kenneth N. Waltz, "The Emerging Structure of International Politics," *International Security*, 18, 2 (1993), pp. 44–79.
5 See for example William C. Wohlforth, "The Stability of a Unipolar World," *International Security*, 24, 1 (1999), pp. 5–41; Stephen G. Brooks and William C. Wohlforth, "American Primacy in Perspective," *Foreign Affairs*, 81, 4 (2002), pp. 20–33; Samuel P. Huntington, "The Lonely Superpower," *Foreign Affairs*, 78, 2 (1999).
6 Robert Kagan, *Of Paradise and Power: America and Europe in the New World Order* (New York: Alfred A. Knopf, 2003).
7 Joseph S. Nye, Jr, *Bound to Lead: The Changing Nature of American Power* (New York: Basic Books, 1990).
8 G. John Ikenberry, *After Victory: Institutions, Strategic Restraint, and the Rebuilding of Order After Major Wars* (Princeton, NJ: Princeton University Press, 2001).
9 G. John Ikenberry, "America's Imperial Ambition," *Foreign Affairs*, 81, 5 (2002), pp. 44–60; see also Gert Krell, *Arroganz der Macht*.

10 See Peter J. Katzenstein, "September 11 in Comparative Perspective: The Antiterrorism Campaigns of Germany and Japan," *Dialog-IO* (2002), pp. 45–56.

11 Ulrich Schneckener, *Netzwerke des Terrors: Charakter und Strukturen des transnationalen Terrorismus* (Berlin: Stiftung Wissenschaft und Politik, 2002). John Arquilla and David Ronfeldt, *Networks and Netwars: The Future of Terror, Crime, and Militancy* (Santa Monica, CA: RAND Corporation, 2001); Ronald J. Deibert and Janice Gross Stein, "Hacking Networks of Terror," *Dialog-IO* (2002), pp. 1–14.

12 Karl W. Deutsch et al., *Political Community and the North Atlantic Area: International Organization in the Light of Historical Experience* (Princeton, NJ: Princeton University Press, 1957), pp. 5–6, 9.

13 See also Emanuel Adler and Michael Barnett, *Security Communities* (Cambridge: Cambridge University Press, 1998).

14 See also Emanuel Adler and Michael Barnett, "A Framework for the Study of Security Communities," in Adler and Barnett, *Security Communities*, pp. 29–65.

15 On evidence during the Cold War see Thomas Risse-Kappen, *Cooperation among Democracies: The European Influence on U.S. Foreign Policy* (Princeton, NJ: Princeton University Press, 1995).

16 See for example The Pew Global Attitudes Project, *What the World Thinks in 2002* (Washington, DC: The Pew Research Center for the People and the Press, 2002); idem, *Americans and Europeans Differ Widely on Foreign Policy Issues* (Washington, DC: The Pew Research Center for the People and the Press, April 17, 2002).

17 For the following see The Pew Global Attitudes Project, *Views of a Changing World* (Washington, DC: The Pew Research Center for the People and the Press, June 2003), pp. 19–22.

18 Overview in "Special Report American Values: Living with a Superpower," *The Economist* (January 4, 2003), pp. 18–20.

19 The Pew Global Attitudes Project, *Views of a Changing World*, p. 28.

20 Gert Krell, *Arroganz der Macht*, p. 7; The Chicago Council on Foreign Relations and the German Marshall Fund of the United States, *Worldviews 2002* (Chicago, IL: 2002); Ole R. Holsti, *Public Opinion and American Foreign Policy* (Ann Arbor, MI: University of Michigan Press, 1996); idem, "Public Opinion," in *Eagle Rules? Foreign Policy and American Primacy in the 21st Century*, ed. Robert J. Lieber (Upper Saddle River, NJ: Prentice-Hall, 2001), pp. 16–46.

21 The Pew Global Attitudes Project, *Views of a Changing World*, p. 27.

22 Ibid., p. 97.
23 Data according to Gert Krell, *Arroganz der Macht*, pp. 10–17.
24 Thomas Risse-Kappen, *Cooperation among Democracies*.
25 G. John Ikenberry, *After Victory*.
26 G. John Ikenberry, "America's Imperial Ambition."
27 President of the United States, *The National Security Strategy*.
28 See Bernd W. Kubbig, *Amerikanische Rüstungskontrollpolitik: Die innergesellschaftlichen Kräfteverhältnisse in der ersten Amtszeit Reagans (1981–1985)* (Frankfurt/Main: Campus, 1988); Thomas Risse-Kappen, *The Zero Option: INF, West Germany, and Arms Control* (Boulder, CO: Westview, 1988); Strobe Talbott, *Deadly Gambits* (New York: Alfred A. Knopf, 1984).
29 On the latter see in particular Strobe Talbott, *Deadly Gambits*; idem, *The Master of the Game: Paul Nitze and the Nuclear Arms Race* (New York: Alfred A. Knopf, 1988); Bernd W. Kubbig, *Amerikanische Rüstungskontrollpolitik*.
30 G. John Ikenberry, "America's Imperial Ambition."
31 For a broader analysis of these various strands see Walter Russell Mead, *Special Providence: American Foreign Policy and How It Changed the World* (New York: Alfred A. Knopf, 2001); Pierre Hassner, *The United States: The Empire of Force or the Force of Empire?* Chaillot Papers, 54 (Paris: Institute for Security Studies, 2002); Henry R. Nau, *At Home Abroad: Identity and Power in American Foreign Policy* (Ithaca, NY: Cornell University Press, 2002).
32 On offensive realism see John J. Mearsheimer, *The Tragedy of Great Power Politics* (New York and London: W. W. Norton, 2001).
33 Pierre Hassner, *The United States*, p. 43.
34 Ibid., pp. 28–33; also Ole R. Holsti, "A Widening Gap between the U.S. Military and Civilian Society? Some Evidence, 1976–96," *International Security*, 23, 3 (1998–9), pp. 5–42.
35 See Bob Woodward, *Bush at War* (New York: Simon and Schuster, 2002).
36 President Bush, in President of the United States, *The National Security Strategy*, p. v.
37 Ibid., p. 31.
38 Ibid., p. 30.
39 I have deliberately omitted American liberal internationalists here who share liberal values *and* are committed to multilateralism. This group figured prominently during the Clinton administration.
40 Hanns W. Maull, "Germany and Japan: The New Civilian Powers," *Foreign Affairs*, 69, 5 (1990), pp. 91–106; *Germany as a Civilian*

Power? The Foreign Policy of the Berlin Republic, ed. Sebastian Harnisch and Hanns Maull (Manchester: Manchester University Press, 2001).

41 Immanuel Kant, "To Perpetual Peace: A Philosophical Sketch" (1795), in idem, *Perpetual Peace and Other Essays on Politics, History, and Morals*, ed. Ted Humphrey (Indianapolis, IN: Hackett, 1983), pp. 107–43.

42 Charles Kupchan, *The End of the American Era: U.S. Foreign Policy and the Geopolitics of the Twenty-First Century* (New York: Alfred A. Knopf, 2003).

43 For evidence see Thomas Risse-Kappen, *Cooperation among Democracies*.

44 Peter Rudolf, *Krise der deutsch-amerikanischen Beziehungen? Über den Umgang mit den USA* (Berlin: Stiftung Wissenschaft und Politik, 2002), p. 8.

9

The Bush Doctrine: A Chinese Perspective

Zhiyuan Cui

The Bush Doctrine as the Culmination of the US Post–Cold War Grand Strategy

On June 1, 2002, during an address at West Point, US President George W. Bush announced to the world "the Bush Doctrine." The doctrine consists of three basic elements. First, the United States will no longer rely solely on "Cold-War doctrines of containment and deterrence." Instead, it will actively pursue the strategy of "preemptive strike," "take the battle to the enemy, disrupt his plans and confront the worst threats before they emerge." Second, the United States will work hard to export democracy, since "the requirements of freedom apply fully to Africa and Latin America and the entire Islamic world." Finally, the United States would keep its military supremacy beyond challenge, "thereby making the destabilizing arms races of other eras pointless, and limiting rivalries to trade and other pursuits of peace."[1] In September 2002, Bush signed the "National Security Strategy of the United States," which formalizes these three elements of the "Bush Doctrine": preemptive strike, the promotion of democracy, and military supremacy.

It was widely reported in the Western press that the so-called Bush Doctrine has strong roots in the American neoconservative thinking and movement. Paul Wolfowitz's aborted 1992 "Defense

Planning Guidance" already contained the three elements of the Bush Doctrine mentioned above. In 1997, "Project for the New American Century" was founded by Dick Cheney, Donald Rumsfeld, Paul Wolfowitz, William Kristol, and Robert Kagan.[2] As early as 1997, Irving Kristol, the father of US neoconservatism as well as the father of William Kristol, already predicted that:

> One of these days, the American people are going to awaken to the fact that we have become an imperial nation, even though public opinion and all of our political traditions are hostile to the idea. It is no overweening ambition on our part that has defined our destiny in this way, nor is it any kind of conspiracy by a foreign policy elite. It happened because the world wanted it to happen, needed it to happen, and signaled this need by a long series of relatively minor crises that could not be resolved except by some American involvement.[3]

It seems no accident that George W. Bush awarded the Presidential Medal of Freedom to Irving Kristol on July 9, 2002. Also, it may not be surprising to discover that "preemptive strategy" was a key Roman imperial strategy, as forcefully argued by Cicero:

> how can you believe that the man who has lived so licentiously up to the present time will not proceed to every extreme of insolence, if he shall also secure the authority given by arms? Do not, then, wait until you have suffered some such treatment and then rue it, but be on your guard before you suffer; for it is rash to allow dangers to come upon you and then to repent of it, when you might have anticipated them . . .[4]

Certainly, there are no shortages of classical scholars among the neoconservatives.[5]

How did Chinese intellectuals perceive and respond to the Bush Doctrine? Of course, there are many divergent viewpoints, but the main perspective can be identified easily: they emphasized the continuity of the Bush Doctrine with Clinton's foreign policy, and considered the Bush Doctrine as the culmination and maturation of the US post–Cold War grand strategy.

We can better appreciate the Chinese view by contrasting it with the pronouncements of some leading opinion-makers in Europe. For example, a leading German public intellectual and philosopher, Jürgen Habermas, emphasized the novelty of the Bush Doctrine: "The United States has, with the Iraq War, . . . given up the role of a guarantor of power in international law; with its violation thereof she sets future superpowers a disastrous example . . . Let's not kid ourselves: America's normative authority lies shattered."[6] In other words, Habermas and many other European intellectuals tend to perceive the Bush Doctrine as a break with President Clinton's foreign policy.

Why is the Chinese view of the Bush Doctrine different from that of Europeans? Is it simply because China opposed NATO's intervention in Kosovo as well, while Habermas and many others supported it? Of course, for many Chinese, there never was the "normative authority of America" that Habermas talked about. In this chapter I want to outline some deeper geopolitical and philosophical reasons behind the Chinese perspective on the Bush Doctrine as the culmination of the US post–Cold War grand strategy.

Geopolitical Reasons for the Chinese Perspective

The Cold War ended in Europe, but it has not yet fully ended in East Asia. Few Western newspaper readers know that the Korean War has never ended – there was only a cease-fire agreement, no peace treaty. The distrust among all major powers in the region is deep. Many states worry about China as a rising economic and political power. China worries that Taiwan will seek independence with the backing of the US and Japan. In this geopolitical environment, China naturally is more sensitive about American aggressive unilateralism than Europe.

The Chinese view about the continuity between the Bush Doctrine and Clinton's foreign policy seems to be confirmed by the neoconservatives themselves. For example, Kaplan and Kristol stress that "Bush would hardly be acting without precedent if he acted unilaterally against Saddam. After all, President Clinton resorted to force without U.N. approval on several occasions, each time receiving the support of Daschle and his fellow Democrats." They also quote Richard Holbrooke as saying: "Act without the Security Council, or don't act at all."[7]

The Chinese cannot fail to remember Madeleine Albright's proud words: "We are the indispensable nation, we stand tall – we see further into the future." Zbigniew Brzezinski, a former democratic national security adviser, explained the purpose of the US grand strategy as follows: "to prevent collusion and maintain security dependence among the vassals [Europe] . . . to keep barbarians from coming together." From the Chinese perspective, the Bush Doctrine is only one step further along the same direction of American grand strategic thinking.

What are the Chinese counterbalancing efforts to set against the unipolar power of the United States? At least four of them can be identified:

1 using China's power in the UN Security Council to seek peaceful solutions;
2 supporting the euro by diversifying China's foreign currency holding;
3 developing Asian trade and monetary cooperation;
4 developing trade and security cooperation with Russia and the neighboring states in Central Asia (Shanghai Cooperation Organization or Shanghai Six).

Of course, the Chinese counterbalancing effort is very limited so far. Indeed, China has generally been keeping a low profile in international affairs for the purpose of not being perceived as a "threat." This can be seen vividly in the UN Security Council's resolution veto records (see table 9.1).

As indicated in the table, China has used her veto power only five times since she became a member of the UN Security Council (and almost all her vetoes are in some way related to the Taiwan issue), in contrast with the frequent use by the Soviet Union/ Russia (120 times) and the US (76 times).

However, China's "low profile" policy does not mean that her view of the Bush Doctrine and US grand strategy has no real

Table 9.1   UN Security Council veto records

Country	Vetoes	Comments
USSR/ Russia	120	Soviet Union vetoed 79 times in first 10 years of UN. Only 2 vetoes since collapse of Soviet Union in 1991: Cyprus (1993), Bosnia (1994)
US	76	Blocked 35 resolutions criticizing Israel. Blocked resolution alone 53 times
UK	32	23 of UK's 32 vetoes have been on resolutions also vetoed by US. Vetoed a resolution alone only 7 times. All solo vetoes were on Rhodesia (later Zimbabwe)
France	18	13 of France's 18 vetoes have been on resolutions also vetoed by US and UK. France vetoed 2 resolutions alongside UK, both on Suez crisis (1956)
China	5	1946–71, Republic of China (Taiwan) occupied Chinese seat, which used veto once to block Mongolia's application for UN membership. In 1972 China vetoed resolutions twice: Bangladeshi membership, and Middle East. In 1997 blocked the sending of 155 UN observers to Guatemala to verify a cease-fire. In 1999 China blocked extension of mandate of UN Preventive Deployment Force in Macedonia

policy effects. Indeed, the increasing cooperation between China and the EU may be the most important response to the Bush Doctrine on the part of both China and the EU.[8]

Philosophical Reasons for the Chinese Perspective

The Chinese view on the continuity between Clinton and Bush is based on the observation that neoconservatism shares with liberalism the vision of the United States as a "Redeemer Nation" with "Special Providence." Moreover, both Clinton and Bush based their foreign policy on the theory of "democratic peace" and "human rights trump national sovereignty," as evidenced by the second element of the Bush Doctrine mentioned above.

To appreciate the continuity between neoconservatism and liberalism, we need to realize the forward-looking nature of American neoconservatism, which is in sharp contrast with British conservatism. In the words of a leading British conservative thinker, Michael Oakeshott:

> What is esteemed [in conservatism] is the present; and it is esteemed not on account of its connections with a remote antiquity, nor because it is recognized to be more admirable than any possible alternative, but on account of its familiarity. . . . To be conservative, then, is to prefer the familiar to the unknown, to prefer the tried to the untried, fact to mystery, the actual to the possible, the limited to the unbounded, the near to the distant . . . the convenient to the perfect, present laughter to utopian bliss.[9]

It is revealing that Irving Kristol, the father of American neoconservatism, explicitly rejected Michael Oakeshott's respect for the present. Kristol declared that Oakeshott

> is irredeemably secular, as I – being a Jewish conservative – am not . . . It is impossible for any religious person to have the kinds of attitudes toward the past and the future that Oakeshott's conservative disposition celebrates. Our Scriptures and our daily prayer book link us to the past and to the future with an intensity lacking in Oakeshott's vision.[10]

Therefore, US neoconservatism is in fact forward-looking, even revolutionary! It is no surprise that it shares with American liberalism the so-called democratic peace theory.

The "democratic peace" theory was proposed by Princeton political scientist Michael Doyle in the 1980s and gained prominence among US policymakers in the early 1990s as a justification for exporting democracy. It holds that "Liberal States do maintain peace among themselves" while "these republics would engage in wars with nonrepublics." The reason that democracies do not go to war with each other is that "Institutional features lead to caution," since the consent of citizens is required under democracy.[11] Doyle claimed that his "democratic peace theory" originated with Kant's 1795 essay "Perpetual Peace." However, he fundamentally misunderstood Kant's thesis. As Kant explains:

> the consent of the citizens is required to decide whether or not war is to be declared, it is very natural that they will have great hesitation in embarking on so dangerous an enterprise. For this would mean calling down on themselves all the miseries of war, such as doing the fighting themselves, . . . having to take upon themselves a burden of debt which will embitter peace itself and which can never be paid off on account of the constant threat of new wars.[12]

It is clear that Kant's reasons for maintaining that republics are more reluctant to go to war are twofold: citizens had to fight themselves and they had to bear the burden of public debt. Neither of these two reasons fits today's "democracies," which have large professional armies and the capacity to issue debt to foreigners. Kant's theses cannot explain, especially, the foreign policy of the United States, given its status as the largest professional military power in the world and the largest debtor country.

The "democratic peace" theory is wrong empirically. As Kenneth Waltz pointed out, the fact that the US have toppled or undermined democratically elected leaders (such as Salvador Allende of Chile and Juan Bosch of the Dominican Republic) "cast[s] doubt on the democratic peace thesis."[13] But, more importantly, Doyle's claim that "liberal states do maintain peace among themselves" while at the same time "these republics would engage in wars with nonrepublics"[14] totally misrepresents Kant's idea: Kant's two reasons for the republics' reluctance to wage war do not tell us anything about the nature of the enemy.[15]

It is rather surprising that Doyle's dubious interpretation of Kant's ideas has gained such a wide acceptance in academic and policy circles. Perhaps the only answer to this puzzle is that the "democratic peace theory" may be used to justify the imperial project. Doyle himself noted that "the protection of cosmopolitan Liberal rights thus bred a demand for imperial rule that violated the liberty of Native Americans, Africans and Asians."[16] But, as Georg Cavallar points out, Kant in fact argues against the European imperial project by asserting that the cosmopolitan rights of hospitality must not be enforced: "The natives can turn strangers away on condition that this does not cause their death. The [European] strangers in turn are obliged to behave 'in a peaceable manner', and if they don't, the natives act 'wisely' if they place restrictions on them."[17]

Doyle ignores Kant's fifth thesis in "Perpetual Peace," which states that: "No States shall forcibly interfere in the constitution and government of another state."[18] Why? Kant's answer is very clear: "the interference of external powers would be a violation of the rights of an independent people which is merely struggling with its internal ills. Such interference would be an active offence and would make the autonomy of all other states insecure."[19] Though Kant did not consider the Prussian state of his time as a republic, he did not want foreign interference in the internal affairs of Prussia, as indicated by his opinion that "a people which occupies extended territories in Europe may feel that monarchy is the only kind of constitution which can enable it to preserve its own existence between powerful neighbors."[20]

It is interesting to observe that Kant's noninterference principle is remarkably similar in spirit to the Chinese "Five Principles of Peaceful Coexistence." These principles were first put forward by the late Chinese Premier Zhou Enlai when he met an Indian delegation in December 1953. At the first Asia–Africa conference (the Bandung Conference) held in April 1955, Premier Zhou Enlai reiterated these principles, whose spirit was incorporated into the declarations of the conference. In 1982 these Five Principles were written into the Constitution of the People's Republic of China:

1 mutual respect for sovereignty and territorial integrity;
2 mutual nonaggression;
3 noninterference in each other's internal affairs;

4 equality and mutual benefit;
5 peaceful coexistence.

As China's Ministry of Foreign Affairs explains:

> Both history and the current international developments since
> World War II have shown that practices of defining friends and
> enemy according to differences in social system and values through
> forming "camps", "groups", "the big family" and "alliances" invari-
> ably fail. Only by observing the Five Principles of Peaceful Coex-
> istence can normal state-to-state relations be maintained and a just
> international order be established. The establishment of a new
> international order based on the Five Principles of Peaceful Co-
> existence will surely safeguard world peace and promote common
> development and human progress.[21]

Obviously, the Chinese "Five Principles of Peaceful Coexistence" are the opposite of the Bush Doctrine of preemptive strike,
democracy export, and military supremacy. This certainly does not
mean that China should not democratize. China must face the
challenge of democratic innovations both in economic and political spheres. Frantz Fanon wrote: "If we wish to turn Africa into a
new Europe, . . . then let us leave the destiny of our countries to
Europeans. They will know how to do it better than the most
gifted among us."[22] The best response to the Bush Doctrine is for
the new generation of Chinese intellectuals, policymakers, and
common people to develop new institutions of democracy and
market economy, thereby contributing to the progress of human
civilization beyond the narrow horizon set by Bush and his like.

Notes

1 Cited from Lawrence Kaplan and William Kristol, *The War over
  Iraq: Saddam's Tyranny and America's Mission* (San Francisco, CA:
  Encounter Books, 2003), p. 74.
2 See their website: www.newamericancentury.org.
3 Irving Kristol, "The Emerging American Imperium," *The Wall Street
  Journal* (August 18, 1997).

4   Cited in Richard Tuck, *The Rights of War and Peace* (Oxford: Oxford University Press, 1999), p. 21.
5   See Saul Bellow's novel *Ravelstein* (Harmondsworth: Penguin Books, 2000), pp. 58–9, for a story about Paul Wolfowitz's relation with Allan Bloom. Also, Donald Kagan, the father of Robert Kagan, is a leading scholar of the Roman Empire at Yale.
6   See Jürgen Habermas, "Was bedeutet der Denkmalsturz?" *Frankfurter Allgemeine Zeitung* (April 17, 2003), p. 33.
7   Kaplan and Kristol, *The War over Iraq*, p. 90.
8   The policy paper adopted by the European Commission on September 10, 2003, sets out a framework that is intended to guide EU policy and action towards China over the next two to three years. The paper identifies six priorities for relations in the coming years, including sharing responsibilities in promoting global governance, supporting China's transition to an open society based upon the rule of law and the respect for human rights, and promoting China's economic liberation domestically and externally. The paper also contains a number of concrete proposals with a view to enhancing EU–China relations in key areas, including economic and trade relations and China's internal reform process. See http://europa.eu.int/comm/external_relations/china/com_03_533/com_533_en. pdf.
9   Michael Oakeshott, "On Being Conservative," in Oakeshott, *Rationalism in Politics and Other Essays* (London: Basic Books, 1962).
10 Irving Kristol, *Neo-Conservatism: The Autobiography of an Idea* (New York: The Free Press, 1995), p. 373.
11 Michael Doyle, "Liberalism and World Politics," *American Political Science Review*, 80 (1986), pp. 1151–69.
12 Immanuel Kant, *Political Writing*, ed. H. S. Reiss (Cambridge: Cambridge University Press, 1991), p. 100.
13 Kenneth Waltz, "Structural Realism after the Cold War," in G. John Ikenberry, ed., *America Unrivaled: The Future of the Balance of Power* (Ithaca, NY: Cornell University Press, 2002), p. 34.
14 Doyle, *Liberalism and World Politics*, p. 1159.
15 See Georg Cavallar, "Kantian Perspectives on Democratic Peace: Alternatives to Doyle," *Review of International Studies*, 27 (2001), p. 233.
16 Michael W. Doyle, *Ways of War and Peace* (New York: Norton, 1997), p. 272.
17 Cavallar, *Kantian Perspective*, p. 241.
18 Kant, *Political Writing*, p. 96.

19   Ibid.
20   Ibid., p. 183.
21   "Build a New International Order on the Basis of the Five Princi-
     ples of Peaceful Coexistence" (November 17, 2000), at www.fmprc.
     gov.cn/eng/ziliao/3602/3604/t18016.htm.
22   Frantz Fanon, *The Wretched of the Earth* (New York: Evergreen,
     1966), p. 255.

10

Waiting for Armageddon: The "Mother of All Empires" and its Middle East Quagmire

Abdelwahab El-Affendi

In a well-known Yemeni joke from the 1970s one frustrated Yemeni politician hits on what looked like the perfect solution to that country's chronic underdevelopment.

"We should declare war on America," he suggests to a group of colleagues. "We will be defeated, and America will then take over the country and shoulder the burden of its development."

"Brilliant idea," one interlocutor agreed. "But there is a snag."

"And what would that be?" everyone asked.

"What will happen if we were to defeat America?"

Since one gentleman of Yemeni descent recently declared war on America from another country, this does not sound like a joke any more. Predictably, the United States won that war hands down, and is now busy developing the offending country, Afghanistan. And since spring 2003 Iraq, which has not declared war on America, has also been enjoying the benefits of American attention. Interestingly, though, the America which is dispensing these imperial favors does not look very much like a victor. In fact, it all but conceded defeat in Iraq when it agreed in early September 2003 to table a new UN resolution offering to share control with prospective partners ready to provide troops, a possibility that the victors were loath to contemplate in the run-up to the war. Already Afghanistan has been handed over to a loosely structured combination of born-again warlords, UN peacekeepers and NATO forces. The arrangements there, like those in Iraq, look precarious and far from sustainable.

The Real Paradox of American Power

The developments in Afghanistan and Iraq, and the escalating violence in Palestine, not to mention the long trail of terrorist attacks from Jakarta to Rabat (literally this time), point to one of the central paradoxes of the current American ascendancy. One distinctive and revealing aspect of the "paradox of American power" in its Middle East manifestation is its amazing ineffectiveness. While this region has seen the most formidable displays of American power in instances of what Kaldor calls "spectacle wars,"[1] American influence here is far from proportionate to its muscle. In the Middle East, American power exhibits itself at once at its most ostentatious as it seeks to "shock and awe," but also at its most ineffective. Where success had been achieved, as was the case against Iraq in 1991 and again in the spring of 2003, the resulting threat to American interest and influence has become even more serious. The tensions which produced the September 11 atrocities were a direct result of that encounter, and especially of the unnecessary prolongation of American presence in Saudi Arabia. The more recent intervention excited an unprecedented level of popular hostility and resentment, and launched new processes of change that will come to haunt American policymakers for generations to come.

There is a sense in which those events have shaped, even created, the present American Empire. Saddam Hussein's foray into Kuwait has offered a confused post–Cold War America the opportunity to assert itself and redefine its identity and stamp the new world order with its own particular stamp. A dictator with minimal legitimacy created a cause that was at once noble and profitable: America could simultaneously defend its national interest, demonstrate its authority and its awesome firepower, earn brownie points in the process, and even make a handsome profit.

While the war marked the emergence of the world's only superpower, it also reinforced a long pattern of adventures which tended to backfire badly, and where involvement appears to have influenced America more than the reverse. This in part reflects the peculiarity of a region where adversaries can be very tenacious. One can bomb Arafat into two rooms in the rubble of his former office, but cannot get him to sign up to the smallest concession, let alone deliver what he had signed up for. One cannot induce the Saudi royal family to reform and one cannot even prevent close ally Egypt from unfairly imprisoning innocent American citizens. As for Ariel Sharon, forget it. It is not the individual members of terrorist groups who exhibit suicidal tendencies. States and regimes do as well. In a quagmire like this, the world's only superpower is reduced to pleading with its clients, which makes it much more pathetic than the unfortunate subjects of the tyrannies of the region. What we see here is the powerlessness of power in its most spectacular and paradoxical manifestation.

This could also be seen as a reflection of recognized limits of American power, which include the admission that America's liberating and liberalizing project has neither been wholeheartedly pursued, nor should it be.[2] The attempt to expand US influence is also shown as self-contradictory in that its very search for worldwide stability appears to be destabilizing,[3] while the implied pursuit of imperial ambitions risks losing the soul of the republic itself.[4]

This paradoxical situation first reveals clearly the nature and basis of the resurgent American power, as well as the challenges facing it. The two are closely interrelated, since the nature of the challenges are themselves shaped by the nature of American power and the way it interacts with the forces it wants to bring under control in the Middle East in particular and in the Muslim world in general. This in turn reflects the nature of the Muslim world as the "final frontier" for American imperial expansion, and highlights aspects of the crisis of the world system and the irrational responses of entrenched interests to this crisis.[5]

The Last Frontier?

The Muslim/Middle Eastern challenge to American power has come to be defined in terms of a "war against terrorism," a phrase that sums up a wide range of fears (not to say paranoias), assumptions, prejudices, objectives, and aspirations. Terrorism is not a novel challenge in the modern West, since terrorism in its present form is an essentially modern challenge affecting mainly democratic societies. Western democracies have a rich experience in dealing with the challenge more or less successfully, without sacrificing essential democratic freedoms. However, the discourse and practices surrounding the current US-led "war on terrorism" have introduced novel dimensions which see terrorism as a generic phenomenon divorced from its surrounding social and political realities, in particular the existence of a multiplicity of wars and conflicts in which terrorism is employed as a tactic. The "war on terror" thus becomes a recipe for involvement in intractable local conflicts from the Philippines and Chechnya to Palestine and Lebanon. Worse still, one can glimpse in the discourse of some Western leaders, in particular British Prime Minister Tony Blair, a sense of paranoid desperation that seems to regard terrorism as a completely irrational response, and one that is moreover inevitable and can only be countered by equally irrational measures.

The fact that Blair looks at homegrown terrorism in Northern Ireland differently, and seeks rational ways to deal with it, points to interesting questions of inter-civilizational prejudices to which we shall come later. However, the missionary zeal this paranoia instills mirrors the determination of the terrorists, and is disturbingly reminiscent of paranoid feelings that have periodically haunted Western capitals during the past couple of centuries, most memorably in 1930s Germany and 1950s America.

While it may be far-fetched to claim that the terrorist challenge has inflicted a defeat on America and its allies by virtue of creating this very paranoid fixation with the form the challenge to Western power has taken, the near universal consensus that the terrorist attacks of September 11, 2001, have "changed the world" and everything[6] seems to suggest this. If the terrorists can set the agenda for America, and the world, for the foreseeable future, then we may as well start calling this "Osama's Century." For in spite of the pious affirmations we hear about not letting the terrorists win, the truth remains that terrorist outrages, especially when they take the horrendous form they took on September 11, 2001, are so traumatic and disturbing that they inevitably shake up societies and force drastic changes. The international system is also so structured that it responds more readily to acts of mass violence and neglects mass suffering if it is endured in silence. We see this in Palestine, Iraq, Kosovo, Chechnya, and elsewhere, where terrorist acts galvanize a vigorous international response, while the silent suffering of millions goes unnoticed.

This paradoxical rewarding of terrorism is reinforced by the apparent self-defeating nature of US interventionism in the region and the wider Muslim world. It is well known that the US intervention in Afghanistan and its support for the Saudi regime is at the origin of its present troubles. Nothing appears to have been learned from that experience, since the recent pattern of US interventions in the region might as well have been devised by the late Ayatollah Ruhollah Khomeini. Two of the biggest enemies of Khomeini's Islamic Republic, Saddam Hussein's Iraq and Taliban Afghanistan, have fallen victim to US military might in the space of one year. The third most hated regional enemy, Saudi Arabia, is under a serious threat from the combination of American hostility, pressure, and dwindling support. Internally, the Islamic Republic's deadliest and most implacable enemy, the Iraq-based Mujahedin-e-Khalq, or People's Warriors, are now also history, thanks to American diligence.

If this sounds irrational, the whole antiterrorist strategy adopted by the US and its allies at present seems to compound the problem at hand. The emergence of rogue elements like the September 11 terrorists is a direct consequence of a complex crisis in the region, symptoms of which include the erosion of the power and legitimacy of states, a growing sense of frustration, and a long list of grievances which pushed many to take "direct action." Some of these grievances include a sense of national humiliation due to the failure of states to stand up to external enemies. This was compounded by the perception of the failed and ineffective state as distant and unresponsive to popular demands, or even as alien and oppressive, and devoid of legitimacy.

The consequence of US action has been to accentuate these trends by leading a new assault on the Arab and Muslim state, and by focusing on its inefficacy and moral bankruptcy. The attacks on Afghanistan and Iraq, combined with resurgent Israeli militarism, compounded the anger and humiliation of Arabs and Muslims and created an atmosphere that is ideal for the proliferation of rogue non-state groups with no project but limitless destructiveness. They also poisoned the atmosphere and inhibited the essential dialogue needed to contain these and other threats.

In part, the status of the Middle East as a default frontier for the emerging American Empire has been foisted upon it by events beyond its control, including the inexorable logic of imperial expansion and the burdens of history. The Middle East was a frontier that had a particular and enduring fascination for Western empire builders from Alexander the Great to Caesar through Napoleon and down to Lord Cromer, who all regarded the region as their ultimate destination and prize. On arrival, they immediately fell under the spell of the local cultural traditions and "went native." For many, the region was the launching pad for imperial careers. For others, it also became the burial ground of ambitions.

But there is also an element of payback for previous attempts to control events in the region. On the eve of the 2003 campaign in Iraq, enthusiasts and critics alike agreed that this was indeed going to be the "mother of all battles," one that will not only reshape the destiny of the Middle East, but also that of America and the world as a whole. For the duration of the campaign, no mortal, especially one who also happened to be an American television viewer, was left in any doubt that Baghdad had become the center of the universe, and that it would be in Baghdad that America's future would be charted.

This was not the first instance in which a Middle East campaign defined the destiny of a great Western empire. Frontiers and battles to demarcate them define empires through complex processes of inclusion, exclusion, realignments, and dynamic interactions:

The principal preoccupation of the guardians of empire is the frontier: what the Romans called the limes. The frontier separates insiders and outsiders, citizens and/or subjects within from "barbarians" without. This does not mean that barbarians cannot enter the empire: they can and they do and they are often actively recruited – as professional soldiers in Roman days, as industrial workers, as gardeners and house-cleaners, as hospital orderlies, and also as skilled professionals. But the empire seeks to control their flow from the frontiers of antiquity to the fences along the Mexican border.[7]

In the case of *the* major Western empire of the past, that of Rome, this self-definition through drawing frontiers ended in turning the process of identity formation on its head. The empire was turned inside out, with the frontier becoming the center. The "barbarians" took over the empire culturally first and then delivered a left hook and overran it militarily. For Gibbon, the two "disasters" are inextricably linked: it was the cultural and spiritual invasion that undermined the empire from within and facilitated the military collapse. The rise of Christianity and its attainment of supremacy within the empire had adversely affected the virtues which made the empire possible, even if Christianity had also softened the blow by toning down the savagery of the barbarian conquerors who had also caught the malady.[8] In the end, the rise of the so-called Holy Roman Empire was not a mere caricature of the original, but the very embodiment of its twin cultural-military defeat at the hands of the barbarians.

More recent imperial endeavors also came to grief for similar indiscretions. The British Empire met its final and fatal setback in Suez, while it was arguably Iran, rather than Vietnam, which marked the end of the last phase of American expansionism. The French Empire collapsed in Algeria. The argument has been made that the Soviet Union's Afghan misadventure was probably its final and most fatal blunder. It has often been argued that the Soviet Empire met its Waterloo in Kabul.[9] But one can also see the Soviet collapse as the end point in a long process in which the Cold War was fought, lost, and won in the wider Muslim world. This protracted process started with resurgent communism's first major setbacks in Malaysia and Indonesia in the 1950s and 1960s.

The defeats faced by the Soviet-supplied Arab armies in 1967, 1973, and 1982 represented a wake-up call for the Kremlin, whose defeats they were and whose technological inferiority they exposed. The defections of Sudan (1971), Egypt (1974), and Somalia (1978) to the Western camp were major political setbacks that compounded the humiliation. The influence of resurgent traditional oil monarchies, coupled with the rise of noncommunist revolutionary regimes (Libya, Iran) and movements (radical Islamism, Arab nationalism), combined with other trends to stem the tide of pro-Moscow radicalism. Afghanistan finally drove the message home. It was merely the final straw.

There is no denying, though, that encounters such as the ones in Afghanistan, Algeria, Palestine, or Iraq have an epoch-making quality to them. The destinies of the participants become so intertwined that it becomes difficult to determine with certainty who influenced whom. The Afghan encounter, for example, raises the question of whether the accusation against the US of having stoked the fires of Islamic radicalism to defeat the Russians should possibly be seen from the other side. It could be Islamic radicalism that saved the American Empire.

God's Own Empire

America's probable (and of course unintentional) contribution to Islamic revivalism has been the subject of much discussion in recent years. While claims that the US has actually created or substantially helped Islamic revivalist movements in Afghanistan and elsewhere are certainly an exaggeration, the biggest irony remains that developments such as the creation and ascendancy of Israel have contributed significantly to the rising tide of religious radicalism in the region. As a state whose *raison d'être* and very ethos is religious, Israel has put religion at the center of political debates in the region. Israel's successes were cited by Islamic theorists and propagandists as a decisive argument against the claims of radical and liberal secularists who argued that secularism is the only way to permit Muslims to join the modern world. Here is a state, the radicals argued, that had revived an ancient religious dream, and prospered to no end, winning victories against allegedly secularizing and modernizing regimes. We, the Muslims, can do even better.[10]

US and Western policies have also contributed to religious revivalism in many other ways: by backing conservative regimes such as those of Saudi Arabia against radical secular opponents, and by appearing hostile to Muslim and Arab aspirations. By supporting the conservatives, the US has weakened the secularists, and by apparent hostility to national aspirations, it has caused the message of the radicals to resonate with the wider public. Above all, first through support to Israel and conservative Arab regimes, then through Afghanistan and Iraq, the US is being progressively sucked into the ancient religious feuds of this region, and is actually becoming a party to some of them, as the rise of the American religious right and its "Armageddonian" agenda indicates.

America has, since the days of the Pilgrim Fathers, survived on the symbolism of a "New Jerusalem" and the notion of being God's chosen nation. From the 1980s, these metaphors began to be taken rather more literally in some influential quarters. As Gore Vidal noted with alarm in his essay "Armageddon?"[11] increasingly influential political trends from the religious right in the US (who happen to count former President Ronald Reagan in their number) were seriously contemplating actively courting a nuclear holocaust in the Middle East to hasten the Saviour's Second Coming. The idea was that the world was almost at an end, and that this end was going to come with a bang, a nuclear holocaust around the now extinct biblical village of Armageddon somewhere to the north of modern day Tel Aviv.[12] Long before Francis Fukuyama provided the secular equivalent of this messianic historical determinism, Reagan told the American people that the final pages of history "even now are being written." What worried Vidal was the realization "with mounting horror" that Reagan may not have been "what all of us had hoped (even prayed), a hypocrite."[13] He actually entertained the thought that the Second Coming may be just the push of a nuclear button away. This view was also apparently held by other members of his administration, including his Secretary of Defense, not to mention close supporters such as the influential Christian Coalition, led by Pat

Robertson, which became an important actor within the Republican Party.[14]

The drift towards "militaristic messianism" in the Bush camp has alarmed even some moderate evangelicals who would otherwise warm up to his religious rhetoric. This alarm was heightened when influential Republican lawmakers began to describe the September 11 attacks as being "retribution from God" because America has not been supportive enough of Israel,[15] or when the administration's alliance with "Armageddonites" began to have a direct impact on Middle East policy.[16] Some church leaders even branded Bush's supporters among the evangelicals as no more than cheerleaders for a man who has become their "political messiah." In a role reversal, these evangelical zealots, rather than being Bush's spiritual guides, have become "his faithful disciples."[17]

> The president confidently (dare I say "religiously"?) asserts a world-view that most Christian denominations reject outright as heresy: the myth of redemptive violence, which posits a war between good and evil, with God on the side of good and Satan on the side of evil and the battle lines pretty clearly drawn. War is essential in this line of thinking. For God to win, evil needs to be defined and destroyed by God's faithful followers, thus proving their faithfulness.[18]

Against this background, and with polls showing that over 40 million Americans share the belief that the world is "heading into the last days of the final battle between good and evil," concern is mounting about "how the evangelicalism of Bush, key aides such as Condoleezza Rice, and his political constituency might play a role in Middle East policy." This has become a serious concern as "Christian Zionists" and other Armageddonians happily claim that Bush "is with us in his heart and in his soul," and use their influence to obstruct constructive Middle East policy in favor of even more unconditional support for Israel's extreme stance.[19]

Israel is, of course, the theater of this final battle, and also its object. This explained the ambivalence of the fundamentally anti-Semitic religious right towards Israel. The right vehemently supports Israel, not for its own sake, but because, like the hijackers of

September 11, they want to employ Israel as their guided missile which they would love to steer towards inevitable doom, and salvation. "Sensibly and cynically," Vidal remarks, "the Israelis exploit this religious madness."[20]

Israel of course has its own brand of religious madness. In October 2001, the prominent Israeli columnist Meir Stieglitz lamented in *Yediot Ahronot* what he called the demise of pragmatic Zionism and its displacement with "Messianic Zionism." The former aimed to create "a historic haven" for the Jewish people in the "Land of Israel." Messianic Zionism, however, is concerned with religious salvation for the people of Israel through the liberation of the entire "Land of Israel." The former was prepared to kill and be killed to secure a safe (preferably democratic, secular) home for the Jews in Israel; the latter are prepared to kill and be killed in order to ensure the total Judaization (read "holy ethnic cleansing") of the "Land of Israel" which should preferably be governed by religious edict. Under Sharon, this messianism has now moved from the fringe to the mainstream, burying all prospects for peace and compromise.[21]

It is ironic that Osama bin Laden, who should be perfectly at home in this rarefied atmosphere of utter disregard for this world and concentration on the life to come, appears to be the more rational actor among his competitors. While the American religious right and hardline Zionists are bent on using worldly resources to pursue purely religious goals that entail no worldly benefits for them or anybody else, bin Laden's quest for eliminating the US presence in the region appears by contrast as a very rational political objective. While bin Laden's rhetoric pays due homage to religious messianism, his demands are surprisingly specific and this-worldly, and are shared by many who neither approve of his murderous style nor share his religious messianism.

Be that as it may, it would appear that there is a confluence between the rising tide of religious radicalism in the Muslim world, and the similar tide of Christian revivalism in America and Jewish extremism, with the proviso that Islamic radicalism remains a peripheral fringe movement in the Muslim world, while Jewish and Christian revivalism are at the heart of power in Israel and in America.

It is symptomatic of these new developments that influential commentators sympathetic to the present US administration regard with strong approval the display of religious zeal in official circles, and regard this phenomenon as reassuring, rather than alarming. The overt religious tone of President George W. Bush's State of the Union address in January 2003, argues one sympathetic commentator, and his liberal use of "explicitly theological language" conclusively refute those persistent allegations of America's imperial ambitions.[22] By affirming that the "liberty we prize is not America's gift to the world, it is God's gift to humanity," the commentator argues, Bush has laid to rest accusations that America wants to impose its values on the world. As Americans, Bush said, "we exercise power without conquest" and "sacrifice for the liberty of strangers" because it is the right thing to do. These remarks should lay to rest all those predictions and comments about America's imperial ambitions.

> America acts on behalf of freedom not because it is benevolent (though it often is), nor because it wields its power prudently (though it often does), but because defending freedom is the right thing to do. God created people for freedom. America and all other nations are called, by divine mandate, to recognize this freedom. It is a justice instituted by God; so, when we fight, we fight on God's side.[23]

For those who may see in these reassurances a more frightening prospect than the threat they purport to dispel, and feel nervous about such an audacious appropriation of divine sanction, disturbingly reminiscent of past (and present) mischief perpetrated in God's name, the commentator produces further theological quotations from the State of the Union address to dispel their misgivings. "We do not claim to know all the ways of Providence," Bush said, "yet we can trust in them, placing our confidence in the loving God behind all of life and of history." The implication is that:

> any divine favor America possesses is the result not of its intrinsic merit but of God's gift. Such a gift may be taken from us; Scrip-

ture teaches that nations rise and fall by God's command . . . To be
a nation "under God" is to be, among other things, under his judgement – to be held accountable to his standards of justice. Liberty,
for America, is not a divine birthright but a divine challenge. So
we strive to be just.[24]

Those who are still not reassured should content themselves
with the secular version of this theological vindication of the new
Empire of Virtue, supplied this time by enthusiasts who do not
wish to deny imperial ambitions, but see in them the very vindication of America's righteousness. For Michael Ignatieff,

> The 21st century imperium is a new invention in the annals of
> political science, an empire lite, a global hegemony whose grace
> notes are free markets, human rights and democracy, enforced by
> the most awesome military power the world has ever known. It is
> the imperialism of a people who remember that their country
> secured its independence by revolt against an empire, and who like
> to think of themselves as the friend of freedom everywhere. It is
> an empire without consciousness of itself as such, constantly
> shocked that its good intentions arouse resentment abroad. But that
> does not make it any less of an empire, with a conviction that it
> alone, in Herman Melville's words, bears "the ark of the liberties of
> the world."[25]

The notion of an empire that is "the friend of freedom everywhere" is, of course, a contradiction in terms. An empire is by definition an entity which subjugates external political entities to its
hegemony by force. An empire, to quote Gibbon, constitutes a
"perpetual violation of justice."[26] It reflects the "effects of political power at its purest" and can be attained only when unopposed
political power is unleashed, with its tendency towards "fortifying
itself," and with the attendant abuses that are to follow.[27] But for
the proponents of the "virtuous empire thesis" America is "an
empire with a difference," an "empire by invitation," one which
relies more on "soft power" than outright military subjugation: an
empire that is not really an empire.[28] While admitting that the use
of the term "empire" denotes a relation built ultimately on coercion, one that is by definition something distinct from an alliance

or a federation,[29] the proponents of this thesis argue that, whatever we may care to call it, American power remains, on the whole, benevolent, however unpalatable the notion may be to those liberals who distrust empires and imperialism:

> Yet it remains a fact – as disagreeable to those left wingers who regard American imperialism as the root of all evil as it is to the right-wing isolationists, who believe that the world beyond our shores is none of our business – that there are many peoples who owe their freedom to an exercise of American military power.[30]

Exporting Revolution and Revelation

Interestingly, both the messianic and secular claims on behalf of the New Rome/Jerusalem on the Potomac appear to find vindication in its newest conquest on the banks of the Tigris. In Iraq, America has shown itself simultaneously to be an instrument of Divine Providence as well as an empire that liberates by conquest. And here one can argue that significant success has been achieved. There is no denying that America's conquest of Iraq was in one sense an act of liberation. It was seen as such in Baghdad, Basra, and Kirkuk, where relief at seeing the end of Saddam's nightmare regime was palpable and genuine enough. The people were also acutely aware that it was only thanks to American imperialism that they had finally regained their freedom, or some of it at least. Their gratitude may not have been overwhelming, but the joy was.

The fact that this act of liberation continues to be regarded by the usual suspects of idealism as a suspect move of imperialist self-interest is of great significance. That Tony Blair and George W. Bush managed to appear as the villains of the piece in a plot where Saddam became the "victim" is not a simple failure of salesmanship as some spin doctors seemed to think.[31] One explanation can be found in the commodity being exported. There is no denying that the American Revolution, that mother of all modern revolutions, is an eminently exportable commodity, even if the market for it appears to be in a deep slump at home these days. Both Bush and

Blair have sought in the run-up to the war to sell their Iraq campaign as a part of a wider crusade to extend freedom, justice, and compassion at home and abroad.[32] However, observers could not fail to point out that the Iraqi crusade came at a time when the British government was involved in bitter disputes at home with the labour and trade union movement, and at a time when the American President had come out openly on the side of the forces of reaction: opposing affirmative action, appointing controversial personalities to the Supreme Court bench, and pursuing economic policies detrimental to the interests of the less well-off majority. The height of irony in these new tendencies was observed by one commentator who noted that at the beginning of April 2003, the Republican-dominated Congress passed a resolution supporting the troops fighting the war in the Gulf and, within minutes, passed another resolution cutting veterans' benefits.[33] This was also a time when leading Republicans thought it safe (erroneously it turned out, as one Trent Lot found to his expense) to make overtly racist remarks and regret the earlier failure of racist politicians to take charge of the country.[34]

At the time of its export to Iraq, therefore, the American Revolution looked more like a counterrevolution than at any time in its history. It was now led by a class of leaders who could be described as "interventionist isolationists" (others prefer to call them "Reaganite Wilsonians").[35] They combine the least desirable characteristics of both traditional American camps. Like the isolationists, they do not care what the outside world thinks or needs; like the internationalists, they seek to meddle everywhere.

It is true that the American Revolution has been unduly glorified and credited retrospectively with lofty values it neither espoused nor intended to. However, this cannot eclipse the fact that it remains, as Hannah Arendt rightly pointed out, one of the most (if not the only) successful political revolution in human history. Arendt ascribes this unique success to the fact that the American Revolution was not revolutionary enough. Unlike the French and other subsequent revolutions, it did not throw the people back into a "state of nature," but preserved and built on existing institutions, traditions, and practices. Adherence to these norms culminated in the establishment of a new, stable political order centered around a written constitution and an independent judiciary. Together with other representative and civil institutions, these legal provisions guaranteed stability and avoided a relapse into chaos or tyranny.[36]

But it could equally be argued that the American Revolution succeeded because it was too revolutionary. It has maintained itself by ingeniously (if unwittingly) combining the Marxist ideal of eliminating economic exploitation with the Maoist principle of "permanent revolution." By constantly seeking to resolve the tension between its ideals and practice in favor of the former, it can be seen as a series of revolutions which sought to actualize the promise of the original uprising against authoritarian rule and unfair exploitation.[37] After the first revolution (the War of Independence), the second (the Civil War) achieved the abolition of slavery, a step further along the way towards actualizing the principle of human equality, while extending the slogan of "no taxation without representation" to the broader one of "no work without pay." (It was not yet time for "fair pay.") The New Deal was another revolution which sought to confront inequality and its consequences. A fourth revolution came with the civil rights movement and the general prodemocracy eruptions of the 1960s and 1970s. Then to cap it all, we had the counterrevolution, the successful Reaganite attempt to revert back to the original pre–civil rights and pre–New Deal visions of "republicanism without democracy."

What reconciled these two apparently contradictory tendencies was that these "mini-revolutions," including the Reaganite counterrevolution, were mostly "revolutions from above," which consistently built on each other. Just as it was the local aristocrats who led the first revolution, it was usually the elite who launched the subsequent revolutions. The exception may have been the civil rights movement. But even here, the role of men like President Lyndon Johnson was crucial not only in the success of the movement, but also in giving it an impetus. Unlike other revolutions, they did not seek to wipe the slate clean and start from year zero, even if the rhetoric sometimes indicated otherwise. The original revolution preserved the gains of British liberalism, federal institutions, and legal traditions and built on them, while the Civil War did not seek to destroy the federal system. The New Deal and the civil rights movements were only made possible by the outcome of the Civil War and the cumulative gains from capitalist accumulation as well as in areas such as education. It is not only that black people became better educated and more vocal, but their role in the economy became more pivotal. Even the Reaganite reaction could not have succeeded without the New Deal and the existence of the welfare state. The welfare state cushioned the upheavals resulting from the unleashing of unbridled capitalism on the nation and the world, and thus averted what could have been a catastrophic crash of the system amid chaos and conflict. In each case, existing conditions and cumulative gains made the scene ripe for the new transformation.

There were two instances in which attempted revolutions floundered because objective conditions were not ripe for their fulfillment. The first was Jimmy Carter's 1976–80 moral crusade and his attempt to put into practice the long-standing principle of support for democracy and human rights worldwide. This crusade came to grief as it became clear that American interests and power often came into direct conflict with the promotion of these principles abroad. The same fate befell President Bill Clinton's more recent attempt to combine a Second New Deal with revived benign internationalism. His twin revolution hit a wall at home as vested interests blocked welfare and health care reforms, and abroad for the same reason that Carter failed. This set the scene for the Bush counterrevolution.

Being under a sustained attack at home, it is not that easy to package the revolution as an exportable commodity, especially not to the Middle East, where a different revolutionary tradition is on the ascendant. The problem with the Bush crusade can thus be summed up in the fact that what is being exported is a counterrevolution, a hegemonistic project which seeks to roll back the gains of the American Revolution at home and act imperiously both at home and abroad.

Civilization, Barbarism, and other Clashes

More important, the rhetoric surrounding the anti-terror campaign, and the implicit assumptions driving it (that the threat of terrorism comes specifically from Muslims angered by US policies in the region), feed the perception on both sides of the divide that this is indeed a campaign against Muslim peoples and interests. The total reliance on "hard" power in the Middle East (in contrast to other areas such as North Korea) is premised on deeply held assumptions about the region and its peoples, which we need not go into in detail here. But its gist is that the folks down there are, it appears, somewhat immune to the seduction of American "soft power," and only understand communications emanating from the barrel of a gun. There is, the assumption goes, an irreducible gap of misunderstanding marked by a civilizational fault line that could not be bridged or negotiated.

It has been argued that the thesis of "clash of civilizations" is a restatement of old themes of white supremacist aspirations that had animated US and Western perceptions of the world for centuries.[38] This view could find support in the related surge in racism connected to right-wing circles where the thesis is most popular. It is interesting that black Americans, the most "American" group in civilizational terms, have been, and in some sense remain, the preferred victims of the abuse of American power. It is a supreme irony that only when US blacks began to reject Western values and seek refuge in non-American cultural traditions, mainly Islam, did they begin to gain a grudging recognition for their plight. It would appear that whatever may be the nature of the "clash" of which American blacks (and Palestinians) are victims, it has nothing to do with civilization and a lot to do with barbarism in its racist manifestations.

But the clash of cultures remains a reality, if only as a consequence of the trajectory the war on terrorism has taken, metamorphosing into an attempt at total control of the Muslim world in order to safeguard US security. This was the justification marshaled in support of the invasion of Iraq and the US Middle East Partnership Initiative (announced by the State Department in December 2002). The ethos behind all these initiatives is the quest to reshape the region using America's military might, its economic power, and political and diplomatic clout. The aim is to bring about not only political change, but also a cultural transformation in areas such as education, religious values, and political norms. This is a very ambitious and, needless to say, very intrusive project, which is likely to encounter strong resistance and provoke new conflicts. Its chances of success are slim, given earlier and more determined attempts (France in Algeria, Russia in Central Asia, etc.).

Part of the problem stems from the nature of the imperialist project itself, and its contradictory character, unable to live up to the values of equality and inclusion which were used to justify it. The "Reaganite Wilsonians" in today's Washington are even less concerned with shouldering the burden of empire in the way Wilson, or even Clinton, was prepared to do. They are keen to create a "virtual empire," with zero responsibility and maximum privilege. The outcome is a throwback to pre–civil rights days, if not to pre–Civil War America. The new subjects are expected to accept their inferior status and submit to it, and gradually reclaim their rights by pleading with the Caesars of the day and accept what they receive as gifts from them.

War as Surgery

These expectations are buttressed by the secular version of Armageddonian messianism, which believes American military might capable of bringing about the millennium here and now. As a consequence of the formative events surrounding its emergence, the military component of the identity of the new American "hyperpower" became dominant, contrary to the claims by some analysts who suggested the decline in the role of military power in the present era.[39] It is also a military power which sees in the Middle East its main challenge and the area where it should prove itself. This dual character of the hyperpower was further enhanced by the unprecedented militarization brought about by the September 11 events.

As a consequence, American leaders do not see much need to deploy America's most crucial asset: its new role resides in its newly acquired moral authority as the world's leading democratic power, its "soft power," to use Joseph Nye's term. For Nye, this "soft power" is a combination of legitimacy, moral authority, seduction, and diplomatic prowess. Nye assimilates his "soft power" notion to the Gramscian concept of hegemony, without a hint of irony, another sign of the innocence of American political science, but that is another matter. For a while in the 1990s, the Clintonian prelude permitted many dreams and illusions of a new millennium of benevolent internationalism, where for once might and right coincided. Hegemony became a term of endearment, signifying truly the rule of God on earth. Some optimistic analysts have even started to speak of global or "cosmopolitan democracy," which "envisages the limitation of national sovereignty by the direct intervention of democratic publics."[40] This vision assumes the will to empower the peoples of the world through the construction of international institutions which "would not draw their authority from the 'reason of arms' but, rather, from the 'arms of reason'."[41]

In this millennial existence, war is no more. Now we have surgery. The term "surgical strikes" was coined to refer to the ultimate clean war, where divine wrath targets only the iniquitous. People began to speak of "peacekeeping" and even "peace enforcement" as the primary task of the world's mightier military machines. The prospect was seductive enough and many found it irresistible. Some continue to find it irresistible still, even after Bosnia, Somalia, Rwanda, Burundi, Kosovo, Chechnya, Angola, Democratic Congo, Sudan, Tibet, and, of course, Palestine.

Part of the fascination with the latest campaign in Iraq is this enduring seduction of "war as surgery": a relatively short and "painless" campaign that roots out the evil of a murderous dictatorship with only minimal "collateral damage." It is the dream of all utopians come true, like cancer surgery, or like chemical and radiation therapy: the malignant tissues are targeted and the healthy body is spared and actually helped to prosper.

The fact that it was the opposing view (the one which saw the war as evil, imperialist meddling) that caught the imagination of idealists everywhere in the run-up to the campaign in Iraq was not due only to the ineptitude of the "Surgeon-in-Chief" who lost the "soft power" battle. At bottom, it was a visceral mistrust of absolute power, especially one which lays a simultaneous claim to virtue while deploying itself unashamedly as naked unapologetic power, which animated those mistrusting America and its pretenses.

The result is a paradoxical situation where the might of American imperium, in spite of its claims to universal benevolence, appears as devoid of legitimacy and moral authority. And it is lack of moral authority that renders American intervention there ineffective. In spite of winning lightening wars and imposing submission on regimes and peoples, America is no nearer to achieving its goal of securing wholehearted cooperation. In a rather symbolic manifestation of the paradoxical situation of the "powerlessness of power," American leaders and their Israeli allies spent a long time blaming five men for their troubles in Afghanistan, Iraq, and Palestine: a wheelchair-bound octogenarian (the Hamas spiritual leader Sheikh Ahmed Yassin); a virtual prisoner in the rubble of his office (the PLO chief, Yasser Arafat); and three fugitives with unknown addresses (Saddam Hussein, Osama bin Laden, and Mullah Omar). When the world's greatest superpower is threatened by disabled elderly men and fugitive criminals, you can tell that there is a problem here somewhere.

Conclusion

American power thus displays itself in the Middle East intriguingly at one level as an unprecedented phenomenon of self-proclaimed and unchallengeable virtuous might, and at another as a familiar imperial colossus suffering from the limitations of empire and its dependence on brute force. At this most challenging "frontier," not only is the "soft" component of this power underused, but the "hard" component appears utterly inefficient as well, given the intractable nature of this region's feuds. The US has contributed to ongoing conflict and has also internalized the feuds to an extent unprecedented in earlier empires.

Gibbon has blamed the collapse of the Roman Empire partly on the intolerance inspired by monotheistic Christianity which destroyed the "religious harmony of the ancient world." Christianity could in turn be blamed on the Hebrews, and the "sullen obstinacy with which they maintained their peculiar rites and unsocial manners," and which set them apart from the rest of the empire's subjects, who were quite happy to live and let live: "Neither the violence of Antiochus, nor the arts of Herod, nor the example of the circumjacent nations, could ever persuade the Jews to associate with the institutions of Moses the elegant mythology of the Greek."[42] Gibbon's somewhat archaic comments about the "obstinacy" of the Hebrews and their inexplicable refusal to conform are nowadays being polished and reproduced with amazing frequency, both in the press and in "learned" literature alike, not to mention policy circles. Only the more fervent and more recent heirs of the Abrahamic tradition, the Muslims, are named in the new comments instead of their cousins and rivals. The charges of "obstinacy" and refusal to "fit in" are not without validity with regard to Muslims. However, the people making these charges are more open to Gibbon's charge of harboring an "implacable hatred of the rest of mankind."

Gibbon did not raise the question about why Rome could not have saved itself by leaving the Hebrews alone, and in any case, this precaution may be too late to commend today. Walls or inoculation would probably not save the New Rome on the Potomac, where the Caesars have already contracted Gibbon's plague. Unlike their Roman predecessors, who inadvertently stumbled into the trap, the new emperors vehemently believe (and hope) that their Middle Eastern adventure will not only spell disaster for the region, but hasten the end of the world as well. In a supreme irony, the roles are reversed, as today's Romans are outdoing the homegrown zealots in promoting completely irrational agendas that include the re-creation of an ancient religious kingdom and offering Heaven unsolicited assistance in bringing about a speedy end to this world.

In the end, Armageddon may not come because many suicidal groups in and around Washington are busy courting it, or because rival Middle Eastern fanatics crave it, but because the very logic of empire demands it. As in the older case, it is always the general who decides that the security of empire or personal glory (or both) demand the extension of the frontiers just one mile further, who will stir up the hornet's nest that is best left alone. Perhaps someone has already done so.

In the meantime, the New Rome looks much more like old Jerusalem (or even modern Tehran) than ancient Rome. And while Rome came to adopt one of its more obscure cities as a model only in its final days, the New Rome has taken the guise of its more despised colonies at the very beginning of its ascendancy. This could indicate that the beginning and the end of this imperial reign may not be far apart.

Notes

1 Mary Kaldor, "American Power: From 'Compellance' to Cosmopolitanism?" *International Affairs*, 79, 1 (2003), pp. 1–22.
2 Tony Smith, "Making the World Safe for Democracy in the American Century," in Michael J. Hogan, ed., *The Ambiguous Legacy: US Foreign Relations and the "American Century"* (Cambridge: Cambridge University Press, 1999), pp. 30–51.
3 Charles S. Maier, "An American Empire? The Problems of Frontiers and Peace in Twenty-First-Century World Politics," *Harvard Magazine*, 105, 2 (November–December 2002).
4 Michael Ignatieff, "The American Empire: The Burden," *The New York Times Magazine*, January 5, 2002.
5 Abdelwahab El-Affendi, "Islam and the Future of Dissent after the 'End of History,'" *Futures*, 31 (1999), pp. 191–204; Immanuel Wallerstein, "Islam, the West, and the World," *Journal of Islamic Studies*, 10, 2 (1999), pp. 109–25; Benjamin R. Barber, *Jihad vs McWorld* (London: Corgi Books, 2003).
6 Barber, *Jihad vs McWorld*, p. xxxiv; Nicole Gnesotto, "Reacting to America," *Survival*, 44, 4 (Winter 2002–3), pp. 99–106.
7 Maier, "An American Empire?"
8 Edward Gibbon, *The Decline and Fall of the Roman Empire*, ed. Hugh Trevor-Roper (London: The New English Library, 1966), pp. 273–82.
9 Ali Mazrui, "Islam and the End of History," *The American Journal of Islamic Social Science*, 10, 4 (Winter 1993), pp. 512–35, esp. pp. 529–30.
10 Muhammad Jalal Kishk, *Al-Naksa wa'l-Ghazw al-Fikri* ("The Setback and the Cultural Invasion"; n.p., n.d., 1968?). Witness Kishk's own statement of the thesis: "They [the Jews] proceeded to

establish in the heart of our land a religious state based on national fanaticism, and for the service of this religious state, and for the service of Jewish nationalism, they hired in our countries some people to argue that the age of nationalities is at an end, and the era of peoples and humanity had dawned, and that religion is superstition, ignorance and backwardness, and renaissance can only be achieved by secularism and by waging war on Islam."

11 Gore Vidal, *Armageddon? Essays 1983–1987* (London: Grafton Books, 1989).
12 Ibid., pp. 103–7.
13 Ibid., p. 110.
14 Paul Boyer, *Fallout: An Historian Reflects on America's Encounter with Nuclear Weapons* (Athens, OH: Ohio University Press, 1998), pp. 140–53.
15 David Corn, "Not on Our Side: The Right Blames God and Bush for 9/11?" (April 19, 2002), at AlterNet.com.
16 Julia Duin, "Zionist Meeting Brands 'Road Map' as Heresy," *The Washington Times*, May 19, 2003; Russell Mokhiber and Robert Weissman "U.S. Hires Christian Extremists to Produce Arabic News," (May 2, 2003), at AlterNet.com.
17 Fritz Ritsch, "Of God, and Man, in the Oval Office," *The Washington Post* (March 2, 2003).
18 Ibid.
19 Duin, "Zionist Meeting"; Jane Lampman, "New Scrutiny of Role of Religion in Bush's Policies," *The Christian Science Monitor*, March 17, 2003.
20 Vidal, *Armageddon?*, p. 110.
21 Meir Stieglitz, "Messianic Zionism is Ready to Commit Massacres to Complete Judaisation," *Al-Quds al-Arabi*, 26 October, 2001, translated from *Yediot Ahronot*, 25 October 2001.
22 Gregory Dunn, "God and Empire: Some Theological Reflections on the State of the Union," Editorials, Ashbrook Center for Public Affairs, Ashland University, 2003, at www.ashbrook.org/publicat/oped/dunn/03/stateofunion.html.
23 Ibid.
24 Ibid.
25 Ignatieff, "The American Empire."
26 Gibbon, *Decline and Fall of the Roman Empire*, p. 274.
27 Robert G. Wesson, *The Imperial Order* (Berkeley, CA: University of California Press, 1967).

28 Geir Lundestad, "Empire by Invitation in the American Century," in Hogan, *The Ambiguous Legacy*, pp. 52–91; Joseph S. Nye, Jr, *The Paradox of American Power: Why the World's Only Superpower Can't Go it Alone* (Oxford: Oxford University Press, 2002); Maier, "An American Empire?"

29 Maier, "An American Empire?"

30 Ignatieff, "The American Empire."

31 Abdelwahab El-Affendi, "In a Picture Where Saddam is Victim, the Villains of the Piece Have an Image Problem," *The Muslim News*, 166 (February 28, 2003).

32 Tony Blair, "The Price of my Convictions" (an edited extract of Blair's speech to delegates at the Labour Party's spring conference in Glasgow on February 15, 2003), *The Observer* (February 16, 2003).

33 Paul Krugman, "Behind our Backs," *The New York Times* (April 15, 2003).

34 Jon Meacham, "A Man out of Time," *Newsweek* (December 23, 2002), pp. 43–9.

35 Nye, *The Paradox of American Power*.

36 Hannah Arendt, *On Revolution* (London: Faber and Faber, 1963), pp. 157, 164–8, 199–204.

37 El-Affendi, "Islam and the Future of Dissent."

38 Gerald Horne, "Race from Power: U.S. Foreign Policy and General Crisis of 'White Supremacy,'" in Hogan, *The Ambiguous Legacy*, pp. 302–36.

39 Kaldor, "American Power."

40 Daniele Archibugi and David Held, eds, *Cosmopolitan Democracy: An Agenda for a World Order* (Cambridge: Polity, 1995), pp. 14–15.

41 Ibid., p. 15.

42 Gibbon, *Decline and Fall of the Roman Empire*, p. 88.

Index